For Sue:
with love!

Jim Garfunkel fP

How to Protect Adolescents
from Bullying, Harassment,
and Emotional Violence

and
words
can
hurt
forever

James Garbarino, Ph.D., and
Ellen deLara, Ph.D.

FREE PRESS   New York   London   Toronto   Sydney

FREE PRESS
A Division of Simon & Schuster, Inc.
1230 Avenue of the Americas
New York, NY 10020

Copyright © 2002 by Dr. James Garbarino and Dr. Ellen deLara
First Free Press trade paperback edition 2003

FREE PRESS and colophon are trademarks
of Simon & Schuster, Inc.

For information regarding special discounts for bulk purchases,
please contact Simon & Schuster Special Sales:
1-800-456-6798 or business@simonandschuster.com

Designed by Karolina Harris
Manufactured in the United States of America

10 9 8 7 6 5 4 3

The Library of Congress has catalogued the hardcover edition as follows:
Garbarino, James.
And words *can* hurt forever: how to protect adolescents from bullying, harassment, and
emotional violence / James Garbarino and Ellen deLara.
p. cm.
Includes bibliographical references and index.
1. Bullying. 2. Aggressiveness in adolescence. 3. Bullying—Prevention.
I. DeLara, Ellen. II. Title.
BF637.B85 .G36 2002
373.15'8—dc21   2002021629
ISBN 0-7432-2898-7
ISBN 0-7432-2899-5 (pbk)

To our children: Lynne, Josh, Eric J., Joanna, Eric S., and J. R.
Also to Taylor, Isabelle, Blake, Piper, and Seldoen—
the next generation of schoolchildren.
And to the safety of all children.

Contents

Preface

Parents around the country are increasingly concerned with school violence, their fears amplified by media images of kids killing kids at school. While there are more plans and attempts to inflict harm than there are real incidents of serious violence, the actual number of school shootings with multiple victims has increased in the last decade. The number of children who die at school can seem modest when compared with other sources of lethal injury, such as automobile accidents or child abuse and neglect; however, school shootings testify to the existence of a much more far-reaching phenomenon—emotional violence at school.

Every school year, literally millions of teenagers suffer from emotional violence in the form of bullying, harassment, stalking, intimidation, humiliation, and fear. Gunshots may be rare, but psychological stabbings are all too common in the daily lives of kids. Sticks, stones, and bullets may break their bones, and words can break their hearts. This book is about these teenagers, and how parents and other concerned adults can help their children, their schools, and their communities overcome this problem.

And Words Can Hurt Forever results from our research with adolescents from around the country, conducted from our base at Cornell University's College of Human Ecology. This research reveals the extent of the emotional violence that occurs in the typical high school. What do we learn from listening to kids talk about school safety? We learn that even in schools that adults consider physically safe, many children feel threatened. And we learn that adults are often oblivious to this fact. How can adults remain oblivious in the face of significant and indisputable evidence? Part of the answer is that kids don't disclose their fears to adults, and another part is that adults either don't know how to or aren't willing to listen to kids. In interviewing teens, we found clear indications that despite the good intentions of teachers and administrators, many schools inadver-

tently support and enable hostile and emotionally violent environments. This is a surprising finding for parents who expect the schools
to be doing everything in their power to provide a safe setting.

In their political rhetoric, our country's leaders have emphasized
the importance of school safety for many years. And since the events
at Columbine High School in April 1999, protecting children at school
has become a high priority for policymakers at every level of government. But based upon our research, we conclude that much of this
rhetoric and policy initiative misses some of the basic experiences of
kids at school.

Parents have always been interested in this topic, of course, and the
families of children in urban schools have had to face issues of school
violence for many years. But not until the tragedy at Columbine did
most Americans feel an intense need to investigate questions of safety
at their local schools. Further, our research reveals that even the best-
intentioned parents are in the dark about the realities of emotional violence in the day-to-day experience of their kids at school.

Our book is distinctive in that it comes from listening to the voices
of kids—regular kids in regular schools—that is, schools that parents
and educators would typically consider safe. And it is critically different in that, by focusing on the experiences and voices of teenagers, it
demonstrates that they themselves have surprising answers and *solutions* to the problems of school violence. Because we have started
from the premise that teenagers can be articulate about their own
experiences, our analysis and solutions are grounded in their day-to-
day reality. The book also stands apart in recognizing that the strategies parents and other caring adults may employ in helping young
children or preteens (for example, talking to the parent of an eight-
year-old bully) may not work with adolescents.

In fact, *And Words Can Hurt Forever* goes beyond the simple categories of bully and victim. This book embraces the perspective that
the whole system and culture of the school is responsible for the con-
tinuing harassment and emotional violence there. Because we think
schools are unwittingly enabling hostile environments, we look at all
the participants in the system—the students, the teachers, the
administrators, and the support staff. By looking at how all the players interact, we get a picture of how the social system of the school
creates the climate in which bullying and victimization thrives. Based
on this full picture, the book identifies how parents can change the
social system by calling adults in the school to a higher standard of

responsibility. Finally, *And Words* Can *Hurt Forever* is unique in that it focuses on the broadest range of emotional violence (not just physical assault) as it exists in the lives of our adolescents.

Even if your child has an easygoing temperament, he or she goes to school with children who are sad and angry, and who show this all too often through emotionally violent means.

This book is our attempt to make sense of the atmosphere of emotional violence that pervades our nation's schools, not just in the inner cities, but also in the suburbs and small towns of mainstream America. In writing *And Words* Can *Hurt Forever,* we have listened to the words of many teenagers, and have made an effort to understand what they have to say. Based upon our understanding of research on child development, moral development, educational theory, and the working of social systems, we then propose strategies to improve our teenagers' emotional lives at school, and in so doing better every other aspect of their existence.

As authors, we bring to our task decades of experience working with children, youth, and families. In 1986, Jim published *The Psychologically Battered Child,* one of the earliest book-length studies of psychological maltreatment. Now, almost two decades later, the issues raised in that book have taken on a new importance as more and more teenagers are reacting—sometimes violently—to the psychological maltreatment they experience on a daily basis at school. Since 1993, Ellen has been interviewing teenagers specifically about their high school experiences, and working with families and school districts to correct dangerous practices.

For more than twenty-five years, Jim has been working to understand and offer a helping hand to parents, teachers, school administrators, politicians—even CEOs of multinational companies—about issues of children, youth, and violence.

Jim: I have been seeking solutions to emotional violence in our schools since my earliest days as a young teacher in the late 1960s. Working in a junior high school I was struck by the way my young students dealt with violence in the halls, in the cafeteria, and on the bus. But I was even more shocked by the hostility some of my fellow teachers oozed when they spoke of students in the faculty lounge— and when I overheard them in the classroom. I was also moved by the toll that bullying took on some of the boys and girls I taught. The hostility among cliques and groups of students was often intense, and it was emotionally costly for everyone. As a teacher I did what I could to improve the climate, but I was inexperienced, and the leadership in my school wasn't helping much. It was partly this frustration that led me to go back to graduate school and take up a doctoral program in human development. Now, more than thirty years later, I return to this topic of the emotional life of kids at school, where I started.

This all came to a head when I interviewed the parents of Dylan Klebold, one of the school shooters in Littleton, Colorado. Their sensitive son was driven to desperate violence by the relentless bullying and emotional violence he experienced at Columbine High School. The horrible consequences of his tragic life and death strengthened my resolve to do something about this problem.

Similarly, for over twenty-five years, Ellen has worked with children, families, and schools. In interviews and in counseling, she has seen the profound impact of bullying, so-called harmless teasing, and emotional violence on individual children, on families, and on the schools themselves.

Ellen: When the school climate consists of elements of emotional violence—or, worse, it becomes the prevailing atmosphere—children, teachers, and everyone else are harmed by this toxic soup. Children come home from school sad, angry, depressed, "tired," needing to be left alone, or simply relieved to be on safe ground for a few hours before the cycle begins all over again. And we, as parents, often have virtually no idea of why, other than to think it was a hard day academically. Sometimes this is the case. But how often do we mistakenly believe their emotions are due to academic pressures, or to normal adolescent development, when in fact they may be directly attributed to "a hell of a day at the office" with their peers?

As a researcher talking to kids, I have been struck time and again by their profound sense of helplessness about their school experiences. Most children go to school happily enough each day, hoping that the new day will be a good one. At the same time, most encounter some form of harassment or intimidation much of the time, if not every day, at school. Often it is not aimed at themselves, but at some of their friends or peers. They see it and have a full range of feelings and reactions to the bullying. Many children, including teenagers, say the same thing:

Yeah, I see kids get bullied or teased everyday at my school. Nobody
stops it. It makes you feel kind of bad inside. You can feel it in your
stomach. Most of the time, I think I *should* do something, but it's like
you're not supposed to. Anyway, I don't know what I could do. I try to
stay away from those kids—the ones who do it.

As a therapist, I have worked with hundreds of children and families. Some of these children are the victims of bullying, and some are
the friends of chronic victims at school—the bystanders. Sometimes
whole sessions are filled up by a teenager trying to explain the pain
he feels at seeing his friend being threatened constantly at school,
trying to figure out what he can do, what he is capable of doing to
intervene. He cannot comprehend why this continues to happen day
in and day out at school when, as he sees it, the teachers and other
adults know what is going on. The bystanders are filled with anxiety,
helplessness, and shame. They feel, at some level, that it is their
responsibility to intervene. And they know two things—that they
don't know how to intercede and they don't have enough power to
make the bullying stop.

For me, this book really began almost a decade ago with disclosures by my children and their friends about violent events occurring
in what I had always considered our safe local schools. I was stunned
by much of what they shared with me and shocked by the various
adaptations they made to try to deal with the atmosphere at school.
As a parent, an educator, and a concerned citizen of the community, I
knew that I had to look at the problems and begin to advocate for the
children. Otherwise, their situation and sense of helplessness would
stay the same. Their right to a peaceful and productive day would be
a wistful hope instead.

Our book focuses on several themes in the search for solutions:

Institutional Caring: How do caring and authoritative adults in
the school contribute to a safe atmosphere? Do administrators and
teachers have a narrowly "academic" view of their role, or do they
consider it part of their job description (or part of being a professional) to intervene in bullying, harassing, or violent behaviors they
see at school? What kids and teachers have to say about this is intriguing.

Peer Predictability: Adolescents demonstrate a critical need to be able to predict the behavior of their fellow students in order to feel safe and minimize aggression at school. When kids sense a lack of adequate adult supervision, they feel compelled to take safety into their own hands.

Interpersonal Respect: How does respectful behavior among students (and between students and staff) serve as a deterrent to bullying and emotional violence, thereby reducing the threat of physical violence?

Human Rights: How does a focus on the human rights of students as part of character education programming help change the school climate and reduce emotional violence? How can all students in a school be empowered by their administrators to feel they can truly contribute to greater safety?

Teenagers' Own Solutions: Why are most of the current strategies in schools for reducing the possibility of violence inadequate? Because these adult-created institutional interventions—including conflict resolution, metal detectors, and surveillance cameras—are insufficiently attentive to the school as a social system. Students speak frankly about these approaches and how they contribute to an atmosphere of fear, how they don't work, and why. Teenagers believe other, more prevention-oriented strategies could and should be put into place in all schools to increase safety.

Our book looks at safety and violence at school from the perspective of the day-to-day emotional life of adolescents, envisioning schools as places where the entire system contributes to creating a psychologically safe environment. Many other books have focused on the experience of "high-risk," "antisocial," and "violent" kids (including Jim's 1999 book, *Lost Boys*). Here, though, the interviews are primarily from youth who would be called mainstream American teenagers. We conducted the interviews and discussions with rural and suburban high school students living in "all-American" communities. This does not mean the only participants in the study were the adolescent elite, however. We also have interviews from "marginal" teenagers, adolescents who are at the fringe of acceptance in their high schools. Referred to by the other students as "hicks" or "scrubs" (and by their teachers and administrators as "at-risk" or "high-risk" students), they are more susceptible to problems such as school failure, drug use, dropping out, and adolescent pregnancy.

Many themes emerged in the interviews, through our review of the research and programs of others, and in our own direct experiences working with youth, families, and educators over the past quarter century. Each theme becomes the focus of a chapter, and each chapter concludes with a section entitled, "What Can You Do?" That section provides concrete guidance in dealing with the issues raised in the chapter. We conclude with an extensive resource list of books, articles, websites, organizations, and model programs to turn to for support and guidance.

In collecting information for this book, we used a method called Action Research. This style of looking at problems and questions basically means that we did not see ourselves as the experts when we were in each school. We left it to the students, teachers, and administrators to tell us their views on safety and what was important to them. They were our research partners.

The action research model is well suited to working with adolescents, and its use has good potential for effecting change in the school environment. After the formal research itself is over, the students and adults have many opportunities to continue working with the ideas raised during the information-gathering stages. The names and other identifying characteristics of specific locations have been changed to protect the anonymity of our research partners—the teenagers and others who participated with us in this discovery.

We have received much support in preparing our book. Our spouses (Jim's wife, Claire Bedard, and Ellen's husband, Thom deLara) have provided ongoing encouragement and intellectual assistance throughout. Their emotional support has been considerable and unfailing. Our agent, Victoria Sanders, has been there for us as our unshakable advocate. Our editor at Free Press, Philip Rappaport, has been a challenging partner, chapter by chapter and page by page. We express our appreciation to Catherine Bradshaw for her assistance with references and the resource guide, and to Lisa Rose for managing the manuscript thoroughly its many drafts. Thanks also go to our colleagues at the Family Life Development Center and to Patsy Brannon, Dean of the College of Human Ecology at Cornell University where we make our academic home. We want to thank gifted educator and colleague Diana Wolan for her contributions to one of the survey instruments and its initial implementation. Our appreciation is also extended to the principals and educators who shared their time and allowed us into their schools. Our research was

funded, in part, by a grant from the United States Department of Agri-
culture.

We owe special thanks to the many kids who opened their hearts
and minds to us in the intense process of writing this book. They did
so specifically in the desire to make a contribution to improving the
safety of schools for all children. It is our hope that by bringing the
voices of these kids to you, your understanding of the depth of emotional violence will allow you, in your own way, to be an advocate for
all of our schoolchildren.

Chapter 1

Emotional Violence Can Kill

S ticks and stones may break my bones, but words can never hurt me." It's an old rhyme, taught to generations of children as a tactic for deflecting taunts and teasing. Usually it comes with the instruction by a parent or teacher that the child chant it back to those who taunt him or her, like some kind of verbal amulet to ward off the evil spirits of teasing. But the essence of this childhood verse has never really convinced children, not in their hearts. Without denying the importance of physical pain, they know that what other children think and say about them *does* matter. Perhaps even more than broken bones, words can hurt forever.

No child is a stranger to teasing, for the roles of victim, perpetrator, and witness can be fluid from day to day and one school year to another. A survey conducted for the National Institute of Child Health and Human Development (NICHHD), published in the *Journal of the American Medical Association* in April 2001, reported that almost a third of American children in grades six through ten are directly involved in serious, frequent bullying (which includes many forms of harassment, intimidation, and emotional violence)—10 percent as bullies, 13 percent as victims, and 6 percent as both. Other national surveys report even higher figures. The U.S. Department of Education reports that 77 percent of middle and high school students in small midwestern towns have been bullied.

But these numbers tell just a part of the story, because the vast majority of kids at school experience bullying as bystanders. Most acts of bullying occur in front of other children, who rarely come to the aid of their classmates. A very small number of these witnesses may take pleasure in the suffering of others, but most are simply relieved that it is someone else's turn to be the target. Most children watch the bullying of their peers with a sense of helplessness, frozen in fear, with guilt and, ultimately, shame for doing nothing to help.

What is more, the NICHHD survey focused only on situations in which the bully was more powerful or older than the victim, excluding so-called equals in age, gender, and size. But damage is done not just when one child is older or more powerful than the others. We are convinced that emotional damage is done also through bullying by equals or by peers.

This is why, right from the start of our book, we want to be clear that our concern includes bullying as it is typically defined—aggressive acts by older kids toward younger ones—but goes beyond to include harassment and all other forms of verbal and nonverbal emotional violence. Warren, a fifteen-year-old in New York, taught us as much:

> Some people are really rude and disrespectful. A lot of people . . . they make fun of people. Sometimes they try to push people around. You can get a nervous feeling in your stomach. There are people that it happens to everyday. I see a lot of people who are picked on all of the time. I don't know if they feel unsafe. A lot of people just try to ignore it. *I think it takes a really mentally strong person to just try to ignore it and forget it immediately.* And I don't think many people do.

Why Does Paying Attention to Bullying and Emotional Violence Matter So Much?

No one can deny that American kids have faced a series of challenges to their sense of safety and security. The events of September 11, 2001, were one such challenge. In the space of one day, kids around the country were confronted with cataclysmic images of disaster that threatened their confidence in the ability of their society to protect them. But the sight of planes crashing into the World Trade Center towers was not the first such assault.

Two years earlier, America was aroused to a fever pitch of concern by the school massacre committed in Littleton, Colorado, on April 20, 1999. Indeed, surveys show media coverage of this story led virtually all others for the entire year; and adults put what happened there at the top of their list of important stories in 1999. But what are the lessons of Eric Harris, Dylan Klebold, and Columbine High School? How do they speak to the importance of emotional violence as an issue facing American teenagers? Such instances of serious school violence are part of the emotional life of adolescents now.

> Last year with that Columbine thing—it really freaked me out. The month after that, I stayed home from school, 'cause I had this really bad feeling. I stayed home 'cause I felt something bad was going to happen. And it did . . . there was a school shooting at Conyers, Georgia . . . it freaked me out. (Crystal, age 17)

> After Columbine, I had dreams of people with masks coming in. I had to try to protect my friends. I'd get all the kids under the tables. What would I do? I have brothers, cousins, friends in this school. I'm friends with everybody in this school. I'd have to do something, but I don't know if anyone else would. (Ashley, 17)

> I generally feel safe at school, but after Colorado I know that that is an illusion. Very little can stop that sort of thing. Teachers had no control. (Paul, 16)

Imagine going to school with the belief that feeling safe at school "is an illusion"! That is very sad commentary on the state of our schools and the state of mind of our schoolchildren. For most of us, it was not how we experienced our school days, and it is certainly not how we want our own kids to live.

Columbine changed everything, or at least it should have. The tragedy offered to open our nation's eyes to the pain so many of our kids feel as they confront emotional violence at school. The fact is many eyes were closed until that day in April 1999. As the principal of the high school, Frank DeAngelis, said two years later, "If someone had asked me on April 19 if it was possible that there were boys in my school so angry and troubled they were planning to kill us all, I would have said it was impossible. And then the next day it happened."

School shooters act in a terrible way and with a sense of outrage and even justification that many kids around America felt—and still feel. They believe that they have to endure a school dominated by emotional violence and that no one, particularly no adult, will do anything about it. In that belief they represent but an extreme form of something quite common. Molly, age sixteen, is from a small, rural high school in the Northeast:

> If you're bullied, that can really add up. And high school is such an environment to fit in and when you're bullied, you know, that hurts! But nobody could really stop that. No officials could, really.

Dean, age fifteen, is a sophomore from a suburban high school in New York of more than 1,500 students:

> If you get pushed and pushed, sometime you're going to fight back. The teachers see it, but they don't do anything about it. When there's a fight going on, they just walk by. If you're there, you don't know what to do.

Another sophomore, Robert, age sixteen, attends a suburban high school in Massachusetts of approximately 1,000 students:

> Everybody in middle school and high school gets teased or whatever. You have to just learn to deal with it. Sure the teachers see it, but they don't do anything about it. For one thing, they can't always tell what is serious teasing, like a threat, and what is just fooling around, you know? Some kids get it worse than others; I don't know why. Sometimes it makes you feel bad inside to see it.

We must pay closer attention to the insidious role played by bullying, harassment, and other forms of emotional violence in our children's lives. Even those of us who thought we knew how truly scary school could be (because we remember our own adolescence, or because we work with kids) have been surprised to discover the extent to which bullying and its companion problems influence our children's everyday lives.

It is eye-opening and disturbing to see the environment of school for what it really is. But we must do so if we are to respond effectively. For some of us this means to respond as parents and as citizens, demanding that schools do a better job of creating and maintaining a humane, caring environment. For others it means responding and intervening as professionals—educators or mental health workers charged with the responsibility of taking care of other people's kids. Whatever our role, *we are responsible.*

Now That We Are Aware, What Can We Do?

We will give you the very best information available—the same studies and true-life stories that we and other experts draw upon in providing advice and consultation to schools around the country. Then we must use this knowledge to make things better. Our teenagers deserve no less. We start with an appreciation for their basic psychological needs, most notably the need for acceptance.

More than twenty years ago, two researchers surveyed the psychological landscape of kids from very different perspectives but with a common aim. Ronald Rohner started his journey as an anthropologist, interested in culture and its treatment of universal human issues. He studied 118 cultures around the world in an effort to understand how the phenomenon of rejection worked in the lives of children and youth. He found that although cultures differ in how they express rejection, in every one, rejected kids turned out badly (with the meaning of "badly" differing from culture to culture, just as the form of rejection did). Rohner concluded that rejection is universally a "psychological malignancy," a form of emotional cancer.

Psychologist Stanley Coopersmith studied young people in the United States to understand how and why they experience acceptance, the mirror image of rejection: what it means to them, and what its consequences are. His conclusion, which parallels Rohner's finding, was that children need acceptance to feel good about themselves. They crave it, and will go to great lengths to get it.

Specifically, they will desperately seek to look and act like "the popular kids" to be accepted. Or children will endure the agony of becoming addicted to smoking. (Though when they start, they don't believe they will be among the unlucky ones to suffer any consequences from smoking.) They will shun their parents. Or they will suffer through painful initiation rituals like being "jumped into" a gang, being tattooed and pierced, or breaking the law.

The need for acceptance runs deep. A prisoner serving a life sentence once said, "I'd rather be wanted for murder than not be wanted at all." Everyone has to be someone, someone whom another person can embrace. Does misery love company? Human beings love company, and if it takes being miserable to get it, most are willing to pay the price.

Understanding bullying, harassment, and other forms of emotional violence starts with understanding the power of acceptance and rejection in human motivation. And not just on an individual level, since part of the meaning of acceptance and rejection lies in what groups you identify with. Race, gender, social class, sexual orientation, physical appearance, religion, and ethnic heritage are all categories relevant to this process.

For example, parents who reject homosexuality are rejecting individual gay or lesbian children, whether the children are their own or other people's. Denying gender equity portrays a dismissive attitude about girls. Ignoring poverty necessarily means rejecting poor kids. Ethnocentric adults cannot help but disdain children of other cultures. Rejecting any *category* of human beings means rejecting real live kids who are in that category.

The issue of acceptance versus rejection stands at the core of bullying, harassment, and other forms of emotional violence. Acceptance is the cornerstone to any true prevention program. Rejection is the principal motivator—and consequence—behind the many forms of abusive behavior that children encounter at school that diminishes and torments them.

Rejection is perhaps the most important and most fundamentally destructive form of psychological maltreatment, but it is not the only form. At least four others, which Jim laid out in *The Psychologically Battered Child,* deserve mention here: terrorizing, isolating, neglecting, and corrupting. All are relevant to understanding emotional violence at school, and we will spend some time on each later on.

Terrorizing is the use of fear to torment and manipulate. This is an important element of bullying and harassment. Perpetrators use the fear they incite in the victim either to achieve dominance or to obtain specific payoffs, including money or other material items, status with peers, or even sexual gratification or power. Bill, a seventeen-year-old from a large, rural high school in New Hampshire said this:

> I see a fair amount of bullying at my school. There is this one small kid who always gets picked on during lunch by a couple of bullies. I think they are all juniors. One of the bullies will go up to the kid with his fist in the air until the little kid flinches, and then the bully starts laughing. It's a regular thing. I'd like to do something. But there is kind of like a

social norm to *not* do anything. If it was anything more than verbal bullying and threats, then I would do something.

Kids are social creatures, and they need to be in relationships to feel right. *Isolating* involves cutting someone off from essential relationships. Some kids are pushed into a social "no man's land" by the exclusionary efforts of their peers. This isolation is itself a problem, as its victims can easily become disconnected from the moderating forces of mainstream society. Ironically, isolation may bring together pairs of kids who link up in their estrangement from the larger group and begin to develop odd and sometimes dangerous ways of thinking about themselves and their schools.

Michelle feels very isolated and lonely at school. She is a marginal student, at best, who sees herself as never intentionally hurting anyone. Much of the time she is *neglected,* her basic emotional needs being ignored by her peers. When she is not being neglected, she is being explicitly rejected; she doesn't understand why she is picked on to the extent that she is. At the beginning of the school year she had a best friend but that relationship fell apart, and she is clearly unhappy and confused. Despite her best efforts, she cannot figure out what went wrong, and now she just wants to get out of school. Her words give us a direct view into the school day of many students like her:

Do you like school?
Not really. I like the classes, but not the people. If I could be home schooled that would probably be better. The people in school pick on you all the time. Right now, I have a problem with people spreading rumors around about me. I don't really like it. Most days I don't want to even come here. The teachers and guidance—they just know I'm here, and that's all they really care about. People say that I'm, like, fat, which I know I am but they don't need to be picking on me about it. They spread it around that I'm pregnant, and I'm not. Just dumb things. My ex-friend, she used to be my good friend, but then a couple of weeks ago she started spreading rumors. So now she's not my friend no more.

Does your brother like school? Does he know what you are going through here?
Yes, he has a lot of friends. He knows about the girl who is spreading rumors about me because it got around the whole school and everything. He just tells some of them to be quiet; they don't need

to be picking on me. Sometimes, when we drive back and forth to school, we talk about it, but he doesn't really know what to do.

Michelle's isolation and exclusion from friends and peers are, unfortunately, common experiences for many teenagers on a typical school day. They rarely report what is happening to them to a parent or to any adult, but they suffer terribly and in silence most of the time. Generally, exclusion from the group is a form of bullying and emotional violence that tends to be particular to girls (indeed, a very basic way in which girls exert power over each other).

As if Michelle's psychological pain isn't enough, she must also contend with its consequences for her learning. How can she concentrate when she must be wondering and worrying about what rumor about herself she will hear next? Learning in such an environment takes the backseat for many children; for some, though, their studies are their refuge.

As parents and educators, we have to ask, what is our responsibility? What is the school's duty in a situation like this? This issue of who is responsible—adults or kids—is at the heart of the matter.

Corrupting means learning ways of thinking, speaking, and acting that make a child increasingly unfit for "normal" or healthy experiences. Many a parent has been shocked to hear her previously sweet child begin to spout angry and obscene language as she moves into the world of adolescent peer groups. Researchers studying the behavioral effects of this "peer contamination process" report that when peers laugh at and make fun of positive activities and endorse negative activities, positively minded teenagers can start to slide toward antisocial behavior. Because there are always some kids who enter adolescence predisposed to antisocial and self-destructive behavior, there are always negative influences available in middle and high schools to set in motion the process of corrupting.

Who Suffers?

If acceptance is a universal human need, and rejection a universal threat to development, then why do some children suffer more than others? This general query underlies the more emotionally powerful questions each parent must face. Why are some children victims of emotional violence, while others are perpetrators? What happens that turns a child into both a victim and a bully? Is there a "breaking point?" Kip Kinkel, Mitchell Johnson, Andrew Golden, and Michael Carneal, all school shooters from the 1990s, were not the only ones teased and bullied at their particular schools. Why don't other kids resort to extreme measures as these students did? This is a good and important question, one that naturally comes to a parent's mind. Why these children? Why not others?

One answer focuses upon any characteristic of a child that gives a tormentor an opening. Big ears? A stutter? Noticeable clumsiness? All these "differences" can provide that opening. And some children, directly because of their heightened sensitivity, are temperamentally more vulnerable to being the victim of a bully than are others.

Evidence of a truly genetic component in childhood aggression is meager, according to neurobiologists. What part do genes (nature) and what part do environmental factors (nurture) play? It is hard to sort out the contributions of prenatal exposure to drugs, peer pressure, drug abuse, poverty, parental unemployment or criminal activity, and parental and community neglect and abuse. Researchers such as Robin Karr-Morse and Bessel van der Kolk are discovering that many social factors influence the development of a child's brain and increase his or her sensitivity to any stimulation in the environment. According to science writer Craig Ferris, Karr-Morse and van der Kolk's studies "strongly suggest that the most important biological flaws putting children at risk for future violent behavior creep into the brain at certain critical times: developmental windows during which the brain and the nervous system are extremely sensitive to environmental and emotional insults that shape how an organism responds to stress." These factors literally and continually alter the child's brain, and therefore change his behavior and responses to places and people around him.

Some kids are more vulnerable than others to emotional violence—or at least to its effects—because of their sensitive temperaments. Things hit them harder. In her book *The Highly Sensitive Person: How to Thrive When the World Overwhelms You,* psychologist Elaine Aron identifies some of us as being wired from childhood to be more sensitive to everything. For these children, emotional violence carries more force than for other children, and they may be particularly prone to be dragged down by it. But their heightened sensitivity does not mean these children are alone in their suffering, only that they feel it more intensely.

Working in Germany, psychologist Friedrich Losel and his colleagues found temperamental differences in bullies, victims, and kids who were neither one nor the other. One indicator of temperament is the basic heart rate of a child. The families they studied were classified into two groups: "normal," well-functioning families and "high-risk," abusive families. Bullies in normal families had average heart rates of 65 beats per minute, while victims in similar families averaged 75. Kids who were neither fell in between these groups, with an average heart rate of 70 beats per minute. In the high-risk families, all three groups had heart rates of 70 beats per minute.

This was presumably because in the high-risk families, the abusive parents were powerful enough to create anxiety in the "cold-blooded," bully-type kids and thus raise their heart rates. Meanwhile, in the threatening families, the temperamentally sensitive kids had to disconnect themselves emotionally to survive (what psychologists call "dissociate")—a response that brought down their heart rate.

An Example of How Bad It Can Be

On February 14, 2001, millions of kids woke up dreading to go to school because they feared they would face emotional violence. Most of them decided they could or would have to live with their feelings of trepidation. Some planned out their route to school to avoid bullies. Some dressed with special care to avoid being teased for wearing clothes that were not "cool." Some used creams to cover their acne. Some felt or faked stomachaches in an effort to enlist parental support for staying home. Some left the house but never showed up at school, preferring to run the risk of punishment at the hands of their parents and the principal for skipping school rather than face the torment they knew awaited them.

But for one boy, all these strategies, which he had used over and over again for years, were no longer sufficient. On this February 14, eighteen-year-old Jeremy Getman woke up as he did every day, feeling hurt and angry. He knew he would face the same agony he had faced daily since fifth grade. What made this day different was that he broke into his father's gun cabinet and took a shotgun and a pistol. To these he added a gym bag full of homemade bombs, and Jeremy boarded the school bus planning to end his pain once and for all.

Fortunately for everyone, two female friends saw Jeremy when he first got off the bus and felt something was very wrong. While one of them talked with the boy, the other ran to get help. By the time the girl returned with the campus police office, Jeremy was ready to give up his weapons. A deadly crisis was averted.

A few months later, Jim sat down and talked with Jeremy about his life and the emotional violence that had brought him to the brink of disaster. What he learned was that Jeremy was a casualty of a malfunctioning social *system* in his school, not just a troubled teenager.

Systems Are More Than Just the Individuals Who Inhabit Them

American culture pushes us to see problems and solutions in terms of individuals: bad kids, neglectful parents, apathetic teachers, misguided principals, victims, bullies, and heroes. But it would be a mistake to stop here. Each kid's story is compelling and matters, but there is more to this issue than individual stories, important though they may be.

Winston Churchill once said, "We shape our situations, then our situations shape us." We make decisions about schools—who will be in them, how big they will be, what the policies on aggression will be, how to punish misbehavior, how teachers and administrators will spend their time. But once these decisions are made, once we have created the systems, then these systems have a life of their own. To do something about the problems of bullying demands that we see the systems around the individuals involved.

The study of systems is a complex and intriguing field and has contributed several basic principles relevant to our goals in this book:

1. The system is greater than the sum of its parts. Think of a shiny new car, ready to be driven off the dealer's lot. Then picture a pile of car parts— all the same ones that are in the new car. Given the choice, which would you like to have? We would choose the assembled car because it is more than just a pile of parts; it is a fully operational system.

2. In a system, all people and all parts of the system are interconnected. Everyone in the system has a role in how it functions. In other words, it is not possible that there can be simply "bad" kids in the school without all the other people and components of the system (including parents) making a contribution to their failure or their acting-out, even if that contribution is inadvertent.

3. The system will always work towards maintaining itself, for better or worse. This state is called *homeostasis*—meaning that the system, in this case, the school, will strive for some kind of balance. Systems may sacrifice individuals, even whole groups, to achieve homeostasis.

4. The system will discourage change. In an attempt to keep the balance of the system (homeostasis), the system will discourage change; will discourage differences or unusual and atypical behaviors. Difference is punished, while conformity is rewarded.

5. Interactions between people are circular, not simply a series of causes and effects. To make positive and lasting improvements, we must look at the interactions between and among people in the organization. Expelling a kid who acts out will never bring an end to the problem, because it assumes that A (the acting out) leads to B (getting expelled) leads to C (resolution of the problem), and that is the end of the process. But that is only a small fraction of what is happening in the system. The interactions that happened *before* the child acts out at school and the programs and planning that must be put into place *after* the child is expelled are equally important, and essential to figuring out how the system is functioning.

6. Some systems have scapegoats. Systems that are not working well, or are unhealthy in some meaningful way, tend to produce scapegoats —individuals or a group that everyone else in the system can blame for the problems.

As we proceed in the book, we will always be thinking about what these six systems principles mean in terms of how schools do or don't work. We absolutely must begin using these principles if we are to really make our schools emotionally safer places for our teenagers (and for the adults in the system as well). It's not simply a matter of finding the bullies and suspending them. It's not simply a matter of admonishing teachers and administrators to be more vigilant and emotionally engaged with students. It's not simply a matter of talking in a kind and sensitive way to your children. And it's not simply a matter of teaching bullyproofing techniques, which may be effective with elementary school students but are largely ineffectual by the teen years.

Finding real solutions means getting to know your fellow parents at school, and working with them as well as local community leaders and educational professionals to change the social systems of schools. Your ability to make things better for your child and other children hinges to a large degree upon teaming up with others to improve these systems.

Emotional violence is a national problem that affects most of our kids. For some children the impact is chronic and diffused, reducing their pleasure in life, their feelings about themselves, and their full participation in the many educational experiences school can offer. Others hurt more deeply, and it takes a toll on their spirits and their bodies. And for some, the effects are deadly: Suicide is the third biggest killer of American youth after motor vehicle injuries and homicides. Kids kill themselves (and, as we have learned, on rare occasions they turn their deadly pain against others) when they simply cannot "take it" any longer.

We will ask many questions throughout this book, encouraging you to think about your role in the systems we discuss. How are peer groups of kids implicated in the problem? How do teachers, coaches, and administrators add to the isolating, shunning, and taunting that take place everyday in their school classrooms, corridors, and playing fields?

Functioning as a system, how does the school provide a caring or a neglectful or hostile setting for students? At the end of each chapter, we will suggest actions that you can take, individually, with your family, and with your neighbors and friends. We start now.

What Can You Do?

1. **Accept the fact that there is at least some degree of bullying, harassment, and emotional violence in your teenager's school.** This is the critical first step. Experts agree on this fact, and it is past time to accept it as a challenge that we can meet together. Denying the extent and impact of the problem will render you completely ineffective in making your child's school experience any different or any safer than it is right now.

2. **Come together with your parenting partner.** We mean this to be a highly

inclusive term that covers your spouse or domestic partner, as well as your child's stepparent or any other relative or significant other who is willing to be your partner for the sake of your child's well-being.

3. Sit down and talk to your child. If the opportunity arises, talk to his or her friends as well. School is their "workplace," and like adults, students are knowledgeable about the functioning of their daily environment. We have learned that there may be a tremendous amount of information to be gained from simply talking informally to your child with another student present.

4. Form a community team with other parents and youth. Understanding schools as systems dictates the need for parents and other concerned adults—and youth—to band together in teams to work on the system issues. This means meetings and discussions where you can communicate your understanding with school administrators and school boards. It means getting involved with the PTA and PTO. It also means mobilizing your faith community.

5. Make sure your team really is a team in that it functions like a cooperative working group. Given our history as a society (and the personal history of each of us as individuals in that society), you should not take for granted that everyone sees the world the way you do. In fact, many adults are inclined to minimize the psychological significance of bullying.

6. With your team in place, **talk to your school administrators** (principals, assistant principals, and superintendents) and some of the teachers as well. You might start with a teacher you know through parent-teacher conferences, or one who has been identified to you as being concerned with the school climate. Here, you will be trying to get a sense of the school's perspective on the issues of bullying and emotional violence. Often school administrators only count physical fights and outright threats as problematic in their schools; talk to teachers who may have a different view from the administrators'. It is important to get a clear sense of the principal's attitudes. Does she see the connection between everyday hostility in the hallways and students' reluctance to go to school? Does he recognize that chronic teasing leads to serious retaliation? Or does the principal still believe that bullying and psychological warfare are basically unavoidable?

7. Find out about programs the school has in place and is considering to deal with the problems of school violence. Ask concrete questions, and insist on getting concrete answers back: Where else have they been used? How successful have they been? What is the proof of that?

8. Know the law. All schools in the nation are subject to the Safe and Drug Free Schools initiative established by President Clinton, which mandated that American schools do everything in their power to provide a safe environment for all students by the year 2000. That deadline has passed, but the obligation on the part of the schools is still in effect. Use this document in your discussions with school administrators and school board members.

9. Exercise your right to contact your school board president and members of the board. School board representatives are elected to be your voice in the school district. Any board member should be happy to hear your concerns for the safety and good working climate of your school. If for any reason you encounter a representative who does not seem interested, move on to someone else on the board who is. Be persistent. Some administrators don't feel as though they need much input from the general public, despite the fact that these are the people who employ them. Remember that systems resist change

10. Regroup with your team to share information that each person has collected, and see where the specific problems are for your children and in the school itself.

11. Formulate a plan to make some changes at the individual level (for example, talking to your child about new ways to handle difficulties at school) and at the organizational level (such as talking to your school officials about creating a safer, happier, more caring school climate).

Our goal in the rest of this book is to provide the ideas, information, and tools you will need to take on this important work, on behalf of your child and the other children in your community.

Chapter 2
The Secret School Life of Adolescents

Over and over again parents are surprised, even stunned, to discover the extent and nature of the emotional and physical violence that their teenagers face at school. Have parents been blind to the reality right under their noses, or are they in a state of denial? The more likely explanation is that teenagers and their parents live in different worlds. Jason, who is fifteen years old, attends a large suburban high school in New York. He has a small group of friends who, like him, are in the band. He is not the kind of kid who gets into trouble at school or at home. He believes in "minding my own business" and still does not understand why he was singled out at school. He described his sense of surprise and helplessness this way:

> When I was a freshman, I was attacked by four guys at school. I was coming back from band practice, and they dragged me into the boys' restroom and beat me up. I never knew why. No, I never told my parents about it. What for? There was nothing they could do about it. There's nothing anybody can do about it.

We have heard many other teens talk with the same level of conviction that there is nothing that they or anyone else can do to change their circumstances during the school day. They just have to figure out how to "take it." This resignation breeds silence, and the students' conviction is reinforced by the rest of the players in the system. For example, as parents, when our daughters come home and tell us that the boys are chasing them on the playground or teasing them with sexual remarks, we might respond with, "Well, they're just doing that because they like you."

While this may be true in some instances, it is not enough of a response to help. We need to say more. We need to give girls strategies for thinking through what to do and how to do it. For many of them, every day that they feel tormented by this kind of bullying, their self-esteem is slipping, and their feelings of helplessness are growing. Boys, too, are the recipients of this kind of harassment, particularly those who are smaller, slighter, and gentler than the typical masculine norm.

Teachers and other adults often ignore this kind of "play" between teenagers in the mistaken belief that kids have to figure out how to handle these kinds of interactions for themselves. Some pediatricians have supported this approach, advising parents to allow siblings to work out their rivalries without any intervention. The problem with this philosophy is that the solutions children come up with on their own are not always healthy, and often lead to escalating conflict rather than its resolution.

For some children, of course, the solutions turn out to be good and adequate and healthy. They learn how to stand up for themselves. They learn assertiveness. But often we fail to see the full scope and impact of these solutions immediately, if we ever see them at all. For many children, the "solutions" to being harassed, bullied, and tormented can include becoming a bully in response, staying in the building during recess, feeling "sick" at recess or during gym class, joining a group that is "tough" ("my homies") for defense, and beginning to use some sort of drug (whether cigarettes, alcohol, or pot) to try to dull the pain they experience.

With these attempted solutions come many future repercussions. Instead of a secure child, we see a child who shuns activities that we consider good and wholesome. We see children who are no longer sure of themselves, and we attribute this to "normal adolescence." We see a child who is full of rage at home or seems depressed, and again, we think, "This is how it is to be a teenager, isn't it?"

The sources of anxiety and fear for children are not obvious to adults, and parents are often shocked to find out what their kids have been going through at school. Survey research we conducted with college students revealed that many of them felt threatened when they were attending high school but never told their parents. For example, 51 percent of the males said that while they were in high school they were afraid of people at school, and 46 percent say their parents never knew this.

Most parents are unaware of the fact that in confidential surveys, kids say the rides to and from school on the bus are often the periods of greatest vulnerability for them. Why don't parents know? How can they know more? In this chapter we explore the impediments parents and other adults face in trying to understand their kids' day-to-day life in high school. We offer some suggestions on how to break through the domains of silence and misinformation between kids and parents.

Parallel Lives

Journalist Patricia Hersch spent six years doing research for a book about teenagers called *A Tribe Apart: A Journey into the Heart of American Adolescence*. What did she learn? "Today's teens are a tribe apart. The most striking characteristic of many adolescents today is their aloneness. . . . I've learned how much their world eludes us adults—not necessarily because they are rebelling or evading us but because we are not part of it. . . . That freedom changes everything for kids."

She concludes: "There have always been troubled kids, but today their increased isolation allows pressures to build up with no release, no guidance. There is often little monitoring of how adolescents spend their time, whether it be on the Internet, with video games, music, building bombs, or doing their homework." This isolation is the foundation for the secret life of teenagers, a life most teens experience in common ways but taking its darkest form in the life and death of a boy like Dylan Klebold.

There are millions of kids around the country who are alienated, who feel like outcasts, who echo the nineteen-year-old boy quoted in Mark Jacobson's May 17, 1999, *New York* magazine article about teenagers' reactions to the Columbine shootings: "To be honest, when I first heard about it, part of me feels like, 'Yay!' This is what every outcast kid has been dreaming about doing since freshman year."

Ask almost any adult this question: "Did your parents know about everything you did when you were a teenager that was dangerous, illegal, or dishonest?" For most of us the answer is a resounding no. To test this out, we did a survey of undergraduate students at Cornell University enrolled in a course in human development. The results indicate that many of the respondents had some secret life of which their parents were unaware. Even among this sample of particularly successful and well-behaved adolescents and young adults, there were many with substantial dark secrets. Here are some sample responses when asked to describe the "worst thing, in the sense of most dangerous or troubling" that they had done or considered doing as a teenager in high school that "your parents never found out about":

I thought a lot about death. I thought about suicide, but after much thought I decided that was morally wrong and I couldn't do it, even if I really wanted to. I often prayed that perhaps I'd be in an accident or something similar so that way I could escape from my abusive father.

I was involved in a situation over a girl that escalated to the point that myself and my best friend were threatened with being shot by a guy who had an interest in this girl.

I drank almost every weekend of my senior year in high school, and my parents had no idea. On one occasion I almost died due to my impaired judgment. I was so drunk I jumped on the front end of a car full of my friends, and the car drove off down the bumpy road. After a while I slid off the front of the car and landed in front on the wheels. I heard the brakes squeal, and when the car stopped the right tire was flush against my ribs. I couldn't even get up until the car rolled back because my sweater was still caught under the wheel.

There are too many for there to be a "worst." I had unprotected sex with my boyfriend when I was fourteen and thought I was pregnant when my period was late. I was seriously depressed and contemplated suicide. I hung out with drug dealers.

A group of us broke into an old school during one winter on weekends so we could have keg parties. We vandalized the school and tore up countless records and important documents that were being stored there. Eventually the police found out, but my parents never did.

I seriously contemplated suicide for most of my high school years. Also, I often cut and hurt myself during high school as a way to transfer the emotional pain to physical pain, and probably also as an attempt to get their attention from the scars and bruises. They never noticed.

I considered suicide in high school. My parents never knew. I was diagnosed as manic-depressive my senior year of high school, which had manifested itself through an eating disorder. In retrospect, I can see that my bipolar disorder had been building since approximately twelve years of age. I was very smart and knew that there was something abnormal in my behavior. I used my intelligence to hide it.

These are academically successful young people, responsible and bright enough to succeed in a prestigious elite university, and majoring in human development. If these students have secret lives, then what could we expect of less able, less responsible, more troubled kids? In her work as a therapist, Ellen has heard and seen this firsthand over and over again. Kids and parents sometimes live in parallel worlds, with parents unaware of what their children face at school or what their children are doing to compensate for the pain they are experiencing.

Why Don't Parents Know?

Swedish psychologists Margaret Kerr and Hakan Stattin shed light on the process underlying teenagers' secret lives in a report entitled "What Parents Know, How They Know It, and Several Forms of Adolescent Adjustment." Kerr and Stattin studied over a thousand fourteen-year-olds and their parents. They found that the more parents knew about what their kids did, the better adjusted those kids were—less delinquency, fewer school problems, less depression, more positive expectations of life, more positive peers, and better relations with parents. It sounds like an endorsement of the popular belief that parents who monitor have better kids. However, that is not the whole story.

Kerr and Stattin learned that the spontaneous disclosure of information by children explained more of what was happening than the efforts of parents to track and monitor their kids. The better-adjusted kids simply told their parents what they were doing more often than the less well-adjusted kids. The authors conclude, "There is no direct evidence, then, to link parents' tracking efforts with good adolescent adjustment in a broad, general way." What does all this mean? Kerr and Stattin report that kids who feel that their parents are trying to control them have worse adjustment than kids who feel their parents trust them. Remember that this is a study of fourteen-year-olds. By that age, parents and kids have developed a lot of momentum; there is a history to their relations. Some kids have established a momentum of positive behavior, and their parents rightfully trust them, and so these kids freely disclose what they are doing. Other kids have established a pattern of negative behavior, and their parents rightfully are suspicious (and seek to monitor these out-of-control kids).

For the most part, adolescence is the culmination of childhood patterns, not some dramatically discrepant period of life with little relation to what has gone before. This provides a sensible context for understanding Kerr and Stattin's conclusion: "It would be a mistake to conclude, however, that child disclosure is something completely separate from anything parents do, because parents' actions probably play a role in a child's willingness to disclose. How parents have reacted to information in the past and how accepting and warm they are, in general, are likely to influence disclosure. . . . Parents' past solicitation efforts could influence child disclosure by encouraging the child to develop a habit of disclosing. Very young children could begin talking to parents about their daily activities because the parents ask and listen with interest, and this could become habitual until the disclosure is independent of parents' asking." As always, an ounce of prevention is worth a pound of cure.

Another vital reason that adults do not know some of the secret parts of their children's lives has nothing to do with purposefully keeping adults in the dark. It has to do with teenagers themselves not naming what is happening to them. Because the everyday environment of adolescents is filled with gossip, name-calling, and several forms of harassment, it is often difficult for them to pinpoint which behaviors go over the line into the unacceptable, which behaviors have created the bad feelings they are experiencing. Therapists and other interventionists believe you have to be able to identify or name something for what it is before you can adequately deal with it. If adults fail to react to situations where one kid is emotionally abusing another, it is nearly impossible for kids to label that behavior as abusive. It becomes the norm. Kids, like adults, do not come home and report what they see as mundane or usual. This is true even for kids with the most receptive parents.

Why Can't Parents Discover the Secret Life?

Why is it hard for parents to discover the secret life of their teenager? Like all the tough questions, this one has many answers. For one thing, most parents have a concept of who their child is, and it is difficult to receive information which contradicts that concept. In a sense, it seems disloyal to be capable of thinking the worst of your child. Parental love is strong—and sometimes blind.

Second, parents don't have all the information that they need to draw accurate conclusions. Some of this is because they have no connection with people outside the family who know their child, or because others deliberately withhold information about the child. At times it is because the behavior of children and teenagers differs from setting to setting. Oftentimes, as we mentioned before, it is because children believe that there is nothing their parents can do with the information anyway.

Most of us think kids have one identity, but actually they may have several. Psychologists call this the *fundamental attribution error*—the tendency to focus on one set of behaviors in one situation and naively assume that this one pattern is the sum total of that person. Different settings and contexts evoke different patterns of behavior in the same person, even if he or she is a child. At the "normal" end of the continuum, many kids have somewhat different personalities at home and at school, for example. A shy, polite child at home may be boisterous and loud at school. At the "abnormal" end, some kids actually are different people in the two settings. This is often the case with kids who are so deeply troubled that they are en route to being psychopaths (like the proverbial "nice guy" who turns out to be a mass murderer).

And, of course, some kids deliberately set out to deceive their parents. They create secret lives at home and at school in order to hide their experiences on the dark side of the culture. Writing in *Time* magazine in May 1999, columnist Amy Dickenson put it this way: "Teenagers are good at hiding their true selves—or the selves they're trying out this month—behind the 'grandma face' they wear when they're trotted out to see the relatives. Behind that pleasant mask there can be volumes of bad poetry, body piercing, and tattoos." But this too is not confined to children and youth. Adults sometimes have dark secret lives that they fiercely work to keep private for fear that disclosure will open them to ridicule or legal sanctions.

A word of caution is important here. While it is true that adolescents can have a secret school life (and want to keep it secret due to their growing sense of a right to privacy, feelings of shame, or feelings of helplessness) *it is a mistake to conclude that most kids are involved in serious patterns of bad or shameful behavior.* Unfounded accusations impede future communication, so get the facts before you say anything, and be careful about coming down too hard on kids. Rather, seek to keep the lines open and find out what you need to know.

What is true is that kids keep secrets or perhaps better put, kids don't share information with their parents or other adults, about their school day for many reasons. It is our job to provide room and opportunity for kids to fill in the blanks for us.

Yet another issue in understanding the secret lives of teenagers is the way kids and their parents differ in their interpretation of family events and history. Tough as it is for us as parents to see the world through the eyes of our children, we must do so. Too many families get caught up in denial and distortion of family events as a way to save face or avoid conflict, only to find that in the long run any short-term gains are washed away by the costs of secrecy.

The Impact of Emotional Violence on "Average" Kids

What happens to kids who get harassed or threatened? What are some of the consequences of bullying and emotional violence? While we are beginning to understand that chronic harassment can lead some children to commit serious acts of violence in retaliation toward others or to gain relief for themselves, most adults are not aware of the consequences for their children—the ones who don't act in a violent manner. In *Lost Boys,* Jim wrote about boys who turn violent to deal with the problems they encounter. But how do "average" kids contend with the obstacles they face every day at school?

Consider the following diagram:

RESILIENT KIDS		VIOLENT RETALIATORS
No noticeable impact	Some psychological damage	Fully developed "dark side" (including shame, lessened self-esteem, impaired self-image, learned helplessness)

On this continuum, we see that at one end are the "resilient" children who, though subjected to instances of bullying and emotional violence (even chronically), do not seem to be impaired in any discernable way. That part of the equation is important. As parents and educators, we tend to look at a child's success in terms of academics and social development. We don't tend to attribute academic underachievement or a bit of social disengagement to emotional violence at school. Maybe we should.

Consider Nathan, who never goes to his high school library. When Nathan was a freshman, he made his way to the library on several occasions with the good intentions of a new student beginning his high school career. He knew that good grades were important to his parents, to himself, and for his future. On each and every occasion, he was met outside the doorway by a group who claimed that spot as their territory in the building. They owned it; they had power there.

To get into the library, Nathan had to first get through a series of taunts about being a nerd, then get past a volley of objects being thrown at him. Nathan was an athlete; he was capable and strong on the field. But he was not "strong enough" to deal with the ridicule and bullying of his peers, so Nathan stopped using the library. The culture that degraded him for trying to do his best infiltrated the rest of his high school experience. Though he was quite bright, Nathan's low grades reflected this poisoning of his social experience at school.

Where were the teachers, staff, and other administrators when Nathan was facing this emotional abuse? Why was this group of bullies allowed to prevail, making each student run an emotional gauntlet before reaching the inner sanctum of the library? The answer is that Nathan attended a very large high school, and the staff at this school did not consider hallway supervision as part of their "professional role."

In their work about school safety, Ron Avi Astor, Heather Meyer, and William Behre while at the University of Michigan focused on the ways in which schools have many "unowned spaces"—places that are not supervised by adults or occupied by positive, community-minded students. Students are all aware of where the dangerous places are in the building and on the campus, and some take advantage of these opportunities to bully others. Children are particularly vulnerable in the hallways.

Most kids will bear up under this kind of emotional violence. But some children who are not as resilient will experience psychological damage. The damage can include (but is not limited to) shame, lessened self-esteem, impaired self-image, and learned helplessness. The basic components of learned helplessness are the beliefs that one has no control over what is happening, that a bad event will continue to recur, and that nothing can effectively happen to change the situation. As a result of these damaging perceptions, kids begin to make important choices that hurt them academically and socially, perhaps in ways that affect the rest of their lives.

As we see in the case of Nathan, kids who are ridiculed by peers for their attempts academically may begin to make choices that result in lower grades or reduced academic interest. Kids who are degraded by their peers can end up with shaky self-confidence, damaged self-image and self-esteem. It is not easy to buck the culture of your peers if you are being tormented for being different.

As adults, sometimes we tend to think, "Students, especially teenagers, should stand up for themselves. They need to fight for what is important to them." While that sentiment has some merit, we must always be humble about matters like this. How difficult is it for adults to stand up or to stand out? On some job sites, the eager or quick workers are told by the rest, "Slow down. You're making the rest of us look bad." How can we expect children to do something that most adults cannot do? Adults will tolerate racist or sexist comments at work, even when they find them offensive, because the social costs of objecting are high. Do we expect more of our kids than we do of ourselves?

Every time we are tempted to blame the individual student for not being tough enough, being too thin-skinned, or not making good choices during the school day while being taunted, we are forgetting that kids are operating as a part of a bigger context, the system of the school. What is the responsibility of that system to each child? Each time we say, "If a child is being bullied, sexually harassed or whatever, it is up to that child to say something to an adult," we are basically saying that the adults—teachers, administrators and parents—who should be and legally *are* responsible for the functioning of the system are not really responsible at all. As long as it is up to the children to be the signal-bearers to the adults, nothing much will change in the schools.

Adults Who Ridicule and Harass

And even this is not the whole story. Unfortunately, there are teachers and other staff members in our schools who ridicule and humiliate kids. The research of psychologist Irwin Hyman at Temple University documents that many of today's adults experienced being the target of this particular form of shaming when they were young. A seventy-seven-year-old woman of our acquaintance describes how in elementary school she was caught sticking colored paper on her hands during art class. As punishment, she was made to visit each classroom in the entire school and tell the other children what a "silly and naughty girl" she was. The shame and rage she felt are as vivid today in the remembrance as they were seven decades ago. Many adults today find it difficult to believe that school personnel still engage in this shameful behavior. We may think it is ancient history, but it isn't. We hear about it from today's kids in our interviews.

The saddest part is that although it is the adults who should be ashamed of bullying children in these ways, it is the children who end up feeling ashamed and hurt. It is true that some teachers and other adults do not as yet recognize that what they do is bullying, and that it is harmful. However, it is both of those things and it needs to stop every bit as much, if not more so, than student-to-student harassment.

Here are two examples of the powerful impact of teacher ridicule on impressionable young people. When Tom was in the seventh grade, he walked into his English class and overheard his teacher and a colleague discussing his paper, laughing and commenting negatively. At first they didn't see him, so he heard more than he should have, and certainly more than they intended. Tom was crushed. He had no idea that teachers would ever laugh about a student, or that his work would be the subject of a joke.

After that, he gave up trying and became a mediocre student, even though in elementary school he had received straight A's. Years later, he remembers this event vividly and with pain as the turning point in his academic career. And Tom was just a typical kid, not an "at-risk" kid. But when he stopped trying, it began a ripple effect that cascaded negatively through his life. He made choices that affected his future, including where he went to college. Most of all, his confrontation with adult ridicule diminished his sense of himself as smart and talented.

Though they had a close family, Tom's parents never knew what happened. They never understood why his grades slipped so much, attributing it to the idea that junior high school was just more difficult. That is the explanation that most parents give themselves when they have no other feedback to go on.

At age thirteen, Amy was a very good math student. She loved its concepts and its precision. Her parents were not worried at all that Amy would be one of the many girls who are intimidated by boys into not liking math. She wouldn't be one of the ones who took a back seat to the aggressive boys in math classes. However, one day in an advanced class in eighth grade, Amy asked a question. The teacher turned to the whole class and responded, "Isn't that the dumbest question you've ever heard?" The teacher's sarcasm gave the class permission to laugh at Amy, and she was shocked and humiliated.

This was her first encounter with a teacher's disrespectful behavior toward her. It was early in the school year, and Amy's self-protective reaction was a decision not to ask any more questions in class. This seemed like a reasonable thing to do. She did not want to risk the harassment of the teacher, nor the ridicule of her classmates. Of course, Amy's grades suffered. Math is not a subject where even most good students can afford to stop participating and still do well.

Amy did inform her parents, but when they approached the teacher, they encountered not regret and apology but arrogance and denial. There was no recovery from this bad situation; Amy just had to suffer through it until the end of the year. But, as with Tom, the impact did not end there. Amy's interest in math waned. Her sense of herself as a good math student disappeared, and her ability to ask questions in other classes all but vanished.

Students who are ridiculed by teachers in front of their peers are more likely to stop participating in class and lose interest in the subject, concluding (rightly or wrongly) that "the teacher doesn't like me." These are all coping strategies for dealing with adult bullying.

Luckily, Tom and Amy did not resort to the extreme response of dropping out of school entirely, so in that sense the danger was limited. But thousands of students every year drop out of our nation's schools because they do not feel welcomed and cherished.

Other strategies that kids come up with for avoiding harassment at school include joining some kind of a group or clique for protection, or prematurely getting involved in a romantic relationship to put a stop to sexual harassment. Psychologists have tended to believe that joining a group is a natural part of adolescence. What we have not looked at closely is the critical need of young people to protect their developing sense of self from the slings and arrows of their peers. One of the ways to do this is to have a group that accepts you and does *not* bully or harass you. Your own group may tease you, but they don't do it in a way that is meant to hurt you. Others will "tease" in a way that is meant to get under your skin and make you feel bad.

That is why even middle-class white boys talk to us about their "homies." This phrase, originally part of African-American culture, implies that you have a group of "home boys" from your neighborhood who will stand up for you and "watch your back." To have this certain protection for your physical well-being and for your honor is extremely important to many young people, especially boys during the school day. Interestingly, adults in schools dismiss this as simply a form of kids at play. Even many psychologists think that this is only an example of kids trying on different and new identities. In the meantime, kids are very serious about being part of a group as a means of protecting themselves emotionally.

Other kids have different ways of grouping themselves for protection. These other groups include sports teams (have you ever watched members of the boys' varsity football team walk down a school hallway together?), drama groups (who reinforce their joint "so not-average" and "crazy" self-image by sticking together), and service groups (the school leaders who are trying their best, doing their best, succeeding, and getting adult reinforcement for it).

Many young people get involved in romantic relationships before they really feel ready. While there are many reasons, one is to find an emotionally safe place when the larger social world of the teenager's life seems unsupportive, or dangerous. Often we hear about peer pressure to have sex and how that can influence our kids to act. What we have not known before is that many kids end up in romantic relationships as a means of escaping sexual harassment. We will discuss this in Chapter 6 (Sexual Harassment and Stalking).

Of course, there are many adults, including well-intentioned academics and educators, who still believe that bullying is "OK." Their argument is similar to psychologist Joan Goodman's when she says, "I think people have to experience being picked on. It's a part of life." This is analogous to saying, "Everyone should experience the impact of war. War is a fact of life." If you ask most kids, "Do you think everyone should experience being picked on? Has anything good ever come out of being picked on for you?" most kids say, "No, being picked on sucks." When we see the impact of bullying and an emotionally toxic daily environment on children, we can begin to understand why we need to intervene to help change it.

Prevention Starts with Strong Families and Willing Schools

There are no guarantees, but we can reduce the risk of emotional violence in two ways. One is by motivating schools to do a better job in maintaining a positive climate and keeping the channels of communication open. Once schools are motivated, we can support their efforts by attending meetings, voting for school boards that are committed to the process, and encouraging our own kids to participate in the school's efforts. Much of the discussion in later chapters will focus on how to do this.

Here we will focus on increasing the ability of families to demonstrate social competence for their kids. How do they do this? Research on strong and effective families identifies a variety of successful coping strategies. Each reduces the risk, although no one can say with certainty that the risk will reach zero. One list of characteristics for strong families developed by sociologist Nick Stennet and his colleagues includes the following elements.

Appreciation. The members regard each other warmly, positively, and give support to each other as individuals. This is vitally important for both children and adults. A family that *appears* successful from the outside may not be working well on the inside, in the feelings among its members. As we showed in Chapter 1, psychological acceptance is a wellspring of self-esteem, and self-esteem feeds competence. Rejection, on the other hand, is a psychological malignancy. When parents reject each other, a common unintended side effect is for their children to feel rejected too.

Spending time together. Strong families spend time together and enjoy it. Being a family is not a hypothetical exercise; it takes time to knit a family together and to keep it from unraveling. This is a big issue for today's families, who must contend with commuting, TV, dual-earner marriages, and the like. Eating together, enjoying working together on projects, participating together in community and school activities—this is the stuff of which successful families are made.

Good communication patterns. Family members are honest and receptive toward each other. The process of seeking to maintain equilibrium within the family system thrives on communication. Families with many issues and topics that are off-limits for discussion become vulnerable to serious disequilibria. Conversely, families can handle a lot of change and stress if they keep talking things through, sharing needs, fears, joys, and strategies for coping. The result is a common social map that helps the whole family know where it is.

Commitment. The family unit is important to its members, as are the interpersonal relationships within the family, so energy and time need to be directed inward toward the family as a unit. Being a successful family today requires some hard choices. There are many things competing for the time and energy of family members (including work, school, friends, hobbies, and recreation). When there are no options, being committed to family is easy: it's the only show in town. In the modern world, though, you can't do everything. Particularly now, commitment is a clear and present element in successful families. Being committed means living your life with the needs of family high on your agenda.

Religious orientation. Strong families seem anchored in a sense of purpose that is religious or spiritual in its foundation. The strength required for commitment has to come from somewhere, drawn from a well of the soul. Connection with a higher spiritual force provides a firm foundation for this commitment, although it is not the only possible source. The point is that families need to be connected to something larger than just existing. Caring for the soul is an important function of a strong family. Children and adults need a sense of purpose, a sense that their lives together mean something more than just getting up, eating, going to school or work, watching TV, shopping, and going to bed. This is a deep spiritual need, and meeting it strengthens the fabric of the family.

Ability to deal with crises in a positive manner. Strong families are able to deal with conflicts, and band together in mutual support when bad times arise. Life always has thorns as well as roses. Almost every family faces painful challenges, such as illness, injury, death, separation, unemployment, natural disasters, and crime. Successful families rally together to meet these challenges, and may even emerge stronger from them. Vulnerable families fall apart or sacrifice members.

Does being a strong family mean the teenagers in that family have no secrets? The only honest answer is no. But it does reduce the risk. As Kerr and Stattin reported in their study, the best defense against adolescent secret lives is a family tradition of openness. While "the earlier, the better" is the rule, it is never too late to start the process.

The opposite of this openness that marks a successful family is what Robert Halpern and Judith Musick call "domains of silence"— topics or issues that are taboo in family discussions. Sex is a common one. Violence is another. Humiliation is a third. All three are implicated in our focus in this book on bullying, sexual harassment, and emotional violence at school, because schools face the same domains as families. Once we recognize this, it should not come as a surprise that parents are often cut off from the secret lives of their kids—even good families.

What Can You Do?

1. **Listen to your children with an open mind.** Try not to make assumptions or jump to conclusions. This is one message from Stattin and Miller's research: Start early with a pattern of hearing, without judgment and criticism. If you listen without interrupting, you will hear who your child really is and what he or she is experiencing at school.

2. **Create ongoing opportunities for your children to talk about their lives.** Talk about issues around the dinner table (of course, this requires having dinner together in the first place), or in the car during many of the transportation opportunities each week. Make it a tradition, so that when negative experiences do occur there is a habit of the heart to rely upon—a habit of disclosing what is troubled and troubling.

3. **Share information with other parents.** Get a second opinion. Are their kids having any trouble at school? Have their kids let any hints drop about being bullied, about hating school "all of a sudden"? The American value on family privacy is a barrier to this, of course. But letting that value prevent parents who have useful information from sharing it with other parents is too costly for all of us.

4. **Seek out information from the school about your children.** Teachers and administrators often complain that parents are resistant to hearing troubling information about their kids. "Not my son!" or "Not my

daughter!" is no way to open the flow of information from the school to the home.

5. Seek out information from teachers and other staff about the climate at the school. How do they see it? Are they seeing more and more trouble at school, more and more "troubled kids"? Are teachers and aides saying they are enjoying their jobs less?

6. Ask teachers what you can do as a parent to provide some help to them during the school day. Often the only thing teachers in middle or high schools get from parents and administrators is aggravation. Most are overworked and operate in overcrowded classrooms. They could use something more substantial from parents and the community than a "Teacher Recognition Luncheon" once a year.

7. Think outside the box. Even though the school has always done something one way, your idea or suggestion might be very welcome—especially if you are willing to put some time into it yourself.

Chapter 3

Taking On the Myths of Adolescents at School

myths of all kinds shroud the experience of kids at school, standing in the way of our efforts to see and hear the reality of what children encounter on a daily basis. Sometimes myths have their root in nostalgia—rose-colored memories of how things once were. Other times, they are grounded in comforting misinformation distributed by self-serving parties about the decline of juvenile crime in general (which doesn't address emotional violence in schools) or the inevitability of bullying and its insignificant impact on most kids. Sometimes these myths have their root in our own need to minimize and rationalize what happened to us as children, because accurate memories of our pain and shame can be too much to bear. And sometimes they have their basis in inappropriately generalizing the experience of some kids to all kids.

Parental response and school policy are, to an extent, often founded on one or more myths. Rather than comforting parents and children who are hurting or even excusing bad behavior, myths about adolescents contribute to hostile school environments. They substitute for reality, and in so doing displace actions and undermine good intentions that would improve the situation. We have identified seven myths that are particularly insidious.

Myth #1: Our Schools Are Safe

Reality: A majority of middle and high school students do not feel safe at their schools. They do not expect to be shot or stabbed every day, yet they feel vulnerable to physical attack or verbal assault (regarding themselves or the things they care about, like coats, shoes, bags, cell phones, or money). In general, our schools as psychological systems are not safe, yet the myth of school safety is perpetuated from one generation to the next. One way this happens is when adults pre-emptively decide their local school is safe, leaving the students no say in the matter. If we want to get to the reality of the situation, we always have to ask, how is "safe" defined, and by whom?

Even people who have years of experience working with children can sometimes fall into the trap of asking simple questions about schools without preparation, or without first establishing a climate designed to encourage disclosure. They ask questions like, "Do you feel safe at school?" or "Is this a safe school?" Many kids will give adults the answer they think adults want to hear. One school administrator admitted to us that he does not spend much time exploring those questions with the kids in his high school, because he is afraid to hear the real answers.

Without digging a bit, adults miss the nuances that prevail in adolescents' perceptions about safety. Researchers, teachers, counselors, and principals can be equally inept at asking the right questions in the right way at the right time. Teenagers can articulate subtle distinctions that adults often miss.

Tyrone, age seventeen, put it this way: "You might feel that the situation is unsafe, like *someone* could get hurt. But not like you'll be the one to get hurt. You might see something from a distance away that is potentially dangerous—a fight starting or what looks like a weapon—but not think that the danger will be aimed at you." Part of this boy's attitude can be attributed to adolescent invincibility, the common belief that "nothing will happen to me." But Tyrone raises an important point. In investigating kids' feelings of safety at school, we can't stop with surface questions and responses. There will be some who need to explain further, who know the school is safe for them but not for others.

It is one thing for adults to determine that a school environment is safe based on their experience of it or their perceptions of day-to-day life. It is quite another thing for the students to declare that same school to be safe. The adults may feel safe, for instance, because they have power. Students overwhelmingly report that teachers and other adults on the school grounds do not have any clue about how many actual incidents of physical and emotional violence and harassment occur in the course of a day.

For many students, the hallways represent a particularly problematic section of the school. In our study, 55 percent of the students thought their peers were disrespectful toward one another in the halls. The comments below express other aspects of feelings of insecurity.

I feel unsafe when I'm walking through a hall and older people I don't know are there. (Jenny, 14)

The number of people in the hallways [makes me feel unsafe]. You get lost and can't be seen. (Janeen, 14)

Rob, age sixteen, from a suburban California school, discussed some of the dilemmas he and other students experience about the hallways. When he was asked, "Do you think the adults pretty much know what is going on in your school?" his answer was an adamant "No!" The rest of his report is interesting:

Most of the time the teachers are in their classrooms, so they are not really in the halls—and that's where everything takes place. So they don't find out.

What's happening in the hallways?
Sometimes, you have people who hate each other, or people who accidentally bump into each other.

From that, you're saying something could happen?
Yes.

How do you feel about it?
It feels weird that the kids notice these things and the teachers don't.

Would it be better if the adults noticed more?
Yes.

How would it help?
You wouldn't have to worry about somebody jumping on your back.

Do you think that you can count on teachers and other adults to intervene if something happens in the hallways?
Probably not. It would take them some time to get there and then to figure out what was going on. It could take anywhere from thirty seconds up to a minute.

Would hall monitors help?
It might help, but where we put hall monitors now is at both ends of the halls. That's too remote. Nothing happens there.

Whether it is "accurate" or not that teachers and other adults in the school are unaware of the problems in the hallways is not the point. What is significant is Rob's perception. Like all of us, kids or adults, Rob bases his feelings and actions on how he perceives his environment. To him, the adults are not aware of what is truly happening in their own building. For him that means extra vigilance, so somebody doesn't "jump on your back." It is also important to notice that thirty or sixty seconds seems like a long time to Rob. And if you are getting threatened or bullied or physically attacked, that *is* a long time—too long to have to wait on a regular basis—for an adult to intervene on your behalf.

In one study we conducted, the school had several wings. One contained the auditorium and several rooms used for music classes. This wing of the building was "restricted," meaning that students were not supposed to be there without a pass, precisely for the reason that there was little adult supervision in the area. Any teachers who were present were fully occupied conducting band or orchestra practice or giving other music lessons. Fifteen-year-old Warren's observation captures the feelings shared by many students about how this space works and doesn't work for kids:

There's lots of places in the school . . . like down by the auditorium—there's no one there ever. Like by the music wing, there's no one there! It's like abandoned except for people who have band or music lessons. There's no one ever there so if something was to happen there, no one would ever know about it.

When Warren related his observation, he was incredulous that there could be such an obvious lack of security in his school. He seemed mystified that the adults in his school would not see what he saw. His voice and body language showed the vulnerability that he felt as a result.

The cafeteria is a problem for students in many schools. While kids eagerly look forward to lunch and break times to see their friends, scuffles and other outbreaks of aggressive behavior occur in the cafeteria unless adult management is intense. These incidents happen often enough that some students are willing to rethink adult supervision in the cafeteria in order to feel safer there:

> There's fights in there [the cafeteria] and teachers don't even notice 'til afterwards. (Stephanie, 17)

> The teachers just stand there in the front of the cafeteria. They can't hear what's going on in a whole room full of children. Sometimes they're not even there for the whole period. (Warren, 15)

> During lunch, there is only one teacher in the cafeteria and over three hundred kids in there. How can she do anything if there's a problem? And anyway, she spends the whole time correcting papers and doing her own work. So she never notices anything, or a fight, until it's already in full swing. None of the teachers want to do cafeteria duty. (Jackson, 18)

To be fair, teachers and principals in schools around the country regard the issue of adult supervision in the halls and other nonclassroom spaces as a big and largely unresolved matter of concern. Teachers generally want the time between classes to prepare. This translates into hallways without adult supervision or, at best, supervision by nonteachers who lack credibility in the students' eyes ("security guards" of one type or another who are not known to students in an educational role). It is a great loss. There was a time in many schools when it was expected that teachers would be in the halls between classes to maintain an adult supervisory presence. From all that we have seen and heard, it is certainly time to bring that supervision back!

Students worry a great deal about being inappropriately touched and having their physical boundaries transgressed. Interestingly, we find that male students can make admissions of physical abuse, such as being punched, without loss of face in a group context, while disclosures of concern over sexual harassment come forward mostly in the anonymity of surveys. About 10 percent of males we surveyed admitted to worries about sexual harassment in the school. The girls in the study seemed to feel more free to report sexual harassment in different areas of the school in both the group and individual interview settings.

> I feel unsafe in the bathroom because someone tried to touch me. (Kendall, 15)

> The bathroom is unsafe because I feel someone will look at me or touch me in private places. (Rob, 16)

These responses are typical of those given by adolescent males in our interviews—those who were willing to mention it at all. They are concerned that someone might approach them in the restrooms or the locker rooms, because then they will be forced to figure out how to deal with some kind of encounter. For the most part, kids do not feel they have the skills to handle such a delicate situation adequately. If approached, they say they would have to defend themselves and defend their reputation in some way. Their fear is that a physical fight would be the result, so they want to avoid any possible encounter. According to a recent survey by the American Association of University Women (AAUW), in adolescent society, the worst thing is to be called gay.

Gay, straight, or bisexual, adolescents do not want to be labeled "gay" because of the extra harassment that they will have to endure. We discuss this further in Chapter 6 (Sexual Harassment and Stalking).

The school grounds can be unsafe as well. Among the concerns that kids talk about are inadequate lighting, lack of adult supervision on the grounds, fast student drivers in the parking lots, students using drugs, and unfamiliar adolescents on the property. The responses that follow are to the question: "Are there any unsafe places at the school?"

> You have to have a flashlight at night for the parking lot; it's so dark, and there's no adults around. (Crystal, 17)

Sometimes on the school property, 'cause there's people I don't know. (Sophie, 17)

Outside is unsafe because there's kids out there doing drugs. (David, 16)

Locker rooms are notorious for problems, whether during use for a gym class or after school for a sports team. They are usually lacking in adult supervision and can be stimulating sexually and aggressively to kids. Many students find the locker rooms to be the most difficult places of all for them during the school day.

The locker room makes me feel unsafe when I'm the only one in there, just being alone in that area. (Patti, 14)

Yeah, the locker rooms can be a problem. I mean the coach tries to watch out for us. There is a window from his office into the locker area, but, you know, he can't watch all the time. Yes, guys can get carried away. Some guys might not know how to handle it. Me, I'm used to it in there. And nobody's coming after me; I'm a senior. (Frank, 17)

When all is said and done, we must give up the comforting myth that except for a handful of "school shooters," our schools are safe. Schools abound with issues of psychological danger and physical vulnerability.

Myth #2: Kids Won't Tell on Other Kids

Reality: Kids will, and do in fact, tell trustworthy adults—even their own parents—about the things that they see during the course of their school day. They do this if they are asked, know they will be believed, and have reason to believe some action will be taken to improve the situation for the better.

Sure, I've gone to guidance before when one boy kept after me. He was touching me all the time in the hall between classes. I don't know what they did but they took care of it. Probably they talked to him. (Suzanne, 16)

You can try to talk to the principal or to the guidance people, but the principal doesn't like me. She doesn't like anybody who dresses different like me. You can tell by her look; she gives you that look. One time I told my guidance counselor about this girl who always says she is going to beat me up—she always threatens me when I'm in the bathrooms—and they just made it worse! And it didn't stop. (Rachel, 16)

There was this girl who kept following me around, so I went to Mr. __, he's our vice principal. He had a meeting with me and this other girl to try to get both sides, but he didn't really do anything. She still kept following me and telling rumors to people about me. Nothing was any different. My father came to school and told Mr. __ he wanted to see it stop. But it didn't. Finally she just left and went to another school. I just had to put up with it, but I was always afraid something bad would happen. (Traci, 15)

All three of these girls took their problems to adults in charge. Suzanne felt there was a good resolution and that she was heard, which is the experience of many children. Unfortunately, Rachel and Traci did not experience positive outcomes as a result of "telling" on their classmates. Though they were very willing to go to an appropriate adult, they both believed that either the situation was made worse or that there was no effect.

What Rachel and Traci told us is representative of thousands of young people every day. Perhaps we can say they didn't really know what went on "behind the scenes," what the administration and guidance did actually do on their behalf. In many instances that would be true. But even then, there is some vital link of communication that is missing for our teenagers. In both cases, some adult needed to get back to each girl and check in with her on a regular basis. Telling Rachel and Traci what steps had been taken to resolve their problems provides important information as well as an insight into how adults go about solving problems. It also would have ensured that both girls felt cared about.

Taking the extra step to inquire a week later, and then again two weeks later, gives young people a clear message: We have heard you, we are working on it, and you are important to us. Whether or not kids "tell" is largely a matter of whether adults persuade them they are listening and will take helpful action.

Myth #3: Kids Will Be Kids; Boys Will Be Boys

Reality: Adults see many aspects of teens' disrespectful behavior toward one another as normal, particularly the physical aggression of boys and the social aggression of girls (that is, hurting each other by spreading mean gossip and cutting them out of peer groups). As a result, adults fail to intervene in instances that could lead to an explosive situation in the future. Safety starts with adults in the school system defining a safe school as one in which every student has the right to be treated respectfully by teachers *and peers.*

Until adults recognize emotional violence in the everyday life of the school, and identify these behaviors as something other than typical for adolescents, the system will not change. Adults will not intervene, believing in the myth that the schools are "safe." As a result, students will continue to feel that they are on their own and must figure out ways to protect themselves during the school day. Until the myth is exploded, kids will continue to reflect back to us through their thoughts and behaviors that the system is broken.

For safety? I put my trust in the other students. We can take care of ourselves when we need to. (Elliot, 16)

The teachers and other staff are too busy. They can't be looking out for kids during class or whenever. Anything can happen, so I just watch out for who looks angry and stay out of their way. Everybody can tell who's angry or in a bad mood that day. (Yvonne, 16)

I feel safe at my school because I bring a gun. (Sean, 16)

I've got my home boys to back me up, so I feel okay at school. (Doug, 15)

Myth #4: There Will Always Be Bullying, and There Is Nothing You Can Do About It

Reality: This may be the most dangerous myth of all. It does its damage by giving a clear message to kids that even adults are helpless to change bad behavior and a toxic environment. Ineffective and halfhearted attempts to solve bullying send the same message: Nothing works, so just live with it. Kids end up losing faith in themselves and in the ability of their teachers and parents to help them.

Teenagers learn many unintended lessons from the failures of pseudo-solutions. They conclude that they have to figure out how to take care of themselves during the school day. Some generate healthy ways to do this (for example, developing good negotiating skills, developing many friendships, and joining several groups for overlapping circles of support). Others do not have the skills or maturity to figure out healthy ways and resort to the best solutions they can come up with. Far from solving anything of consequence, they choose responses that fuel helplessness and victimization.

For example, some children stop participating in organized sports at school because of the institutionalized hazing of new athletes on the team. Some children stop going to the library or even to the bathroom because they can count on being shoved against a locker, pushed into a physical fight, pushed beyond their limits. Beyond the horrible drama of Columbine-type revenge, there are the smaller-scale acts of kids who can't take it any more, from malicious gossiping to fistfights in the hallways or revengeful vandalism. Here is the account of one boy in his first year of high school. It is just one person talking, but his story is the same as we've heard from many others:

When I was a freshman, I played football. But the coach let things go on in the locker room that shouldn't have ever happened—especially to the younger guys. When practice was over, the juniors and some seniors would get a smaller kid. They picked you up and stuck your head in the toilet. I saw it happen many times. It made me sick. It was going to happen to each of us, one by one. And that was just one of the things that went on there. I tried to always get out of the locker room as quick as possible—turn in my equipment and leave. I didn't even stay for a shower; I waited till I got home. My parents never knew about it. But I know one of the guys told his parents and they were mad. They talked to the coach, but he didn't do anything. He said it was a tradition. There was nothing wrong with it. Actually, he thought it was funny. The next year, I didn't go out for the team. I was good at the game, but I didn't want to have to put up with it. And I didn't have respect for those guys who did it, or the coach. I thought they were idiots, and I didn't want to spend my time that way.

One of the ways that this boy did not want to spend his time was worrying. He decided not to be victimized, and given that he could not count on the adult in charge (the coach), he elected to opt out of this organized sport. How many other kids have had a similar experience? How many times has it happened to our own children and we never knew anything about it, assuming our child was just unmotivated or distracted? What is the impact on a teenager who makes a decision like this? And how many coaches still follow this brutal philosophy and tradition of hazing?

Myth #5: School Violence Affects Only a Small Fraction of Our Kids

Reality: The reality is that the costs of physical and emotional violence at school reach beyond the small number of kids who are actually killed, or the thousands physically wounded each year. They go beyond the official statistics on the tens of thousands of kids who carry weapons to school for self protection. They include the 160,000 children who avoid school every day, and the thousands who drop out of school altogether because they are always afraid at school. The true snapshot of school violence must account for the millions of kids who experience diminished learning and peace of mind each day at school. This means most of our kids, in most of our schools. Even subtly hostile environments are damaging to children if they are chronic, even when students learn how to "cope."

Fran, age fifteen, attends a middle-class suburban high school where adults do not know (or believe) that there are gangs:

The gangs are the main things that make it not safe at my school. They fight over dumb things, like getting accidentally pushed in the hall or talking to somebody else's boyfriend or girlfriend. They even put up flyers around school telling when their next party is! And the principals don't take the posters down. Maybe they think it's some kind of school club or something! Anyway, they act tough like gangs you think of from New York City or someplace like that. They make me feel scared everyday. They haven't done much that's serious this year yet, just a few fights in the cafeteria. But the way they act and the look on their faces, you know something could happen anytime.

Myth #6: Kids Have to Learn to Deal With Bullying and Harassment on Their Own.

Reality: Adults have legal protection from bullying, sexual harassment, and emotional violence in the workplace. Why should children and teenagers be any different? After all, the school is the child's workplace. What is more, children and adolescents are immature developmentally. They need adult guidance and protection. It is unrealistic to believe and expect that as soon as kids enter middle school, they will have coping skills adequate to the task of dealing effectively with the interpersonal problems of harassment that they are presented with on a daily basis.

Maybe some kids, their parents may not be there to tell them, you know, like, what behavior's right and wrong and stuff like that. And sometimes teachers need to let kids know. Like the kids need a second kind of parent there to, like, inform them and tell them what they're doing is wrong, because sometimes at home they may not get that. (Shana, 15)

Myth #7: Adopting a "Prison" Approach to Schools Makes Them Safer

Reality: Prisons have more metal detectors, locked doors, and surveillance cameras than any other place in America, yet prisons are the *least* safe places in our society to be. The elements of physical security are important, of course, but they are not what provides the basis for emotional and physical safety. According to the research of psychiatrist James Gilligan, in prisons it is the degree to which inmates feel respected and treated fairly, to which they believe the authorities are in charge and care, that they are psychologically and physically safe. The same goes for schools. To respond to concerns about the safety of students by making schools more like conventional prisons does little for the emotional safety of kids—no matter how much it makes some adults feel better.

We had an opportunity to witness this firsthand when a school in which we were involved responded to a death threat posted on a bathroom wall with a security exercise called a "lockdown drill." How did it work? During the last class period of the school day, the principal came on the loudspeaker to inform the students that their classroom doors would be locked and that no one was to leave for any reason. The teachers were told to explain to the class what they should do in the event a school shooter was on campus. The students were then instructed to line up against the windows and sit down below them. The rationale given was that in this way, the police could see them from outside the building and from inside the hallways. How did it work emotionally for kids? We asked some of those who participated.

Seventeen-year-old Steven seemed happy to offer any help on this subject and seemed relaxed, for the most part, during the discussion. However, some of that apparent calm was probably attributable to the fact that he was a graduating senior and would be leaving the school in a matter of weeks.

Charlie, also seventeen, at first tried to appear blasé about the discussion, as so many other adolescents want to do, but as the discussion proceeded (after twenty minutes) he abruptly left to go home. At various points his bravado slipped away, and he had facial and body language that demonstrated a feeling of vulnerability. He moved from the typical invincibility posture of a late adolescent male to one more typical of a child who feels helpless and fearful

This is what they both had to say about the "lockdown drill" and its effects:

CHARLIE: There were some things about it that I found disturbing. We talked about it for about fifteen minutes in our class before going on to our other work.

What did you find disturbing?
STEVEN: Just how it was done. I think there are a lot of loopholes in the plan. For example, they told us that if it was for a real attack,

the principal or some other appointed person would get on the loudspeaker and tell us to go into lockdown. Well, I know the principal's voice, but I probably wouldn't recognize someone else's. It makes you wonder.

What does it make you wonder?
STEVEN: How can you trust it? Now anyone who is at our school who might want to do this [be a perpetrator] knows the whole plan! The other thing is, if I were going to do something awful like that, I would immediately take out the communications center at the school. Then no one would know what to do or what was going on.

There are a lot of really smart kids at our school. It would be easy to come up with a plan that got around this lockdown strategy. For one thing; what about the kids who would be out in the quad? Or in the cafeteria? Would they just be left there? Would they be banging on classroom doors to get in? Would the teachers let them in or not? How would the teachers know if they were the "okay" kids or the shooters? Then once you opened up the door . . .

The other thing is, you are supposed to sit in a row under the windows. It's like being sitting ducks. Somebody can just break into the classroom and then get everybody. The whole plan is for the benefit of the police somehow, so that they can see where everybody is.

Also, we have windows in all the doors to the classrooms. Somebody could easily break the window and lob a bomb in there, and then get the whole class.
CHARLIE: Yeah, I think the plan might be able to work, but only if the police got there and had control of the situation in a matter of a few minutes, which I don't think would happen.

At your school, is it possible to get out of the windows?
BOTH: Yes, but only on the first floor.
What about the second floor?
CHARLIE: Technically you can get out, but it is a twenty-foot drop; so you can't do that.

If you were on the first floor, would it make more sense to you to get out of the building by the windows?

STEVEN: I can understand that the police would have trouble figuring out who was who—who was the shooter, with a thousand kids running away from the building. But honestly, even if the police shot one or two people by mistake, I think there would be fewer fatalities than just sitting there waiting for the perpetrators. There are too many loopholes and potential problems with it. . . .

Since Columbine happened, you always think about it. It's not like you're afraid every day at school, but you're aware. Before I might have said to somebody, "I'm going to kill you!" you know, just fooling around. But now you don't do that.

CHARLIE: But some kids still do. They'll say things like, "If I was going to do anything [like Columbine], I'd put a sniper here and one there." [gestures to indicate the places on tops of buildings]

STEVEN: Immediately after the shooting at Columbine, everyone looked around our school and determined who was capable of doing the same thing here. And there is a core group like that— that could. I'm friends with some of them, but not all. So there's some worry there.

CHARLIE: Now you always know it can happen anywhere.

STEVEN: I think the teachers have to get to know each one of the kids. That's key. So there wouldn't be anybody who was a loner, or feeling so unhappy that somebody didn't know about it.

The teachers often respond to that idea by saying that they have so much material to get across to meet state requirements that they simply don't have time to get to know everyone.

STEVEN: I can see that. It's true; maybe more true for the Regents-level courses. That's a tough problem, but still there has to be a way.

What about the school social workers and psychologist?

STEVEN: They are usually not brought in, in my understanding, unless there is a known problem. They see the kids who are referred to them, mostly behavior problem-type kids. So they aren't likely to see the kids we're talking about, who just may be lonely, feel rejected, picked on—like that.

Clearly the kids didn't trust the lockdown plan. Contrary to the school administrator's expectations, it made them feel *more* uneasy and less safe at school, since this flawed approach was apparently the best that the adults could come up with to protect them. Because the school implemented the lockdown during the last period of the day on a Friday afternoon, there was no chance for any debriefing for the students. This is a problem from many perspectives, of course, and has implications (as noted above) for many students. It is striking that kids have incorporated their fear of this level of attack into their humor, but the anxiety is real. In this instance, none of the mental health professional staff in the building were consulted for the planning or execution of the lockdown drill.

We found students' reactions to the use or possible use of technology in a school building such as metal detectors and surveillance cameras to be primarily negative. They didn't feel safer for their use. Those expressing a positive view about metal detectors were definitely in the minority.

This anti-technological stance was a bit surprising in an era of adolescent immersion in sophisticated technology. Their attitude was predicated on the belief that technological devices are not useful and can easily be foiled. Further, they create a mini-prison effect that is uncomfortable for both students and teachers.

> I'm glad we don't have cops or metal detectors here. That would actually make me feel less safe, because it would mean there have been people with guns [or] knives, and other problem-causers. (Danielle, 16)

> I don't like all the ideas about the metal detectors . . . or locking the doors. It's stupid. (Samantha, 14)

> I think the metal detectors and cameras are what our school is trying in order to keep up with the safety standards of everybody else . . . like at Columbine . . . to show that we are doing something, but it's not really. I think character education is the best thing. (Tom, 16)

> You can always get by the metal detectors; there are ways to do it. And anyway, I think it encourages some people to try. You know, to see what they can get away with. Bring something to school, like a weapon, and see if you can get over. (Phil, 15)

The kids' feelings have important implications for school district budgets. The message from the students is this: Don't bother to deploy expensive electronic mechanisms; they can be foiled, and they invite adolescent attempts to challenge them. Based on the opinions and experience of these students and others, school safety cannot be bought. According to researchers James A. Fox and Jack Levin of Northeastern University, school personnel are employing "short-term politically expedient solutions" rather than strategies that have a good chance of being effective. For example, schools are spending thousands of dollars on technological devices that "pacify nervous parents" but do not make genuine improvements in school safety. The school culture and climate remain the same, with no effect on bullying, exclusionary cliques, and intolerance of diversity.

Technology is not a kid-friendly resolution to the problems of school violence, and it may not be a wise investment for some school districts. The inference we draw from listening to the teenagers is that depending on technology for safety is placing the emphasis at the wrong end of the continuum.

What Can You Do?

1. **Insist that adults take responsibility.** We must explode the myth that school safety is primarily the responsibility of the children. Many school districts are focusing their violence prevention on measures that kids are supposed to put into place, such as dispute resolution, anger management classes, and hotlines. While it is important to teach children conflict-resolution skills and other means of civil behavior, it is up to adults to be in charge at school. When they do not take charge, the school as a social system is thrown into a state of disequilibrium, and the most likely result is that kids will do too much to achieve some kind of balance. It is primarily the responsibility of school administrators, teachers, and all the other adults associated with the schooling of children to create and maintain a safe and secure environment for them to learn and grow. Children can make an important contribution, *but it is not their job to ensure safety.*

In a family where the parents are not in charge, children feel anxious and fearful for their well-being and safety, because in effect there is no adult present. They will often attempt to assume leadership as best they can. From a systems perspective, it can be said that the children are overfunctioning in the school to compensate for the adults who are underfunctioning.

All adults need to contribute to a healthy atmosphere in the school. Teachers, administrators, and other staff need to decide that it is within their realm of professionalism to interrupt abuse among students, and between students and school personnel.

2. Challenge the myths of school safety when you hear them. One purpose of this book is to provide the ideas and information you need to make a difference in the discussions and debates that take place over the dinner table, at church, over coffee, in school board meetings, at the PTA meeting, and on teacher conference day. Knowledge *is,* indeed, power. At this pivotal time in school history, it is not acceptable for an adult to just let pass what might seem like a casual remark, such as "I was beat up a couple of times at school" and "I don't know what all the fuss is about. So what if you get picked on a little at school?" After reading this book, you should be armed with the information you need to answer those statements. Letting them go by is the same as agreeing with them.

3. Insist on in-service training for school personnel on verbal abuse and the consequences of bullying, harassment, and emotional violence. How can we combat bullying when we don't even know what it consists of? How can we overcome it if we are not fully aware of its extent and its impact? Training programs for *adults* and strategies for intervention need to be established as soon as possible in all of our schools. In this way, we will be taking the problem seriously, and everyone will have a more accurate idea of what the problem is. You can not cure any problem until you can name it.

4. Find out your school's policies on bullying and lockdowns. You may be very surprised when you talk to your school administrators or teachers to hear what your district considers a good policy on bullying or for lockdown procedures. In the example above, Steven and Charlie were able to see the problems and loopholes in the plans at their school. In their case, no adult administrators had consulted a single student or any of the mental health professionals in coming up with the lockdown plan. The students we talked to and the school social workers were unhappy about the plan—how it was conceived, and how it was implemented. As a guardian of your children, you need to know what your school does when bullying occurs, what it considers to be bullying, and what it plans to do if there is a major security threat on the campus. You may find that you are not in agreement with the ideas that the district has come up with. The only way to know and have input is to ask or read what is available. If you feel dissatisfied with the plans, it is important to meet with your team and discuss how to proceed.

5. Offer to volunteer your time at school in new ways. One of the ironies of parenting and school life is that while schools seem eager for parental presence in the classroom when children are in elementary grades, by the time our kids go to middle school, it can feel like our presence is no longer welcome. After being a classroom helper every year while her own children were in grade school, Ellen experienced this phenomenon when they graduated to middle school. She went from every-week involvement in the classroom to no class time. The clear message from the middle school was either that help was not wanted in the upper-grade classes, or that the school felt parents were not competent helpers past the elementary school level.

Given what students are reporting, schools can certainly use the help of parents and other concerned community members to super vise and be another adult presence in the building or on the grounds. Maybe kids would not have to be as worried about the hallways and cafeteria, or the buses, if adults were in these areas for the specific purpose of keeping them safe. Right now, some schools have police and other security teams to serve this function. For some children, this is comforting; for others, though, it is disconcerting. Adults who could be counted on to show up on a regular basis, pay attention to the task at hand (monitoring the kids, not visiting with one another), and be available for the kids would make a difference in our schools.

Typically, schools ask for parental involvement in a variety of ways. Some of these functions (such as the PTA or PTO) are essential components for effective communication between families and schools, along with the many other services that they provide. However, it is important for parents and other adults to be creative about what they can offer the schools along the lines of additional supervision or security of the environment.

One girl told us that if the school building and the classrooms were more attractive and less cluttered, she believed kids would feel more comfortable and safer in the school. She is right in many ways. It is

true for all people that a more pleasant physical space tends to promote feelings of attachment and ownership of the property. A more
beautiful or comfortable workspace tends to produce feelings of
security; this is what we want for our children. If you have ideas about
how to accomplish this, perhaps you can meet with teachers or officials at your school to implement your thoughts. Remember that if
what you propose means more work for the teachers or staff, your
ideas may not get far. They often have too much to do as it is. However, if your project includes volunteering your own time, then you
will have a better chance at implementing your inspiration. Are you
talented artistically or organizationally? Let your own brand of creativ-
ity work for you and for your children's school.

   6. Vote! One of the most important things you can do for your children is vote on the school budget, as well as during school board
elections. In many school districts, a surprisingly small percentage of
registered voters actually vote in any given election. Why? Maybe we
think it doesn't make any difference. Maybe we think the school or
other people know better than we do about the issues. As concerned
parents, we need to make it our business to know about the issues
that directly affect our kids every day at school. How a district spends
its money affects your child. If you have people on the school board
who like kids—or people who don't respect kids and their opinions—that affects your child, too. Parents need to attend some meetings of the school district, especially those focused on school safety
and violence prevention. You will not only hear a lot from the school
personnel but also get a feel for how other parents are thinking in
your district. You may meet others who feel as strongly as you do that
better solutions need to be put into place to protect our children.

Chapter 4

Ins and Outs:
Issues of Power and Groups

a ll the usual issues that divide adults—race, sexual orientation, social class, and gender—operate in the lives of kids. But there are also additional divisions that adults rarely have to deal with at work or in the neighborhood, such as "hicks" and "scrubs" versus "preppies" and "jocks." Social groupings and power relations of teenagers have been a topic of study for psychologists and sociologists for many decades. One of the early pioneers in this field was James Coleman, who in 1965 published a classic study titled *Adolescents and the Schools*. Almost four decades later, the issues of in-groups and out-groups are just as powerful.

Perhaps it is inevitable that kids will differentiate themselves into groups. Some scholars believe this is an innate process that has evolved as a survival mechanism, much as it did among apes and other mammals. But what is *not* inevitable is how fluid movement is up and down the hierarchy, how much groups cooperate or compete, and the degree to which they trample on the emotional development of the kids who don't "fit in" as well as those who do.

Indeed, some of the most interesting research in social science deals with efforts to integrate social groups. Decades ago, sociologist Mustaf Sherif conducted the famous "Robber's Cave" experiment. He set up a summer camp for kids and then explored various ways to generate cohesion versus division among the kids. He found that when he created groups (cabins in this case) and then instigated unregulated competition among the groups (such as games with no referees and ambiguous rules), negative feelings and behavior between the groups arose. Soon the groups hated each other and ascribed all kinds of negative characteristics to "the others." Conversely, when Sherif arranged a situation that demanded cooperation (like breaking down the camp's water system in a way that required everyone's efforts to fix it), he instigated a positive cycle that resulted in improved interactions, feelings, and beliefs among all the groups.

Social scientist Elliot Aronson applied the powerful lessons from Sherif's experiments. He spelled out the costs of corrosive competition and rejection in school for vulnerable children in his book *Nobody Left To Hate.* Aronson went beyond describing the problem to propose a well-grounded solution. Building upon what Sherif learned decades earlier, he argued in favor of the systematic introduction of cooperative structures in the classroom. Aronson's approach is called "the Jigsaw Classroom," and his research demonstrates success in transforming the social relationships among children in a more accepting direction by involving them in teams that demand and reward cooperation.

Power in the School

Who has power, and who does not? Does a child feel at the bottom? How can parents help empower kids at school? Do adults have the power to take charge? Is the school a battleground? These are the essential questions we ask in understanding how kids experience their schools. Empowering students requires active efforts by school administrators and teachers, as well as parents and teens themselves. Despite the fact that they can contribute astute analyses of what is going on, students often feel they have very little power to change anything at their school.

Do kids have power? The teenagers we interviewed didn't seem to think so:

I don't really know. I think it would be kind of hard to get something changed with some of the people around here. (Josh, age 15)

No. I don't think our class president has the power to either. I don't like it, but there's nothing I can do about it. (Warren, age 15)

As a group, athletes have several kinds of power, such as their physical prowess and their unofficial leadership of the school. But "dangerous" students have power too—the power of being unpredictable and threatening. Who are these groups of dangerous students? From the student perspective, the list includes Goths, kids who are different, "hicks," "scrubs" (all groups that we will consider in this chapter), and bullies and "druggies" (two groups we will return to in subsequent chapters).

Goths

Anyone who appears quite different from the norm, like Goths, are feared —unless or until you get to know them, according to more mainstream kids. This fear of the unfamiliar brings us to the need for predictability, which we discuss in Chapter 9. What does it mean to be a Goth? For some, it is style: dressing in all black, with chains and upside-down crosses. For other kids, it is a means of self-identification, and includes not only a style of dressing but also a range of behaviors. Listening to teens talk, you can hear the struggle they have over how to think about their classmates:

Yeah, people that are like different. Different from me. They think they're normal, but people that dress in black like Marilyn Manson and stuff like that kind of freak me out. Some of them are nice—like there's a girl in my grade, she dresses like that but she's a sweetheart. She's really nice. The people I know that dress like that don't scare me, but the people I don't know who are bigger that dress like that kind of freak me out. I think they dress like that to be different. Being average is boring; I hate that, too. (Traci, 14)

Some of the people that are different scare me. When the whole Trench Coat Mafia thing happened at Littleton, then I'm coming to school and it's like, "Oh my God, there's people here wearing the trench coats and everything." Then I realized, I know these people. And I didn't think they would do something like at Littleton, but you never know. Some of them are different and they have the right to be different, but I don't see why they have to be all dressed in black, with upside-down crosses and stuff like that—that kind of worries me a little bit. (Crystal, 17)

They're not just Goths . . . they also do their schoolwork. They just dress differently. (Tom, 16)

One teenager who is a self-described member of this group shared thoughts on lethal violence at school in a national survey conducted by Alfred University:

> . . . stop targeting the "trenchcoats," "freaks," "goths," whatever. I AM ONE! And they think that if anyone is going to [commit an act of lethal violence at school], it's us. They are sooo far from the truth it's not even funny. If it's anyone it'll be the kids that are ostracized, picked on, and constantly made fun of. Oh and by the way EVERYONE has a plan to shoot up the entire school, it's what we do when we're bored. It doesn't mean we're going to do it, it just means we have no school spirit (usually because our school doesn't like us) and we're bored.

Kids Who Are Different

Like most adults, kids can be uncomfortable around people who seem very different from themselves. Hopefully, as adults, we have learned to appreciate differences and the richness that diversity brings to our lives. We have learned a "live and let live" attitude in our daily dealings with others. For many children, however, school is their first and only exposure to people who are unlike themselves and their families. Parents, school personnel, and community members need to make the most of the educational opportunity this presents. If we as adults neglect to talk to our school-age children about "differentness," they will come to their own conclusions, and their behavior will reflect those conclusions, erroneous or not. Here are some examples of kids' thinking about "kids who are different" and safety at school:

> Some of the weird people at school make me feel unsafe. I think they might get ideas like the kids in Littleton or someplace else. (Kara, 15)

> I feel safe, but I don't think I would if I was black or some other minority at this school. (Jenny, 14)

> Some students who are different from us are aggressive. (Rachel, 15)

Rednecks picking fights make me feel unsafe at school. They are jerks. (Tony, 16)

The poor kids make me feel unsafe, seriously. Not all of them. They don't like me, 'cause they think I think I am better than them. Some kids say they will beat you up but they won't. Some will, though; that's the problem. (Tyler, 15)

The kids, the people that talk about violence and seem to enjoy it, make me feel unsafe. They talk about video games, and it sort of freaks me out why they enjoy bloody and weird stuff. (Jackie, 15)

Well, any of the minorities . . . like whether or not you feel different about them . . . a lot of times I think when *they* feel different, like that people don't like them, they feel that they have a need to act a certain way. Like with Columbine, those kids were different and so maybe . . . Or maybe the kids who don't know people who are different or just don't like them, they're scared of them because they don't like them. (Greta, 16)

Maybe those kids who feel different are the ones we have to worry about. (Helen, 15)

Hicks and Scrubs

"Hicks" and "scrubs" can be basically the same kids. Some students lump them in together; some see them as separate. Hicks, according to the teens we interviewed, can be from a rural area, the suburbs, or the city. They can be poor or wealthy. The main thing that differentiates the "hicks" from most of the other kids is that "they don't know how to dress." They wear the wrong shoes and the wrong, or outdated, styles of clothing. So these kids, basically, don't know how to fit in.

This group of students is as feared as are the druggies in school. Suburban and rural students believe that the hicks have the easiest access to guns. Their experience of these kids is that they are the least averse to making outlandish, rude, and harassing remarks. Also, the hicks participate in fights and are often seen as bullies. In fact, many kids in the "hicks" group identify themselves as bullies of their school. Listen to how the kids try to sort out the differences:

Scrubs, trailer trash kids, are unpredictable. (Jordan, 16)

I am afraid that one of these days, since we live in a hick town, that one of the hicks is going to go postal and kill me. (Todd, 15)

Scrubs are people who are annoying, or they could be poor or just not know how to dress very well, they don't wear the right clothes. The scrubs try to be something they're not. (Marianne, 15)

Their parents [the hicks'] were hippies and they live way out in the country, and they live on a farm. The parents have jobs like postal workers or farmers. Then there's the lower-class people in that group, too. (Courtney, 16)

The hicks say these things to you just to be out to impress their friends. They'll just be really rude and really obnoxious, you know. (Ashley, 15)

They [the hicks], I would say, do it the most, are rude and obnoxious. They're more open about it I guess. (Heather, 15)

I think a reason that the hicks kind of scare us somewhat is because the multiple school shootings that have taken place, there's been five kids who have had that kind of background, and they're like the hicks in our school. So I think that's why we're more terrified of them then. (Suzanne, 16)

I don't think you'd ever see a farmer hick come in and shoot up the school. I think it'd be more likely—I don't want to insult anybody—but more likely to be one of you guys, 'cause your parents don't teach you anything about guns. When I grew up I was taught about the use of guns, so I know how to respect them. (Judd, 16)

On Power and Helplessness

Kids often feel helpless or powerless at school. When they do, it is the result of a silent but potent message: "We are not interested in what you have to say, and will do nothing different based on it." Harvard social scientists Steven Brion-Meisels and Robert Selman believe schools will continue to send this message so long as they adhere to what educator and philosopher Paulo Friere called a "magical conforming strategy" wherein "problems are denied or avoided; difficulties are accepted as fate—a part of existence." If the institution believes problems (like bullying, group exclusivity, intolerance, and feelings of powerlessness) are not problems or are "a part of existence," then it won't do much to change things.

Children and adults learn to feel helpless when they repeatedly run into uncontrollable events and do not have the means to escape or master the troubling situations. Kids think, "There is nothing I can do to change this." This attitude of learned helplessness, first described by Martin Seligman, comes to dominate the way they look at all social interactions, including those at school.

We'll Handle It Ourselves

Kids speak poignantly of their sense of helplessness when they think about a major catastrophe, like a school shooting, and when they think about other day-to-day violence at school. Our research supports Jim's earlier findings that children in our society are aware of the difficult situations they have to navigate, and that they typically feel powerless to change them. Clearly, some students take charge when and where they feel the need—often in ways we would rather not see—and then they *do* feel powerful. They take the control they need through initiating a fight, either verbally or physically.

The minority of students who take their own initiative in wielding power tend to be in one of two groups: either the at-risk group (or those identified by other students as the "hicks") or the schools' athletes. The "hicks" or at-risk adolescents take care of themselves in the school through their identification with a group of friends who are not afraid to fight others. Athletes are another group that sometimes exercises power over other students in ways that are not seen by all kids as appropriate. We address the reasons why these particular groups engage in verbal and physical violence in Chapter 5 (The Many Faces of Bullying) and again in Chapter 9 (The Puzzle of Peer Predictability).

How Do Kids Think about Helplessness?

Many students who speak about the phenomenon of helplessness do not label it this way. They talk about being unable to get what they want, having to put up with things like sexual harassment, feeling as though their appointed representatives are not helpful (for example, those on the student council), and talking with adults to no avail. They demonstrate all of the basic components of learned helplessness in their sense of having no control and thinking that nothing can effectively happen to change a bad situation.

The feelings associated with helplessness are uncomfortable. In trying to deal with them, adolescents show the full range of behavior from passive to aggressive responses. The passive responders merely say, "This is the way it is; I can't do anything about it" and accept that position as their reality. The aggressive responders fight with others in the environment in order to gain control over their particular problem or situation (such as over boyfriends, or against those they perceive as too different). The assertive responders first try talking to adults about their concerns. If there is no satisfactory change as a result, then they retreat to a position of helplessness. This position is characterized by such statements as, "I tried to talk to [the teachers, the principal, or the dean of students] about it, but nothing happened. That's how it always is."

Some kids do not talk about groups and power or helplessness in these ways at all. This is due to not seeing this phenomenon for what it is. Teenagers (as well as most adults) hold a belief system that says, "This is just how high school is." Seventeen-year-old Natasha summed up the "truths" of high school as she saw them. She was a popular girl in her school, and her outlook was that there would always be class distinctions and group hierarchies in any high school. These distinctions may or may not lead to problems, but in her accounting it wasn't fair to expect adolescents to figure out how to solve the problems. The sense in listening to her is that the problems of groups and cliques are too much for her to take on. Someone else besides teenagers must handle this concern if it is going to be resolved.

> I think with students it's nice to say, "Oh, well, if everyone just tried to get along better, not pick on each other so much, the world would be a better place." But the truth is there will always be those social levels. There will always be people who put other kids down to make themselves feel superior. There will always be the popular group. There will always be the nerds, you know. It's always going to happen, you know, and I don't think it's fair to put it in the hands of teenagers who have so much else going on. They're not thinking about other people's feel-

ings at the time, you know—it's just, there's always going to be that separation there.

Helplessness Expressed in Anger

Students who are angry frequently experience a sense of helplessness that is portrayed in their belligerent attitudes and behaviors. Teachers and school personnel often observe adolescent anger, but they are not always aware of the profound feelings of helplessness or hopelessness that underlie much of the anger they see. This finding is corroborated by research conducted by psychologist E. Paula Crowley, in which aggressive students reported feeling angry as a result of being "rejected, misunderstood, ignored . . . outcast(s) of society . . . helpless, and unable to change the situation for the better." Statements such as "You can't count on the teachers" and "My faith is in the students" depict the need for more appropriate mechanisms for students to approach adults and to feel empowered to change bad situations.

Lack of power or control is uncomfortable for anyone and is particularly problematic for adolescents, because they bring to any situation a whole host of issues about power, authority, and control. Challenging authority is one of the natural activities of this developmental phase. A wise parent understands this and offers freedoms where appropriate (sometimes before they are requested). Wise school administrators could profit by doing the same.

What Does It Mean?

Many psychologists and others who study kids and their behavior believe that kids, like all of us, just naturally tend to gravitate to groups. We like to be around others who are like us. Primatologists who study bullying behavior among the great apes and monkeys describe the group cohesive effect that occurs as a result of the bullies' intimidating the scapegoats. Ethologist Frans de Waal, from Emory University, has found that the high-ranking members of primate groups tend to harass the low-ranking members (the scapegoats) when the group is under strain, or when the hierarchy is being questioned. Identifying the victim unifies the group, according to de Waal. We explain more about the function of scapegoats in the system in Chapter 7 (Warning Signs).

For a long time, sociologists have studied the questions of social hierarchy and power that are demonstrated by different groupings of people in organizations. But it is increasingly clear that more is going on when kids group themselves. As Ellen found, kids protect themselves during school by being able to predict the behavior of their peers. It is all the better if your group and kids in other groups are predictable in their behavior patterns. A National Center for Education Statistics survey found that 20 percent of sixth through twelfth-grade kids say they try to stay in a group as a strategy to avoid harm or harassment while they are at school. This is more common at public schools than at private schools. If 20 percent admit to this strategy and are aware of it, though, we need to ask other questions. What percentage of kids tries to find a group for security but are not consciously aware of doing so? What happens when a child can not find an "acceptable," wholesome group to accept him or her? What happens to his sense of safety? What group does she end up in?

How and when do we begin to understand that a child's selection of a group we might label "bad influences" might represent his or her only choice for friends? These are often the other kids who have been selected as targets to be harassed for one reason or another. These kids then proceed to live up to the expectations of their peers and their school administrators. They are seen as "other" and so make the most of it, dressing the part in terms of clothing, hair color, hairstyle, and makeup. We need to ask ourselves, "What made this particular kid choose this manner of presenting himself?" rather than thinking, "He [or she] is clearly a troublemaker, rebellious, or on drugs. I can see that just by looking at him [or her]." Which is the chicken, and which is the egg?

What Can You Do?

1. Start at an early age. If you truly want your child to be tolerant of others and not to be a target of bullies, start talking about the similarities that we all share as people. Little children are innately interested in differences they see in the people and the world around them. Use these opportunities to talk about the richness of difference. Talking about "different" as interesting, rather than as something to be feared, is critical to growing healthy, accepting children. When your child is old enough to view a movie that shows some form of racial prejudice, talk to him or her about how sad and strange it is to judge someone based on the color of skin. Talk about how in our history, we have taken chances and opportunities away from other people based only on the fact that they had brown skin, or black skin, that they were Native American, or that they had once lived in an Asian country. Talk to your child about how this is wrong and why. By the time your child gets to middle school, he or she will have a solid basis for thinking about accepting or rejecting others. Your child will be able to judge others based on their heart and actions, rather than on their clothes or skin. Teaching your child to be tolerant and accepting will not turn him or her into "some kind of bleeding heart," as sometimes people fear. What this kind of teaching does is make your child into a strong and self-accepting person. Why self-accepting? Because you are giving the message that people may look different, but it is what is on the inside that counts—and this message is true for your child, too. Self-accepting, self-confident children are the least likely children to be bullied or to bully others.

2. **Know where your child fits in.** Knowing what groups your child participates in or is "assigned to" by peers is an important step. Of course, many kids are reluctant to identify themselves this way, particularly if that identification has negative social conventions (like being a "druggie"). How can you find out? One way would be to talk to your child's counselor at school. More information comes from visiting the school and simply observing the kids. One caution: You may often be wrong if you "judge a book by its cover" in the sense of judging some kids by how they dress. Remember, kids are trying on new identities while they try to discover who they are. You will really learn more about your child's group and friends by providing opportunities for them to congregate at your house. Provide several evenings for your child to invite friends over for dinner or pizza. This is a wonderful opportunity to get to know his or her friends.

3. **Ask school administrators to hold meetings with parents** to talk about the social structure of the school. The response itself may be enlightening. Frank DeAngelis, the principal of Columbine High School, claimed after the violence there that he was unaware of the existence of the Trench Coat Mafia at his school. In a large school (Columbine High had about 1,900 students), that kind of ignorance is somewhat understandable as a cost of bigness. But the ignorance is not accept-

able. Someone in charge should be aware of the social structure of peer groups at the school.

4. Ask what the school is doing to promote social integration across groups. For most schools, the answer is probably "very little," and almost everywhere "not enough." Further, most school administrators believe that (a) it is inevitable that kids are going to group themselves and be exclusive, and (b) kids have a right and are entitled to form groups for their comfort. No administrator is going to admit that it is okay for kids to actively exclude others, but as long as they carry the attitudes mentioned above, school personnel will do very little to try to produce a change. While most school people believe in the benefits of inclusivity for all kids, administrators who hold beliefs (a) and (b) will do little to change how kids cluster together.

5. Offer acceptance at home. There are things you can do to help your child directly. Remember that while every child wants to belong to a peer group, you can make a difference in the intensity of that motivation in your child. How? For one thing, you can offer a lot of acceptance at home. The more a child feels accepted and validated at home, the less likely he or she is to be desperate in seeking out peers. Desperate needs to belong can lead to dangerous behavior and result in unhealthy choices on the part of a child. In addition, you can cultivate your child's spiritual life. Research shows that kids who are involved in nonpunitive, loving religious or other spiritual experiences on a regular basis (particularly if there are other kids involved) are to some degree buffered from the nastiness of today's adolescent peer culture. Kids have spiritual needs—a strong need to know they live in a meaningful universe. Meeting those needs can stand as an alternative to having nothing but peers to build identity. Jim Garbarino and Claire Bedard's book *Parents Under Siege* offers some background and suggestions for accomplishing this important but difficult task. They highlight the finding from the Search Institute (based in Minneapolis, Minnesota, and accessible via the Internet at www.search-institute.org) that kids who have lots of "developmental assets" in their lives are more inclined to embrace diversity rather than bigotry.

6. Help kids have power at school. Kids can and need to participate at all levels, and not merely in a nominal way. When teens are listened to and feel they are heard, they have an incentive to contribute toward positive change in their schools. And all of the kids—the hicks, Goths, preppies, and athletes, not just the "stars" of the school—must have some way of having their voices heard by the school administration. All kids need to feel that someone at school is truly interested in their opinions. They need to see true change based on their ideas and input. How can this be accomplished? For schools to really value differentness and diversity, they must make room to hear from a representative from each major clique or group. Holding meetings on a monthly basis with this cross-section of students will help principals or consultants hear "what is really going on" in their schools.

7. Help kids get to know each other to minimize the fearfulness of difference. One effective and positive way of increasing the chances of kids' getting to really know one another is through positive group activities. Service learning projects are successful in bringing kids together from different groups and cliques for a common purpose. Further, young people feel good about themselves when they can make a real contribution to their community. Service learning is a means for promoting civic responsibility, moral development, and better understanding of others by working together cooperatively. (For more information about service learning projects, check the Resource section at the end of the book.)

8. Consider uniforms for your school. For some schools and some children, a standard outfit or uniform is conducive to safety. It takes away the element of competition among economic classes that kids use to taunt one another. Poor kids stand out from the others because they cannot afford to buy the latest trend in clothes and shoes; uniforms omit that struggle. Kids who are labeled "hicks" and "scrubs" suffer daily over the state of their clothing. Other kids who just "don't know how to dress right" also receive bad treatment from some of their peers. Again, having a uniform to wear eliminates the need to get the latest designer clothes or to figure out what the "right" thing is to wear. Research is not definitive at this time about the effectiveness of uniforms for reducing violence at school, but we believe that they can reduce taunting, teasing, and bullying based on clothing.

9. Support character education and its various expressions (for example, "respect and responsibility classes") help children learn how to navigate interpersonal relationships at school. Suggest that your

school district provide character education for school children beginning in the elementary grades. Teens we talked with said, "It's too late
to begin character education classes in middle school. By sixth grade,
you're already who you're going to be." While we might not agree
that a person is fully formed by middle school, their point is well
taken. It is easier to instill virtues of respecting others and taking
responsibility for one's actions in young children than it is to try to
undo bad attitudes and habits of teenagers. For more information
about character education and its principles, you can contact the
Character Education Partnership at 1-800-988-8081 or visit their website at www.character.org.

Being respectful toward others, even those who are different from
how we see ourselves, is the best way to provide a safe and caring climate for students and staff at school.

Chapter 5
The Many Faces of Bullying

S ean was the kind of little kid who always had a smile on his face. He was good-natured and happy. He loved to do new and different things and was a natural explorer of his environment; he was a perpetual action machine. His mother knew she had her hands full with Sean, but she loved his exuberance and his joy for life. When he was only two, he could just as easily be found jumping from the top of the refrigerator as building a precarious tower of soup cans. As a result, Sean had more than his share of bumps and bruises, but that never stopped him from his next adventure.

Sean was also outgoing and extremely friendly. He would talk to anybody. When his mom took him to the grocery store, not only did she have to keep him from pulling everything he could off the shelves, but as he got older she had to worry about his walking away with strangers if she turned around for a minute.

School was a challenge for Sean right from the beginning. Despite his love for investigating anything new and different, sitting in one place for a lengthy amount of time didn't fit well with Sean. He was constantly in trouble with the teachers for talking and walking around the classroom. His smile and winning personality kept him from being sent to the principal's office, but he began to feel unhappy at school. He couldn't do it right. The other children got smiley-faces on their papers for finishing on time, and stickers for sitting still during circle time. Sean never got those coveted prizes.

The worst part of school was that the other children began to make fun of Sean for getting yelled at by the teachers, always in trou-

ble, always in time out. The boys teased him and laughed at him
every time the teacher had to correct him. The girls called him "baby"
because he couldn't sit still and didn't get his work done. Even
though his infractions or "crimes" were minor, they set him apart
from the rest of the class. Sean began to feel the difference; he began
to feel sad and angry. Then Sean began to take out his anger in small
ways on his friends. He started to take their papers and hide them or
rip them up. On days when he felt really bad, he would hit another
boy or push someone on the playground. By age eight, Sean was acting in ways that caused his teacher to use the label "bully" on her
reports to Sean's parents.

When Sean's mother heard these reports from his second-grade
teacher, she talked to her doctor, and they decided to put Sean on
medication to help him sit still and focus better in school. Sean's
mom felt sad and conflicted about doing this because at home he was
the same smiling child, happy to explore and entertain himself. The
medication helped Sean focus at school, but by that time Sean was
already the target of his classmates. He was better able to sit still in
class and do his work, but instead he was teased and taunted about
the clothes he wore or his shoes. He had become an easy scapegoat.
Sean continued to feel bad and continued to strike out in his own
ways.

By middle school, Sean could readily do his work but was bored
and inattentive. No one recognized that Sean was not challenged by
his academic work, and thought his inattention was due to his early
diagnosis of Attention Deficit Hyperactivity Disorder (ADHD). Since
he was a bright child, he learned how to bully and intimidate others
through words. He no longer needed to strike back by hitting when
he felt angry or sad. He had learned, instead, to do the same thing
that had been done to him. He taunted and teased, humiliated and
harassed. He was no longer teased or taunted himself. His tongue
was sharp, and the other kids (as well as some of the teachers) were
afraid of his ability to hurt them through intimidation. He could
make incredibly demeaning comments about his peers. He knew
their greatest vulnerability—insecurities about their own bodies.
Sean had a group of boys who wanted to be his friend. Some wanted
to share the power that Sean had; some wanted protection by Sean
from other bullies in the school. Most hoped that Sean would not
target them. Sean was once the victim, now the bully. It had all come
full circle.

In Sean's case, he rarely got the chance to be a bystander—the other face of bullying.

Who Does the Bullying?

In the previous chapters we have seen the effects, but not the causes of why so many kids become bullies. What are bullies made of? Theories abound, and while there is no single pattern, several themes are clear. Some kids bully to pay back what they themselves experienced at the hands of bullies. They act from their own sadness and anger, feeling a need to get even and wanting to reclaim a sense of lost dignity.

> Those of us who are larger in size don't get picked on. We get made to be bullies. Nothing can scare us. If somebody calls us a name, so what? (Jason, 16)

> Now people are afraid of me; I don't know why. I've yelled at people and I don't back down, but I've never been in a fight *here*. People don't mess with me. (Marianne, 15)

Some kids bully as a reaction to the punishing lessons that they learn at home at the hands of their parents, siblings, or other relatives. At school these abused and much put-upon kids demonstrate with their peers the lessons they learned the hard way: Might makes right.

Fourteen-year-old Jamie's story is that of a self-described "gang" member. Administrators and teachers consider her to be in the at-risk group—that is, vulnerable to academic, social, and emotional problems. The other students think she is a "hick," and therefore unpredictable. Her experiences of being abused at school, as well as at home, inform us about how she came to act in violent ways at school, and about how she came to see the school as an unsafe place.

> In first grade, my teacher was a child abuser, so she would like lock the doors and hit us with a ruler if we didn't spell "because" right. I spelled something wrong, and she hit me with the ruler. I got in a lot of trouble that year.
> One time, she took me by the neck and dragged me all the way up

to the gym. My mom was picking me up that day and she saw the marks on the back of my neck, and she got right out of the car and said, "Don't you ever touch her again."

There were a lot of violent kids in that class. We used to kick the teacher and hit her—because she used to do it to us.

Then this year I got into a fight because a girl was telling my best friend lies, so I told that girl that she better knock it off. So she went behind me and pulled my hair and told me I'd better watch myself. So I went up behind her and grabbed her necklace. And we fought. She slapped me and I, like, hit her head, but my boyfriend broke it up.

I am . . . I think I was so violent when I was little because . . . my mom and dad got a divorce because my dad beat my mom. He was an alcoholic. It kind of rubbed off on me. He did it right in front of me. I don't remember a lot of things. My life has been really weird. When I was little I'd throw things if I didn't get my way. I'd punch the wall. I'm not like that anymore.

My friends are very supportive, and my mom has helped. The last couple of years at the middle school if I didn't get my way, I'd be very violent. I'd swear at my mom, and we would get in huge fights. Now that I'm going out with my boyfriend, he's calmed me down a lot.

Besides the violence that Jamie encountered at school, her story describes the secondary traumatization that she experienced in a violent, alcoholic home. It is common for children from this kind of environment to act out the family drama in other social settings—in Jamie's case, the school.

Some bullying is almost cultural in nature, in the sense that it is a kind of tradition in the school. One example is the practice of hazing that exists in many boarding schools. Another is the "traditional" bullying of freshman by older students. Molly, age fifteen, describes the plight of freshmen at her rural school. This is not ancient history for today's kids, but a fact of everyday life:

Here the freshmen are treated really badly. The seniors and a portion of every grade like to pick on the freshmen. That's just what goes on. Freshmen are picked on.

Who Gets Bullied?

Getting picked on is something kids think is inevitable. They can't see any way around it, though they say it makes them feel bad much of the time. They seem to feel badly that they cannot envision any way of changing this pattern. They are stuck, and in our interviews they were very aware of bullying's place in the Columbine incident. They can see how constantly being picked on could lead to "just snapping" one day.

Students are able to agree on who gets picked on every day and who does the bullying. They are clear that picking on others can make you feel good because it gives you a sense of power. For a short moment you are better than someone else, and sometimes you can impress your friends if you do it. But then they express a sense of sadness that some kids get picked on every day, even though they are "so annoying" they "bring it on themselves."

Teenagers told us that "autistic kids" and other "handicapped kids" get it the worst. Kids with "mental problems" or who are "slow or dim" are targeted for harassment. In focus group discussions kids felt guilty, saying that these children should not be bullied because they have "an unfair disadvantage." Boys particularly were clear in their opinions that these kids should not be continually victimized, but they were unsure that it could ever actually stop.

Much of the victimizing for disabled children takes place in the cafeteria, partially because this is the place where all groups of students come together, and also because the level of adult supervision is often low. Students at one school told us about a boy who is bullied at the table where he eats lunch every single day. These kids felt that there were no bullies per se in their school, just people who harassed some particular individuals. This is an interesting distinction that kids make, and is worth thinking about. If you ask kids, "Are there any bullies in your school?", from the example given above we see that they may answer no. If you ask them, "Does anyone get bullied or teased at school?" you will probably get a different answer. This is a good example of how important it is to listen to kids without preconceptions.

Here's something ironic. All of this "picking on" and bullying that the kids describe often takes place in schools where there are banners and posters all over the school and in each classroom denouncing it. We have to recognize that anti-bullying programs and slogans are no substitute for changes in the underlying school culture and social environment.

Athletes

Let's also remember that not all bullies are "losers" or outcasts. Some are very popular. Research reveals that some of the most intense bullying that takes place at school comes from dominant social groups—like athletes—who may have the implicit tolerance of adults in what they do, and sometimes may even have their overt support. In a sense this is "pro-social" bullying in that it seeks to maintain the dominant power relationships in the school as a society. The larger culture beyond the school rewards those who succeed or win at all costs. As school and military consultant Jackson Katz notes, "The bully is a kind of hero in our society. Our culture defines masculinity as connected to power, control, and dominance. The concept of power we admire is power over someone else."

Evan Ramsey, currently serving a term of 210 years in prison for shooting an athlete and the principal of his high school at age sixteen, said, "The principal told me to just start ignoring everybody. After a while, you can't take it anymore [the constant taunting]. I felt a sense of power with a gun. It was the only way to get rid of the anger." Evan experienced his peers taunting him as power *over* him. His response with the gun was not to even out the power distribution, but to have power over his tormentors.

Most of the time, even if you have a friend who tends to bully or persistently tease and give a hard time to other kids, as long as you know that he is not going to do the same to you, you can feel safe and confident in that relationship. That seems to apply with particular force to student athletes.

Josh, a fifteen-year-old athlete, was struggling with a moral dilemma. He knew that the other athletes he was friendly with sometimes engaged in threatening and bullying behaviors. It was obvious that he realized his friends' actions toward others would be at least unpleasant for the recipients. His body language testified to his discomfort with this situation as we spoke about it.

Yes. I can think of one who is always causing stuff. He's an athlete. I'm friends with him; he's good to me. I don't have a problem with him.

Other students at the same school make a similar observation:

> The boys who play sports—the athletes—make fun of the other boys,
> the weird ones. And the athletes hate them [the weird boys] for what
> they do. It's really strange. (Lizzie, an athlete, 15)

> The athletes at our school—some of them—have a major problem
> about alcohol. I mean you always hear about how much they're drink-
> ing. They're supposed to be really healthy and all that, be fit, so they
> can win, but then they do all this partying. Not all of the teams, but
> some of them. (Sam, 16)

Clearly the athletes in this school were involved in some behaviors
that are not deemed safe by everyone, such as harassing freshmen
and the use of alcohol during the season. However, few kids were
willing to talk about it directly. The major athletes (such as football
players) hold positions of enormous power in all schools. And they
are often the behavioral standard bearers, the norm enforcers, for
adult mainstream society. Students who reflect on this are uncomfortable with this fact of life for them at school.

The New York Times of April 8, 2001, cited an example of the ath-
lete-bullying phenomenon at Mountain Lakes High School in New
Jersey. Eric Koch, a senior at that time, complained that the new zero
tolerance for bullying policy "had upset the school's social hierarchy."
Eric was an athlete who participated in three varsity sports. He said
that during all of his underclass years, the seniors had dominated the
school through physical and emotional intimidation. Once zero tolerance was established at his school, he felt the freshmen students
were "getting out of hand." They were not deferential to the seniors,
like he was forced to be.

"Now, kids get away with whatever they want," according to Koch.
Another student added, "Senior year is supposed to be your time.
Now we're on the same level as anyone else."

With the zero tolerance policy for bullying in place, some of the
athletes were angry at what this did to their power base. They felt it
upset the school's "natural" social hierarchy. Unfortunately, many
students agree with this idea, that seniors should have the right to
intimidate others based on what they suffered as underclassmen.
Still worse, to this day, many adults agree also, including some
school personnel.

Of course, not all athletes feel similarly entitled. But the problem continues because it is a cultural problem that runs deeper than whether particular athletes are kind or mean. Listen to the following student's comments about athletes and their actions at his school:

> The athletes here are pretty nice, most of them. I do think they have a privileged status, though. For example, last year when the hockey team won the state championship, we had a special program in the auditorium and the mayor came over. When I was on a tech team that won the *national* championship, we had to go to the Board of Education and beg for money to go. When we won, there wasn't any special school or city recognition.

At his school, the athletes are not bullies in particular, but they get the benefit of special funding and recognition.

Elsewhere, a student who attends a small rural high school commented on the athletes she knows and observes:

> At this school, the athletes are the ones who are trying to keep their grades up. They don't want to get suspended for bullying or anything. So it's not really the athletes who are picking on people.

However, at Columbine High School some of the athletes took it upon themselves almost as a holy mission to ridicule Eric Harris and Dylan Klebold. School principal Frank DeAngelis, who himself had spent many years as a football and baseball coach, made the following telling remark: "This harassment by athletes on Eric and Dylan that has been printed time and again—I never received a call indicating that these people were harassing them. At no time did Eric or Dylan walk into my office and say, 'Mr. DeAngelis, I'm concerned.'"

This is a peculiar and alarming statement for a high school principal to make. Do high school principals expect that adolescents will walk into their offices and complain if they are being bullied at school, especially by the athletes? Do secondary school administrators really have such little understanding of adolescents? The sad answer, all too often, is yes.

Adults Who Bully

Adults who misuse their power make the majority of kids feel uneasy, unsafe, and powerless. Consider the case of Bill, an easygoing, likable eighteen-year-old senior. Outwardly, he gives no appearance of a kid who is upset or angry or uneasy about anything. He seems very comfortable with himself. He has many friends and is well thought of by his peers. He is an all-around "good guy."

However, in discussing his experiences over four years at his large suburban high school, he talked about feeling powerless. He believes that teachers and school administrators regularly misuse their power over students. He lives each day with the apprehension that one misstep could cost him any foothold he gained in his attempt to be a success at school. He could go from "a good kid" to somebody with a stain on his "permanent record." And worst of all, this fall from grace would likely have very little to do with anything he had control over.

This was a persistent theme in the students that we interviewed. Their perception is that decisions made at school reflect arbitrary power. As the students see it, major consequences from administrators and teachers can flow from very minor infractions. They fear being caught in a disciplinary action instigated by somebody else's bad behavior. This is Bill's take on his time in high school, despite his good grades and good attitude.

You're saying that you sometimes feel powerless at school?
Yes, at least two or three times a month. The teachers, security people, and administrators all have so much power, and they could abuse it any time. Then it could all be taken away from me—everything I have worked for all these years. It wouldn't matter than I have worked for my grades and to get where I am. It could all be gone by somebody deciding to give me ISS [in-school suspension] because I didn't have the right pass to go to my car and get my gym bag.

What do you do when you feel powerless?
I listen to music, talk to friends, I write, I have a therapist.

We must explore this issue of power and its misuse as part of our understanding of the functioning of the school as a social system, as a way of maintaining the authoritarian system in our schools. The ques-

tion we need to look at is: How does this authoritarian system promote or quell violence?

In April 2001, the day after the second anniversary of the
Columbine shootings, there was a serious threat to the safety of Bill's
school. In the interview that followed this threat, Bill was asked, "Did
you go to school that day? How did you decide?"

> I didn't go. I tried to weigh up all the risks. I talked to my brother and
> to some of my friends who were taking it seriously. My brother said, "If
> you don't absolutely need to be there, why take the risk?" That seemed
> to make sense to me. I talked to my mother, too. When it got to be 2:30
> that day, I felt relieved that I didn't hear of any thing bad happening at
> school. So then I was glad I made the decision. The next morning,
> though, I felt a little weird.
>
> Then it didn't help any when I went into school and my English
> teacher yelled at us, the whole class, for what she called "taking a vaca-
> tion day." Just like we couldn't have taken any of it seriously ourselves.
>
> She said we just wanted a day off and should admit it. I felt she was
> being very condescending to us about it. She always says, "You don't
> know what life is." She always implies that the teachers work so much
> harder than the students do. That's just not right.
>
> At the high school, it is such a condescending environment.

Bill offered another example of how he and other students are
treated by the same teacher:

> She tells us all the time, "You don't know what life is. I came over to
> this country on a boat from Europe and it took weeks, and I was sea-
> sick the whole time." By implication, whatever you have gone through
> in your life to this point is nothing by comparison.
>
> What do they think we are doing after school? I have a job, *and* I
> have three or four hours of homework to do each night, too.

The teacher is, of course, shaming the students by her behavior,
and she is being verbally abusive. What's in it for her? We can't know
exactly what is going on in her head, but it is clear that what she is
doing meets some need of hers to dominate and diminish kids. It is a
blatant misuse of her power, and also one of the reasons Bill ends up
feeling angry and helpless at school. This misuse of the classroom
platform, of course, does not take into account that there are chil-

dren in the class who do suffer from many of life's difficulties already.
For Bill, it is divorced parents and a father he never sees.

Another way that adults stimulate aggression at school is by using
intimidation:

> Adults make me feel safe because they intimidate troublemakers. (Ed,
> 16)

Regrettably, some teachers and other adults directly contribute to an
unsafe climate through their intimidating behavior. Not all the bullies
in a school are kids. Here we must emphasize that the damaging
effects of adult intimidation are far-reaching because adult bullies
amplify the effects of peer bullies. They do this by depriving kids of a
sense of adults as allies. We asked students, "What are some of the
things that make you feel *unsafe* at school?" Kids from suburban and
rural, large and small schools shared responses similar to these:

> The teachers. (several students)

> One of the teachers—he threw a kid up against the wall, and that was
> scary. (Shannon, 16)

> Teachers and administrators not taking notice of violent or threatening
> behavior make me feel unsafe. Teachers and parents need to be look-
> ing for warning signs in kids. (Molly, 15)

> Stories about Mr. ___ molesting kids and stuff make me feel unsafe
> around him. (Amy, 16)

> Mr. ___ is a sick person. He has problems that he should look into help
> for. (Sandra, 15)

> A certain teacher makes me feel unsafe. There's a lot of rumors about
> stuff he did. (Camille, 14)

> Adults and teachers scare me sometimes. (Cherise, 16)

> Surly aides who have nasty rumors spreading about them make me
> feel unsafe. (Conrad, 15)

What is the purpose of intimidation? Does it, in fact, serve the same function as "I can hit you, but don't get the idea that you can hit anyone else"? Unfortunately, researchers like psychologist Irwin Hyman have found that all too much of the time, teachers who are emotionally brutal to their students are replicating a pattern of emotional victimization they themselves experienced when they were students. Thus the cycle continues.

This is not some new development in education, of course. Jim remembers, as a young teacher in the late 1960s, being told of a colleague in another school who complained to the assistant principal about a troublemaker in his class. The assistant principal showed up for the next class and sat in the back of the room. When the same fifteen-year-old "acted up" again, the assistant principal punched him in the face, knocking the boy unconscious. Then, as he dragged the boy out of the class, the man said to the others, "anyone else who gives this teacher a hard time can come on down to my office for a meeting." Need we say that intimidation as an action plan typically does not contribute to the development of a caring community? Intervening quickly and with clarity of consequence is certainly needed, but the type of interaction that intimidation implies is simply a form of bullying on the part of the adults. It is not a good model of conflict resolution to provide for adolescents.

The Connection Between Teasing and Bullying and the Potential for Serious Violence at School

Josh Sneed, a "country boy" or "hick" from Powell, Tennessee, snapped after constant bullying and attacked one of his bullies at school. He says, "Everybody's hollering that they need to get rid of guns, but it's not that. You need to find out what's going on in school." His mother believes he was made fun of because he was from the country, poor, and small.

In a series of five videotapes that they made before their shooting spree at Columbine High School, Eric Harris and Dylan Klebold spoke bitterly of verbal harassment that they had been subjected to for years by other students as the main precipitant of their violent rage. Harris, from a military family that moved many times during his school years, talked about how people constantly picked on him and made fun of him—"my face, my hair, my shirts." Similarly, for Klebold, he described his brother, a popular athlete, as well as his brother's friends, as having repeatedly "ripped" on him. He felt his parents treated him well, but that was not enough. He expressed hatred for the "stuck-up" kids and said, in the video, "I'm going to kill you all. You've been giving us shit for years."

On the other hand, the justification offered by one of the students who engaged in the "teasing" and verbal harassment of Klebold and Harris was that in so doing, he and others were upholding some kind of school or social norm. It appears that he felt morally compelled to treat these two "rejects" in the ways that he did:

> Columbine is a clean, good place except for those rejects [Klebold, Harris, and friends]. Most kids didn't want them here. They were into witchcraft. They were into voodoo dolls. Sure, we teased them. But what do you expect with kids who come to school with weird hairdos and horns on their hats? It's not just the jocks; the whole school's disgusted with them. They're a bunch of homos, grabbing each other's private parts. *If you want to get rid of someone, usually you tease 'em.* So the whole school would call them homos, and when they did something sick, we'd tell them, "You're sick and that's wrong." (A Columbine High School athlete; emphasis added)

What Is the Norm?

What is this school or societal norm? Is it about homophobia, or fear or hatred of anyone who is different (xenophobia)? Is it about the school making it okay to belittle others—the hands-off, "there's nothing we can do about it" approach to children's interactions and to school management?

We believe the statement by the athlete above holds a great deal of significance for understanding the problems inherent in providing a safe environment for children at school. Parents, teachers, and administrators need to look closely at the implications of such a sentiment. Sadly, we do not think his analysis is unusual. If school personnel, families, and the community fail to do anything about this way of thinking, and the behavior that follows it, then all adults are complicit in enabling inappropriate and dangerous behavior in the school.

Shame, Violence, and the School System

This athlete's statement is part of a social system, not just the offensive thinking of one arrogant teenage boy. Researchers who study social systems (whether they are schools, families, businesses, or some other such institution or group) see common patterns. The first is that there is usually some informal mechanism in the institution to regulate behavior. Organizational expert W. Richard Scott recognizes that organizations will utilize "shaming and shunning activities" by various actors in the system to maintain culturally proscribed rules. Because the system is set up to survive and maintain itself, the norms and values of the organization must be preserved, even at great cost, and are upheld by people within the system who take on or are assigned such roles. At Columbine High School, as at many high schools, the athletes are implicitly assigned the task of sustaining the standards of the school. And, the means by which they accomplish their job are rarely questioned.

Researchers like psychiatrist James Gilligan have established a link between shame and violence. Shaming someone involves a loss of face, diminished self-esteem, and induces a sense of rage. For some people, rage and shame are turned inward and may result in self-destructive behavior, such as eating disorders, stomachaches, drug abuse, or even suicide. For others, rage precipitates an explosive action towards others. Of course, the same pattern holds for adolescents. Kids are often blind to their role in bullying and harassment. They simultaneously recognize the alien character of some of their peers *and* minimize the impact of any targeting of kids who are different. They may see other schools as having bullies and other students as being bullies, but rarely do they see it in themselves. This is important in allowing for their sense of safety.

Some kids we talked with realized Harris and Klebold at Columbine High School were "different" and probably "Goths," as determined by their style of dress and other behavioral indicators. At the same time, they were quick to point out that, in their opinion, no one in their own schools gave the different kids or the Goths a hard time equal to what the perpetrators at Columbine must have suffered.

The consequence for these students was that they could feel more secure about the different kids and the Goths not erupting into some form of serious violence. We posed it this way to students in one discussion group: "The shooters at Littleton said that the reason they did what they did was because they were sick of getting disrespected for four years. What do you think?" Here are some of the responses:

Well they probably said that because they got it worse than anything here.

Yeah, they were different.

They were Goths.

We have Goths here, too, but we don't go around and taunt them or anything like that. They walk by us and we don't call them names or stuff; we just go on about our business.

Familiarity Breeds Safety

To the question, "Do you have any kids here who get picked on all the time?" Tom, age sixteen, responded: "Not to that extreme. Everyone here has friends they can talk to. Even if you decided you didn't like somebody for some reason, you'd end up in a class with him and see that he's really cool."

This response points to the connection between familiarity and safety. When Tom says if you spend time with somebody in class you are going to find out that he is "really cool," it is evident that proximity and interaction over the course of the school year lead to a different and typically better assessment of a peer by other peers. According to Tom, it becomes more difficult to judge harshly and denigrate a peer with whom you spend considerable time. This philosophy must lead the way for stimulating and guiding change in the schools.

Those who appear to have the most difficult time in the school on a consistent basis are the freshmen and sophomores. They are hassled and teased, bullied and ridiculed for two major reasons. First, they are the newest to the hierarchy of the school organization. Second, they have less power, and those who give them a hard time believe they can get away with it. Kids and adults accept this as a harsh reality of school life: "That's just how it is for freshmen and everyone knows it," they say. Consequently, it is an ongoing problem.

Students, teachers, and administrators seem to be aware of the phenomenon and can speak to it in one way or another. One girl put it this way:

> I think that's one thing also, like seniors are going to feel safer than sophomores because they started to get close knit within their friends. They're like a part of their class and I think that if you can feel close to your class, you're going to feel a lot safer. (Janelle, 17)

She sees that the younger students do not have the same base of networks and friendships to carry them through difficult situations. Having a close support system enables students to feel a sense of greater safety at school. This sounds too much like what inmates say about being in prison, and that is frightening to acknowledge. In prison, you need your buddies around you to be safe. In fact, kids have repeatedly told us the same thing: "I have my homies to watch my back. So I feel safe here." This, by the way, is how some kids can answer, "Yes, I feel safe at school" to questions put to them by adults or on surveys.

We asked, "Do you see a connection between kids' being bullied and teased and eventually becoming violent?"

> Yeah, sooner or later you're going to crack. You can't keep it all inside forever. (Steve, 16)

> I think it kind of depends on the type of person who bullies you. If it was someone that you suspect could be violent, then that could be unsafe. But if it's someone you used to know, then you know they could be a good person and that's different. There are people in the school that I think could be capable of serious violence. (Courtney, 16)

Suicide

One of the ways in which kids "crack" is by exhibiting violence toward themselves. This can take any number of forms, but the worst is suicide. Chris Joyner, a twelve-year-old boy, committed suicide in the restroom of his middle school in North Carolina. He had been one of the many targets of "teasing" by others in the school. Administrators had difficulty grasping his violent reaction, saying, "No one considered the teasing more than an adolescent rite of passage." After all, they thought, isn't teasing and bullying merely a fact of life for children at school? This "rite of passage" phrase expresses an all too common belief.

After Chris Joyner killed himself, the vice-president of the PTA asked, "In hindsight, who was responsible for this child?" The answer should be obvious: Everyone in a child's life has a part of the responsibility for his or her healthy development and safety.

In Atlanta, Georgia, Brian Head killed himself at school with his father's handgun. He was a fifteen-year-old sophomore constantly teased and ridiculed by the popular kids or the athletes, according to his mother, for being overweight. He was their target until he made himself a final target. In his poetry, Brian said, "They see me as an insignificant 'thing,' something to be traded, mangled, and mocked. . . . In the shadows, I can sleep without dreams of despair and deception." After his suicide, neither the school nor a single classmate was held accountable in any way.

In the 1998–1999 school year, 2,700 kids between the ages of ten and nineteen took their own lives according to the Centers for Disease Control (CDC). For every one that died, many, many others tried. Every year, one in thirteen high school students makes some sort of suicide attempt. By far, the majority of those who attempt suicide are girls, but the greater percentage who complete their attempts are boys. The CDC further states that teen suicide rates have tripled since 1960. Suicides at school are at their peak in the spring, while homicides are highest at the beginning of each semester. Sociologists and mental health experts believe the increase in teenagers' self-destructive behavior has to do with the instability of the American family, parental abuse, poor impulse control, depression, and a general sense of isolation and alienation from caring adults both at home and at school.

Suicidal feelings and homicidal behavior can be all mixed up for some kids. Several of the school shooters have either committed suicide in conjunction with murdering their classmates and teachers, or have hoped they would be killed in the act. This "suicide by cop" phenomenon is described by the United States Secret Service in their Safe School Initiative, and it corroborates Jim Garbarino's earlier work in *Lost Boys*.

Many of our teenagers are living with thoughts of suicide. According to the 1998 Wisconsin Youth Risk Behavior Survey, fully 50 percent of all high school students have "seriously considered" suicide before they graduate. Many kids are living with despair. Much of the despair they feel is not so-called normal adolescent unhappiness. It is the result of the unrelenting daily emotional violence they experience in their schools. At this time, though, only 20 percent of American schools have suicide prevention plans in place.

Preventive strategies for suicidal teenagers must include a holistic approach to looking at the problem. In systemic terms, suicidal desires in teenagers are symptoms that not only are they in pain, but also that the system is malfunctioning. From the examples of Chris Joyner, Brian Head, and the school shooters, we can safely conclude that here is another way that bullying is taking an unacceptable toll in the lives of children—unacceptable for the teens who die and their families, and for the grief and guilt it leaves on the young people left behind.

At this point, no one is really sure how many young people actually kill themselves due to the rejection and humiliation they experience at school among their peers. Social scientists are certain that the rates for suicides among school-age kids are underreported and underestimated. Often coroners do not know what to look for and many times they, along with the victims' families, are unwilling to list "suicide" on a death certificate. Where kids have left clear-cut markers, like a suicide note or videotape, we can be certain about the link between terrible treatment at school and the child's conclusion that death was the only escape. Other instances are not so obvious. We have anecdotal evidence of the terrible toll on kids through the suicides of the boys described above, and through the murder-suicides of the now-infamous shoot shooters. This price—the loss of any young and as yet unformed life—is too high a price to pay for our failure to rein in bullying at school.

But many adults do not see the connection between ridicule and bullying, on the one hand, and serious violence on the other. Since bullying and teasing have always happened in schools, they have difficulty seeing its role in school violence beyond an occasional fight in the halls or in the schoolyard. The failure to see this connection is a critical breakdown in any attempt to build a systemic solution to enhance safety and reduce violence. Why are adults reluctant to see the systematic connections? Some of it is the result of their own psychological self-defense mechanisms.

As long as adults view those kids who commit serious acts of violence at school as merely unstable or mentally ill, the school as a system does not have to make the connection, and thus it does not have to intervene in the consistent bullying that some students experience daily.

But there is more. Often, adults in the system are not aware of the cyclical nature of the victim-bully interaction. It is discouraging to hear educators and mental health professionals asking, "Is he a bully or a victim?" The national survey research conservatively documents that at any given time, at least 10 percent of kids are both bullies and victims. For sexual harassment, this percentage is much higher. If we look at it over the long haul and across situations (home, neighborhood, *and* school), we can see that there are few kids who are exclusively bullies. Most have experienced both roles in one way or another, at one time or another in their lives.

Often, when a child is victimized by a bully, his or her response may be to bully back or to harass someone else. School personnel need to understand this dynamic in order to effectively intervene and eliminate bullying behavior in the school. It is necessary to do this for many reasons, not the least of which is to eliminate adverse psychological effects (among them being secondary traumatization) in those children who are innocent bystanders. They witness bullying and thus feel unsafe. Further, our research indicates that upward of 75 percent of children say they themselves feel "ashamed" when they witness someone else being bullied. Other studies indicate that adolescents say they "feel bad" or are "uncomfortable" when seeing someone get the brunt of verbal or physical bullying. This is made worse if the bullying goes unchallenged by those in authority on whom the children count for protection.

What Can You Do?

1. Be clear in your own mind about the answer to the question, "What is bullying?" You may have a sense of bullying, harassment, teasing, and emotional violence from your own life—both as a child and as an adult. It is important to think about your own experiences. What did or do you still feel like as a result of them? Did they leave you feeling bad or shamed in any way? It is important to pay attention to the voices of the kids in this book. They are saying clearly, in each chapter, that bullying is damaging to them or to others as they observe it. Also, an adult might define bullying differently from how a young person would define it. Two six-year-old boys cornering a six-year-old girl on the playground (or girls cornering a boy) may not look like harassment to an adult observing from a distance. It might be only after talking to the six-year-old child that you would find out about her fears. Unwanted sexual attention, threats both physical and emotional, both with and without weapons, and actual physical harm to people or property are all forms of bullying.

2. Be willing to see bullying in your child. Have you observed bullying of younger children at home? At family gatherings? In the neighborhood? If so, then you must be ready to act to help your child.

3. Take responsibility as an adult if your child is being bullied. We become like a broken record on this, but we cannot say it too often: Telling kids to handle bullying on their own is a dangerous, unfair, and emotionally negligent strategy.

4. Have a discussion with your partner about bullying. Here is an example of a possible discussion you might have with your partner:

YOU: Do you remember being bullied or teased when you were in school?

YOUR PARTNER: Sure, it happens to everybody.

YOU: How did you feel about it?

PARTNER: It's just something that you deal with as a kid. No big deal.

Or:

YOU: Do you remember being bullied or teased when you were in school?

YOUR PARTNER: Sure, it happens to everybody.

YOU: How did you feel about it?

PARTNER: I hated it. I remember that there was this one kid who used to regularly wait for me, and I got it from him for all of seventh grade. The next year, he laid off me. I grew over the summer and was taller than he was.

Then:

YOU: I've been reading this book about kids at school and bullying. It's called *And Words Can Hurt Forever.* It gives examples from kids themselves talking about what teasing and bullying does to them—both boys and girls.

PARTNER: I think too much is being made of this stuff. Kids have to learn how to deal with it. It's the real world.

YOU: It turns out that kids are saying they *can't* deal with it themselves. They need more help. When they try to deal with it themselves, their solutions aren't always very good, like what happened at Columbine and other schools.

PARTNER: Those kids who do that are just crazy. Most kids don't go shooting people just from getting picked on a little bit.

YOU: Yes, that's true, but it turns out that there is a big impact on all kids from the bullying they get at school. Some kids turn violent, but many kids begin to not like school, skip school, or get depressed. Some girls actually get into a boyfriend-girlfriend relationship before they really want to so they can have the protection of some guy while they are at school!

PARTNER: What does all of this have to do with our kids?

YOU: Well, what I've been reading says that most children experience some form of bullying at school, eight out of ten are sexually harassed at school, and a high percentage of them feel afraid every day at school. I don't want that for our kids.

PARTNER: I haven't seen any impact on them.

YOU: How would we know?

PARTNER: Haven't *you* talked to them about it?

YOU: I thought we would talk first, and then decide from there to talk to the kids.

PARTNER: Why don't you go ahead? You're better at that stuff than I am.

YOU: I really need your help. I think the kids may need both of us on this one. They might feel like they can talk more easily with one or the other of us. Also, I think they would benefit from hearing your experiences as a kid. That would get the discussion going.

5. Help your child distinguish among types of bullying. Your children need help figuring out the difference between good-natured teasing and mean-spirited bullying. They need to be able to discern intent. Does this person mean to hurt me? Does this person mean to be mean? Is this person my friend, does she want to be my friend, or is she definitely not my friend? These are some of the questions a child needs to be able to ask him or herself and to be able to sort through. Of course, it would be optimal if kids came to their trusted adults with these important questions. What we know is that most kids don't do that. If they talk about the pain they experience around the issues of bullying at all, they are most likely to talk to a friend. As a parent or caring adult, you can initiate a conversation at any time about the problem of dealing with bullying and "teasing" at school.

6. Decide to be a child advocate. Children need you as their advocate to help them navigate the school years. They need you to help them figure out both academic and interpersonal issues. Irene Claremont de Castillejo said, "How badly the child needs a mediator; someone who can understand both worlds—heart and intellect—and help bring them closer together." Even when teens think they don't need anything from you except money and to borrow the car, they still need your advice, your wisdom, and your occasional intervention on their behalf. Even when they balk at receiving help, or outwardly give you a hard time, inside it feels better to be cared about than not.

7. Remember to look at your school as a system—a system that currently includes bullying and emotional violence as part of its regular functioning. For the most part, school personnel are well-intentioned and well-meaning people. However, the help of the greater community is necessary to fix the problems inherent in our school systems. When mothers got mad enough about deaths due to drunk drivers to form Mothers Against Drunk Driving (MADD), deaths on our nation's highways were reduced dramatically. Mothers, fathers, teachers, school personnel, and other caring adults *can* make a difference in school life.

Chapter 6
Sexual Harassment and Stalking

despite what some of us would like to believe, sexuality has always been part of teenagers' lives. That is not at issue. The question is how and when sexuality will become an active part of their day-to-day lives—and what the consequences will be. Will your child experience a smooth and gradual transition from childhood images and experiences of sensuality to adolescent images and experiences of sexuality, or a transition that is abrupt and traumatic? Will your child's introduction to sexuality be loving, dignified, and grounded in a moral sense? Will your child be able to opt out of sexualized relationships until she or he is emotionally prepared to handle them?

Let's start with girls. Before we can understand sexual harassment of girls in particular, we must understand better how the social and cultural context of that harassment has evolved. In her book *Reviving Ophelia,* psychologist Mary Pipher traces the ways in which it has become harder for girls to avoid dealing with sexuality (what we might call the erosion of non-sexualized social space). When they are not ready for sexuality, it reduces the pressure and stress for girls if they can escape to non-sexualized space.

There was a time, Pipher writes, when girls could retreat from sexual images and not be bombarded with contrary messages—and not be made to feel there was something wrong with them if they did opt out. Then, there were lots of situations that were non-sexual and more focused on childhood. Now sexualized images intrude everywhere, from magazines and newspapers to television, radio, books, movies, and clothing styles.

What is more, Pipher reports, fewer and fewer girls can meet the unrealistic standards of attractiveness laid out for them in the mass media, most notably by pop icons like Britney Spears. For example, the Miss Universe of the 1950s was likely to be six inches shorter and twenty pounds heavier than today's contestants. This is all the more worrying because in the half century since then, the proportion of teenage girls who are obese has increased dramatically. This growing discrepancy between the ideals confronting girls and their physical dimensions puts psychological pressure on them.

Taking on this issue from another perspective, historian Joan Brumberg's *The Body Project* outlines how girls have become increasingly preoccupied with issues of physical attractiveness, rather than with issues of character. Following this trend within the diaries written by teenage girls, Brumberg reports that girls used to write mainly about their struggles to become good people and live up to their ideals. Today, they are more likely to write about their struggles to be thin and live up to the image of some supermodel or television celebrity. Instead of dwelling upon what kind of person they will become as adults, they focus on how sexy they are—like the popular music stars they admire.

How do these issues play out for boys? Amidst a spate of books concentrating on their development, two particularly focus on the struggle with male sexuality. In *Raising Cain: Protecting the Emotional Life of Boys,* psychologists Dan Kindlon and Michael Thompson deal with the pressures on boys to live up to a hypermasculine image. Similarly, in *The Adonis Complex: The Secret Crisis of Body Obsession,* psychiatrist Harrison Pope and his colleagues discuss the impact and stress on young men produced by increasingly exaggerated masculine body images in the media (like Sylvester Stallone and Arnold Schwarzenegger). *The Adonis Complex,* in particular, describes the lengths to which boys will go to hide their insecurities about their appearance and to enhance their size and strength. From weight lifting to steroids to obsessional eating, boys are not exempt from unhealthy responses to media-driven images of perfection.

Both books highlight the effect of cultural stereotypes of masculinity as power, assertion, dominance, and sexual prowess on the emotional life and social behavior of boys. Just as Pipher documents the increasingly unrealistic images of female sexual attractiveness, these writers show how the ideal male body has become more unattainable for boys—who, like girls, are more and more likely to be obese rather than dramatically muscular.

Gay, Lesbian, and Bisexual Teens

Yet another important aspect of the general sexual environment of kids is the corrosive effect of homophobia on kids with same-sex orientation—the gay and lesbian teenagers who comprise about 10 percent of the adolescent population. One of the best treatments of how gay and lesbian kids experience adolescence is to be found in a book by psychologist Ritch Savin-Williams titled *Mom, Dad, I'm Gay: How Families Negotiate Coming Out.* Savin-Williams describes how gay teenage boys and girls struggle to find their way through the minefield of homophobia—on the part of adults as well as peers, and even from within themselves. In our own research with college students, we found that 10 percent of the male students said they had same-sex orientations during high school, but only 63 percent of these males said their parents were aware of it at the time.

In our study of the secret life of teenagers, we found that 10 percent of the female students reported they had a lesbian orientation in high school, and that 90 percent of their parents never knew. The bottom line in all this is that parents should not assume that homophobia at school is "somebody else's problem." If for no other reason than that our own beloved children may be targeted, we should all be concerned that emotionally vulnerable kids are being tormented through this special form of sexual harassment that is rampant in our society and in our schools.

Kids as early as elementary school use "gay" as a kind of conversational or universal insult, even when it does not specifically have a homosexual reference. Even for kids who are not gay or lesbian, homophobic taunting takes a toll. Boys particularly live in fear that any act of same-sex kindness or affection is going to be interpreted as a homosexual gesture and thus invoke homophobic sexual harassment. This is one of the themes that Kindlon and Thompson explore in their work. One teenage girl we spoke with put it this way, speaking of her steady boyfriend:

> Everyone assumes that George is gay, just because he isn't some macho male. He sings and dances in the school plays, and he is kind and gentle. But for years he has been teased and taunted by other kids at school because they think he's gay. He's not, but it hurts him to have to deal with it. (Kinisha, 18)

A two-year study conducted by the Human Rights Watch organization found that schools often ignore harassment of gay students. Some kids become acceptable targets for bullying and all forms of harassment when adults fail to intervene to protect them.

When teachers and other adults at school do not stop verbal bullying of gay, lesbian, or bisexual teens, such abuse can easily move to physical violence. Research finds that homosexual youths are almost five times more likely to miss school for fear for their personal safety or to have been threatened with a weapon at school. And they are almost four times as likely to require medical attention because of a fight at school, according to the results of the important Massachusetts Youth Risk Behavior Survey.

Victimization Experiences of Youth, Grades 9–12

Massachusetts Youth Risk Behavior Survey

	Lesbian, Gay, Bisexual Youth	Heterosexual Youth
Missed school during past month because they felt unsafe	25.1%	5.1%
Threatened with a weapon at school	32.7%	7.1%
Property damaged at school	50.5%	28.7%
Fighting (past 12 months)	8.1%	37.6%
Fighting requiring medical treatment (past 12 months)	14%	4.1%

From R. Garofalo, C. Wolf, S. Kessel, J. Palfrey, & R. H. DuRant (1998), The association between health risk behaviors and sexual orientation among a school-based sample of adolescents. *Pediatrics, 101*(5), 895–902.

Estimates by the American Friends Service Committee Gay/Lesbian Youth Program suggest that homosexual issues affect nearly nine out of every thirty teenagers in any U.S. classroom. They may have a gay or lesbian parent, sibling, relative, or be homosexual themselves. At the time we are writing this, only five states have laws that prohibit discrimination against gay young people in schools, and there is no federal law aimed specifically at protecting homosexual students. (There is a form of protection under Title IX discussed at the end of the chapter.)

Who Am I? What Am I?

During adolescence and into young adulthood, many people struggle with their sexual orientation. Issues of "who am I?" as a sexual person are confusing. While trying to answer this important question, our culture and young people's peers insist on labels. Gay, lesbian, bisexual, and transgendered—these labels and categories are sometimes baffling for parents and other adults to understand. Imagine how difficult they are for young people.

Remember, acceptance is perhaps the most basic psychological need kids have. Parents who want to be supportive to children must be accepting; teenagers are certainly not going to confide in parents who are prejudiced against whole groups of people. A teen who is gay or wondering if he is bisexual is likely to be feeling lonely and afraid. How much worse is his plight when he cannot talk to his mother or father—or his teacher or his friends—about his fears or his joys? If you feel you "just know" that your child is gay or lesbian, or if you feel that "there's something different," raise the subject yourself in a kind and caring way. Educate yourself first by reviewing books such as the one by Savin-Williams, or pamphlets that are readily available. Two good sources on the Internet are the Human Rights Watch report entitled "Hatred in the Hallways" (available at www.hrw.org/reports/2001/uslgbt) and a general website at www.atlasbooks.com/glsen/ordercur.htm

Whether your child is gay or is wondering about his or her sexuality, it is important to give the message that you are always there as support, that your child can always come to you. Together you can find the answers you need. Being brave and kind will pay great dividends in your relationship with your child and for his or her own emotional health. Being scared and hiding will leave everyone (including you), isolated, afraid, and unhappy.

It is impossible to understand any human behavior without understanding the cultural and social context in which that behavior occurs. Having sketched out the sexualized world of adolescents, we can move on to examine the issues of harassment with an awareness of how it fits into the big picture of adolescent lives at school, at home, and in the community.

Harassment Hurts

Just as the larger society has become highly sexualized, so has the world of kids at school. This means that sexual harassment has become more aggressive and blatant. It is no longer confined to the kind of snide and rude verbal comments that many parents can

remember from their own school days. It also includes sexual harassment of students by teachers and other adults. Breaking through sex-
ism and homophobia in the schools is crucial for reducing emotional
violence. What's it like? Listen to fourteen-year-old Anna:

> Oh, sexual harassment happens all the time here! This boy, he went up
> my friend's shirt and her bra and everything. He did it to me last year. She
> was telling me about what happened, and I said, "Suzanne, did you tell
> him to stop?" and she said no. So I said, "Well, that's your problem, then,
> because you're supposed to tell him to stop!" You know? Yes, there is a
> lot of sexual harassment in the school. I see a lot of it. Unless you're go-
> ing out with a guy . . . other boys will go up to you and pinch your butt.

How else does sexual harassment manifest itself? Take a look at the
things teenagers write in each other's yearbooks. One we saw had comments written like, "Sorry I didn't get a chance to f—you in high
school!" And this was the yearbook of a bright, successful girl who graduated near the top of her class and was admitted to an Ivy League university. When asked about this, the girl dismissed it as "just the way kids
are." That's the point, of course—because this girl's cavalier words
could not hide the hurt she felt from the words in her yearbook.

When you really listen to kids, you can hear the pain that many
carry with them every day as a result of the sexual harassment and
other taunting that is their constant companion at school. Natalie is a
tragic example of the impact of this form of bullying. She is fifteen, a
quiet, overweight, and plain-looking girl. After meeting her for just a
short time, you know that she has a good heart and that she truly
cannot fathom why she is treated so badly by other kids. She says she
tries to be nice to everyone, and she has a shy, underused smile. Here
is part of her story:

Do you ever get picked on or bullied at school?
One of my friends—well, she *was* my friend—started a rumor
about me and this guy. She told everybody I had sex with him. And
I didn't. She's telling everyone that I'm pregnant, because I'm fat
and everything. But I'm not.

Does anyone else say these things?
Just a couple of kids who don't like me. They don't like the way
that I look or something.

Does it hurt your feelings?
Yeah.

So what do you do with the hurt feelings?
Nothing really.

Nothing? Do you talk to anybody about them?
No.

How come?
There isn't really anybody I can trust to talk to.

Do you tell your mother?
She knows about this. But she doesn't really know about everything that goes on. She doesn't know the full extent of what's going on.

How come you don't tell her?
Because she is always busy with my little sisters, like taking them to soccer and stuff. So I don't really have time to talk to her.

So do you feel like you just have to handle it yourself?
Yeah.

How are you doing at that?
I don't let it get to me no more.

Is that true?
It *does* really get to me, but I don't want to do anything about it, like get into a fight or anything. I don't want to get suspended or anything. So I just try to let it go over.

You try to let it go over? So that's your strategy?
[nods yes]

That's your strategy, but by looking at your face, I would say that it doesn't always work the best.
No. But most of the time . . .

There's no adult in the school you can talk to?
No.

The sadness on this girl's face and in her voice as she talked about the exclusion that she experienced was palpable. She is another example of what schools call an "at-risk" kid, meaning she is more likely to end up in trouble of one sort or another (dropping out, pregnancy, drug use, academic failure, and so on). As a result of this type of sexual harassment, she also has the burden of trying to hold her head up each day in the face of devastating rumors about her.

Kids say that having sexual rumors spread about them is the worst type of nonphysical sexual harassment that they can experience. It is no wonder that Natalie wishes she never had to go to school. It seems impossible that adults in the school are not aware of what goes on for her, of the type of treatment she receives, or of the sadness she feels. It is evident if you listen to her; it is easy for anyone to see who really looks. But it seems that even if the adults in her life do recognize her sadness, they miss its origins in sexual harassment.

Natalie says that her mom knows some of the problem, but not the full extent. These are scary words for any parents to hear. We want to know what is happening for our kids; we want to be able to help. Natalie's impression is that her mom is too busy with her younger sisters to have time for her. It is easy for parents to let adolescents drift off into their own space and world while they are at home. They are often difficult to reach, and we come to false conclusions that they are "just being teenagers" when they are uncommunicative.

If you have a "Natalie" walking around your home with slumped shoulders and hardly ever a smile, it is important to make time to spend with her alone. Make a regular date that belongs just to the two of you. Sometimes this seems like a lot to add into already overloaded schedules, but the difference it can make in relationships is extraordinary. If Natalie and her mom had a time each week, even an hour for a coffee date, her mom would slowly but surely hear the things we did. With Natalie, at least, all her pain is just under the surface. She wanted to tell someone. It was only a matter of someone taking the time, listening quietly and carefully, and asking a few questions. We think most parents can do this, too, with a little practice and with the determination to take the time. And teachers can too.

From Concept to Reality

In our research we find a high level of student awareness of sexual harassment as a concept. This indicates that the adults in their lives are educating them about this problem, at least at the level of abstract verbal instructions. Like any group of people, however, students have varying ideas about the presence of sexual harassment in the school. Because their definitions differ, some see more than others—and, as we see it, many miss the forest for the trees.

Most of the students we have spoken to believe that adults do not recognize the majority of the sexual harassment that goes on among students. The students we interviewed concluded that adults have very low standards when it comes to how students treat each other. Often what students see as sexual harassment, adults typically see as playful and mutually acceptable interchanges. Here is some of what the teenagers said when asked, "Do you see sexual harassment happening at this school?"

Yes and no. A lot of it . . . that *people would say is just kids fooling around.* It still happens. Usually the person who's doing it doesn't realize that he's doing it. (Tom, 16; emphasis added)

A lot of times it goes unnoticed. Well, the person who's getting picked on knows, but a lot of times the person who is doing the picking on doesn't notice. (Steve, 16; emphasis added)

Maybe every now and then, amongst boyfriend and girlfriend—it's rare. Maybe I wouldn't recognize it. (John, 17)

I've seen it here before, and I guess you could consider it sexual harassment, but they're just like trying to be mean to each other. Like calling some one else a faggot, making a comment about their looks or stuff like that. It doesn't seem like a big issue here. (Warren, 15)

When I first came here, people thought I was a slut, and they called me that. That was their first impression. I didn't know anybody here, and that hurt a lot. (Linda, 14)

There is some. There are some girls that I can't figure out why they put up with what their boyfriends do. (James, 18)

I don't see it: I bet it's probably done, but I just don't see it. Not like those physical fights. (Lizzie, 15)

Lizzie's comments indicate that other forms of harassment and bullying are much more common at her school than sexual harassment, at least in her experience and observation.

A follow-up question asked the students their opinions about adult awareness of sexual harassment at school. "Do adults see sexual harassment happening?"

> If they did, they wouldn't do anything about it, because they would just see it as flirting. 'Cause if you walk down our hall . . . you'd see all the couples kissing all the time. Because we don't have the no-PDA (public displays of affection) rule here . . . so if the teachers saw it, they wouldn't think it was sexual harassment. (Megan, 14)

Megan's observations are very astute. She is saying that as long as the school allows public displays of affection (PDA), it will be difficult for adults to interpret which behaviors constitute harassment and which are mutually acceptable interactions. A no-PDA rule, while difficult to enforce, would inhibit some of the acting-out behaviors that transgress the boundaries. Without such a ban, it is hard for adults to protect kids, because they would have to focus on the motive of the "perpetrator" and the emotional response of the "victim." Neither is realistic for teachers and other adults, who have many functions to perform and face large numbers of students—teenagers who are often highly expressive in some ways, and highly secretive in others. This leads some students to believe that even sexually *inappropriate* behavior is something that they have to figure out how to "take" or manage.

In our research, about one in four girls expressed a concern about sexual harassment. They were anxious about the uncomfortable sexualized attention that they received from the "hicks," who were the "most likely to say rude and obnoxious things." Some were anxious about sexual harassment from a teacher or some other adult in the school. Everyone who knows schools knows that it does happen; even elementary school students are not exempt. The Center for Children released data indicating that 40 percent of fifth through eighth graders say they have experienced sexual harassment by their peers. Fourteen-year-old Stacey shared this story about elementary school harassment and its impact on her:

> In fifth grade, I got in a lot of fights. They started because people were saying that I had sex with this guy, Jonathan. And I was only ten years

old in fifth grade. He asked me to and I said no, but these two girls told everybody that I did. So for four years now I've gotten bull crap for it. Anyone even mentioned Jonathan, and I got really mad.

Teenagers' Reactions to Harassment

In 2001 the American Association of University Women (AAUW) released results from a survey of 2,064 students in grades eight through eleven in public schools. They found that in general, 20 percent of all kids are afraid some or most of the time that someone will hurt or bother them at school. This held true for boys and girls, in suburban, rural, and urban areas. There was no difference among them.

Of the teens who were polled, 81 percent said they had been sexually harassed during school time. The harassment was about equal for boys and girls, a finding that had not changed since their last survey in 1993. Half of the students admitted to sexually harassing someone else. Disturbingly, 38 percent said that teachers and other school employees sexually harass students.

Teenagers have a variety of ways of reacting to being sexually harassed. More than half admit to feeling very upset or somewhat upset after it happens. Most try to avoid the people who harass them; about a quarter decide to talk less in class or try to change their seat so they will be further away from the perpetrator. For teenagers, the most troubling form of sexual harassment is when someone spreads sexual rumors about them—anything from saying they are gay or lesbian to spreading false information about being sexually active or pregnant. Almost 70 percent of kids said that if someone looks at them while they are dressing or showering in the locker room, they find this very upsetting and a form of sexual harassment. Finding their name written as graffiti on bathroom walls or lockers was also very disturbing, according to the kids in the AAUW survey.

Ellen was involved in a case in which teenage girls were afraid based on allegations from the past about one of their teachers. The teacher in question was assigned lunchroom duty, which increased the girls' sense of insecurity in the cafeteria. The administration in the school declined to answer any questions regarding this teacher's past behavior. Nothing was done to alleviate the girls' fears.

In another case, a custodian was harassing junior high school girls for months before any of them was brave enough to report it to a teacher. Although the school administration took speedy action, it left a feeling of dread among the girls that was passed on to others as part of the school's lore.

When boys comment on sexual harassment, they are concerned particularly about the bathrooms and the locker rooms—where, under little or no supervision by adults, anything can and often does happen.

> I don't like going into the bathrooms. I go in there only when absolutely necessary. Otherwise you learn to just wait until you get home. You have to always be looking over your shoulder. The locker rooms are the same way. My brother never used the bathrooms here in his whole four years of high school. (Steven, 15)

Many boys in the high schools say words to this effect: "I don't feel safe in the restrooms. People are looking at your privates, and you don't know what they'll try." Or, "I've had kids grab at me in the locker room. I don't feel safe in there. The gym teacher or coach isn't really watching."

Adult Response to Harassment

Parents and even some teachers across the country have asked us, "Shouldn't kids just accept sexual harassment as a part of life and learn how to deal with it? Why do we have to go to any extra lengths to stop it from happening?" We say put yourself in their shoes, even for a few minutes, and imagine (or, in some cases, remember) how it would feel. Imagine that you are at your place of work, or at a church function, or at your child's sports event. You have just come out of the restroom, where you saw your name scrawled on the wall with the message "————will have sex with anyone," or one saying that you have a sexually transmitted disease. You feel disgusted and shocked to see your name there with these humiliating accusations. And you wonder: "Who could have done this? Who could be that angry at me? Or is it somebody's idea of a joke?"

You leave the restroom resolved to get the graffiti removed from the wall and try to forget about it after that. As you leave you see peers who, though not exactly your friends, are usually friendly enough. Today, though, they avert their eyes instead of saying hello. Some look at you and whisper something to another colleague. Telling yourself that you are being paranoid, you go to the maintenance person to ask that the terrible writing be cleaned off. He tells you it will be there "a while" due to the need to get authorization from somebody to remove it. At lunch you look forward to sitting with a friend, but as you approach the table, nobody moves over to make room. Somebody lamely suggests that there is another table open. Stunned and hurt, you move on to an empty table, where no one joins you for lunch.

Perhaps thinking about this scenario, you can say to yourself, "Well, it wouldn't happen to me that way." If so, that's great. But most of us can identify with the hurt, anger, pain, and bewilderment that anyone might feel in a situation like this. Imagine the impact, then, on a child whose whole universe revolves around acceptance, friendships, and the need for support from peers. It is devastating. That is why teenagers cannot be left to fend for themselves in the midst of this kind of toxic atmosphere. Some adolescents resort to suicide to escape from sexual harassment and exclusion by peers. Others just go "underground" with their true feelings. Some strike out at their tormentors.

There are rigorous injunctions against sexual harassment in the workplace for adults, and many new programs to educate employees about what constitutes sexual harassment are now in effect. The child's workplace is the schools, but these institutions lag far behind in developing and implementing such programs.

Harassment and the Law

Often, instead of a reasonable program to prevent, identify, and combat sexual harassment, children's inappropriate sexual behaviors are being held to ridiculous standards (for example, being expelled for a kiss in kindergarten) or to no standards at all. It is obvious that sexual harassment of one student by others will no longer be tolerated by the courts. But what that means in practice is still often unclear.

A school district that violates the mandate to protect every student's safety is in jeopardy of losing a portion of its federal funds under Title IX, an amendment to the 1972 Education Act. Administrators should be worrying about the withdrawal of their funding if someone is repeatedly sexually harassed in school without appropriate intervention by adults.

On May 24, 1999, the U.S. Supreme Court ruled that "any school receiving Federal money can face a sex-discrimination suit for failing to intervene energetically enough when a student complains of sexual harassment by another student." (Of course this applies to teacher-to-student harassment as well.) The case, *Davis v. Monroe Board of Education,* started as a lawsuit brought by the mother of a fifth-grade Georgia girl who was being constantly sexually harassed by her classmate. Following the Supreme Court decision in the *Davis* case, a young man in Wisconsin brought a suit against his school district. The family argued that his constitutional rights were violated when school officials failed to stop other students in middle school and high school from bullying, taunting, and tormenting him after he acknowledged that he was gay. His school district had to pay him more than $900,000.

Stalking

Few experts have studied the phenomenon of stalking in adolescence. Some high-profile cases reach the mass media, usually when it results in a violent crime. What does it look and feel like to be a parent whose child is being stalked? Here's what a mother told us about what has been happening to her twelve-year-old son, Peter:

> I'm not sure that what's happening is typical adolescent behavior of teasing and picking-on, or something that's indicative of something more scary. I don't want to overreact, but since my child is apparently a target of some violent language, I also don't want to ignore the situation. Last semester I learned that my son was the target of what I would term "stalking" from a peer. He followed him around in school, stared him down in shared classes, made comments about "getting you," and kept a daily log of his activities (what he was wearing, who he interacted with, where he lived, and so on). It was rumored that he had created a web page titled "10 Ways to Kill Peter," but we were never able to prove it was more than a rumor.
>
> We sought the intervention of the school; spoke with the perpetrator's mother, who admitted her son is "difficult in social situations [and] doesn't make friends easily"; and felt confident that appropriate actions had taken place on the part of school authorities. We weren't 100 percent sure of what should be done, but assumed that the school must know how to handle this type of situation.

Yesterday we received a report from the school that another child, whom we've learned is part of a group that hangs out with the original perpetrator, wrote an essay for a class assignment that indicated he wanted to kill my son and his good friend. The fact that he is linked to this first child makes me view what could, under other circumstances, simply be a kid spouting anger and nothing more as something much more serious. I know experts say there is a lot of "hysteria" surrounding the school shootings of late, and that in general, schools are more safe than ever. But I'm wondering whether there are too many little pieces that have scary implications to ignore.

When we met with this woman, she was struggling to decide how seriously to take the threats. Then a six-year-old boy in Flint, Michigan, brought a gun to school and killed a classmate to avenge a conflict the two children had engaged in the day before. Now this mother knows that anything is possible; her son's tormentor really could deliver on his threats. It's statistically unlikely, of course. But statistics like this are not reassuring to a parent confronting the news on television. This mother is demanding that her son's school do more than just hope for the best.

The Principal Is the Problem

Here is an example of how systems perpetuate dysfunction. The problem is that the principal is willing to sacrifice a student's well-being to protect his own reputation for running an award-winning program.

What follows is the story of Tara, a lively and friendly teenager with many accomplishments and many interests. Her harrowing story of being stalked and harassed could happen, it seems, to anyone based on the school's actions and inactions. The story is told first by her dad, and then by her mom; Tara herself is still too upset about what has happened to her to talk about it. In fact, though she doesn't go to the school any longer, neither she nor her parents are convinced that the nightmare is over.

We think Tara's story is worth recounting because it captures both the emotional complexities of stalking and the frustrating process parents may face in trying to get their school systems to respond in a positive and effective manner. No short summary can do justice to this story, so we will tell it in its full, excruciating detail.

Dad's Version

We took Tara out of school, because we feared for her safety. There was a boy named Damian who was threatening her. Tara had very good reasons to be afraid of Damian. We all knew of his problems. He often told tall tales to get attention. He told the kids at school and his own family that he committed a murder, and he told everyone where he had supposedly done it. His mother took him to the police. His story was so inconsistent that they knew the whole thing had been made up, [but] Damian never recanted. He also told the kids at school that he was a vampire and that he was addicted to cocaine. His mother actually had him tested at a hospital, and he was often suicidal. His behaviors and his own request won him a trip to the state mental hospital. He was diagnosed as possibly being paranoid schizophrenic. We knew that he often beat up his younger brother and once stabbed him with a knife.

He also had a penchant for hurting girls. He hurt Tara twice, once at the bus stop and once at school. The school incident happened when Tara was trying to help him. He handed her and some other girl some things that he was holding to free up his hands. He then punched a cinder block wall with his fist. Tara would not give him back the thing she was holding for him until he told her what was wrong. He kicked her in the knee and took it from her. Tara was hurt, [so] she went to the nurse's office. The nurse asked Tara if it was Damian who had hurt her. You see, Damian hurting a girl at school was a weekly occurrence.

The high school [had] implemented a "mediation" program the previous year. Kids that had a problem with another student could request a meeting with that person. A faculty member would be the mediator and be present at all times.

Since Tara was having a problem with Damian, she requested a meeting with him. The mediation did not work. It ended with Damian screaming at Tara that he would "shut her up for good." This was no idle threat from a kid with his history. This was the point when Tara became very fearful of him. From this point on she tried to stay away from him.

It was a matter of weeks later when Tara was asked if she would allow herself to be questioned about some damage done to Damian's locker. She agreed to do it if I could be present. I called the school principal to make the arrangements. It took several days for it to happen, because of trying to find a time when the police, the principal, and I all had time off at the same time. The day before we were to meet, the police showed up at our door with a restraining order.

Damian's mother had filled it out. The document said that Tara was stalking him! It said that Tara had walked our dog past their house. It said that she placed herself within his visual range at school. It also stated that Tara was the prime suspect in a police investigation involving a death threat to Damian and damage to his locker. I went with Tara to the investigation meeting.

After Tara left, I stayed to talk to the principal and police officer about the restraining order. I had the document with me, and I let both of them read it. The principal said nothing; the officer found it to be ridiculous.

The principal's silence got me wondering: Had he told the officer about Damian's history? I told the officer what I knew about this boy. He was shocked. He told me that now that I had brought up the murder story, he was obliged to investigate it. Why hadn't the principal mentioned Damian's history to the officer? My conclusion is that this would reflect badly on the school; Damian was a big troublemaker, and the school had done nothing to stop him. They had documented nothing! We found out that no reports were ever filled out by the nurse's office. No reports were ever written by the principal or by anyone else about all the problems that Damian caused.

The school was not interested in keeping the kids safe as much as they were interested in keeping the school's record clean. No reports, no problems.

The school won an award a few weeks later for their "mediation program" and its effectiveness in reducing teen issues. . . . no wonder, if you don't report anything!

That is why we took Tara out of there.

Mom's Perspective

Two years ago, my husband and I finally removed our two daughters from the public school and decided to home school them. No, it wasn't because we are religious fanatics. The two biggest factors in making this choice were the lack of physical safety for the girls in the schools and a lack of cooperation from school staff and administrators in handling dangerous situations. Our oldest daughter was being targeted by a male classmate, and the administrators refused to recognize how dangerous he was or how frightened our daughter was. When our oldest daughter and one of her male classmates were in elementary school, Damian and she became friends, and I used to talk with his mother a lot. At one time we had similar family situations. Early on

Damian lost his father, and after that he began to display some aggressive behaviors and some antisocial tendencies with members of his
peer group. His mom was concerned, and tried to get some help and
guidance from school officials, but no one seemed to know how to
direct her to the proper people or places to get the help she needed
for him. Finally, his mother removed him from public school and
began to "unschool" him—a form of unstructured home schooling.

Unfortunately, removal from his peer group at that stage of his life
was extremely detrimental for Damian. His mom didn't go out of her
way to make sure that he was involved in extracurricular activities with
other home-schooled children. They didn't take field trips or participate in sports or plays, or any of the things that might have assisted
Damian in honing his social skills. As a result, he never quite learned
how to interact with his peers and, when he finally decided that he
wanted to return to public school, he was a social outcast.

Tara and Damian spent quite a bit of time together. She tried to help
him make friends in the public school, but he got teased a lot and, for
some reason, began to target our daughter with his anger over not fitting in. On one occasion, when he had been teased by other students
on the bus and Tara tried to talk with him about it after they got off the
bus, he got mad at her and elbowed her in the stomach. She told us
about it and when I spoke with his mother, she chastised him. We all
felt the situation was resolved after that, but we were very wrong.

About that time, Damian began running away from home and
threatening to commit suicide. His mother tried to get him some help,
but nothing she did seemed to be working. Then, one day, she found
out that he was telling people that he had committed a murder. She
was fit to be tied. She made Damian go to the local police department
and tell his story to one of the officers there, hoping he would back
down. He didn't, and the police were forced to check it out. No evidence was ever found to suggest that his story had been true, but he
continued to insist that he had done this.

Meanwhile, in school, he had assaulted a number of female students, stabbing one girl in the chest with a pen and kicking our daughter in the knee. He threw science tables across the room and punched
walls when he was angry. The school nurse was getting almost daily
reports about him sexually harassing the girls. He was in and out of
peer mediation because other students were trying to resolve issues
with him, but he would swear at them and threaten them with phrases
like, "I'm going to shut you up, bitch! I'm going to shut you up for

good!" Once, after school officials had called his mother to tell her that he had threatened to commit suicide, she took him to the local hospital for a psychiatric evaluation, and he tried to run away from her. He ended up in the state-run mental health facility. Still, school officials did nothing. They didn't notify the parents of the children he was threatening. They kept no incident reports when he assaulted someone, or when female students complained that he was grabbing them in private places. And they never suspended him from school.

Because in Damian's warped perspective, he believed Tara was responsible for all of his ills, he took out a stalking petition against her and requested a restraining order to prevent her from contacting him. We tried to help the school officials see how dangerous this boy was. We tried to get them to help us protect our daughter. We asked them for incident reports that we could take to the judge, [but] the school hadn't written any. They kept taking his side and blaming her for the troubles, even though there was nothing to suggest that she had done anything wrong and there was plenty to show how disturbed this boy was.

We went to court and, after reviewing all of the testimony and evidence, the judge placed a restraining order on Damian. We felt so relieved! Finally the school would have to see who the real problem child was. But it didn't work that way at all. They worked out schedules—one for our daughter, and one for Damian—to keep them from running into each other in the halls or from being in close proximity to each other on the bus. But as dangerous as Damian obviously was, and as much of a threat as he was to our daughter, they wouldn't suspend him from school. The principal told us that he was entitled to a public education, just like everyone else was.

We let Tara finish out the last three weeks of her academic year at that school, but only after we made arrangements for her to take a different bus to and from school and to have someone with her at all times when she was in school. Then we removed her and began home schooling her.

Damian continued to attend that school. We continued to hear from Tara's former classmates reports about him harassing female students and getting into all kinds of trouble. But he is entitled to a public school education, just like everyone else. School officials won't do anything to stop him. Who knows how far his behavior might escalate, and he is by no means the only student like that in our schools. And just recently, one of Tara's female friends was removed from that school by her parents. The reason? Ammunition was found on the stairs in the school. The school officials called for a lockdown but not until five hours after the ammunition was found, and not until after they had announced that they were going to have a lockdown. That's why our daughters will never attend public school again.

Stalking is about fear and dominance. Anyone who has experienced it will testify to that. When Jim was a young teacher more than three decades ago, he was stalked by a fired employee who blamed him for his job loss (which was true, because Jim had reported the man's sexual abuse of girls in the school to the administration). It was terrifying to feel so exposed and vulnerable, to feel that no place in the community was safe. And Jim was an adult, with resources and choices not available to most adolescents. Stalking is a powerful threat to psychological well-being and a terrible form of emotional violence at school.

Sexual harassment can appear in many guises, from unwanted remarks to dating violence to stalking. In all of its forms, it interferes with healthy social development and academic success. Adults need to decide that the cost of sexual harassment to individual kids and to communities is too high. As community members, adults can decide that schools and the behavior that is tolerated in them should reflect values of respect rather than allowing abuses of power. Schools can and should expect behavior consistent with high moral and ethical principles. Just as we teach respectful attitudes and behavior for one child toward another based on race and ethnicity, we can do the same in school regarding sexuality.

What Can You Do?

1. Take sexual harassment and stalking seriously.

2. Sit down with your child rearing partner and be sure the whole team is on the same page about the significance of sexual harassment and stalking. If you are still facing denial and minimizing, go back to Chapter 2. Once your team has moved beyond that stage, it is time to practice how you will approach the issues with your child. We suggest you sit down and take turns playing the role of the parents and the child in the conversation to come.

3. Once your parenting team is ready, find a quiet time to sit down with your child, in a place that is comfortable for all of you and where you will have privacy. Have as open and respectful a conversation as you can about this topic. Listen to what your child can tell you; he or she is, unfortunately, an "expert" on this topic and how it happens at his or her school. Read Pepper Schwartz and Dominic Cappello's book *Ten Talks Parents Must Have with Children About Sex and Character* for guidance in how to go about starting the conversation.

4. Talk to your children about the possibility that someone will approach them in a sexual way. If an advance comes as a total surprise, they will be unprepared to handle it. Give them some ideas for dealing with such situations in a tactful, healthy, and respectful manner—especially when they are approached by a peer. For the possibility that an adult might approach them, give solid and step-by-step directions like "Say no and run. Tell someone immediately, and call me." Kids need to know exactly what to do to extricate themselves from dangerous encounters.

5. After the conversation with your child, you and your team should take some time to "debrief." Talk over what you learned, what you still don't know, and how to gather more information.

6. Approach the school. Where you start may depend on the school's size and character. In some schools it will make sense to go right to the top—the principal. In other schools—particularly large schools of more than 500 students in grades 9–12 it will make more sense to speak initially to a guidance counselor, school psychologist, school social worker, and an assistant principal.

7. Find out what policies and programs the school already has in place to deal with sexual harassment and stalking. Find out how tolerant they seem to be on this. Do they consider way too much to be "normal" and therefore okay? Do they have a rule against public displays of affection? If not, what do they think they allow? Do you feel that they do not have adequate rules, norms, or prevention strategies in place? Remember Tara's "mediation program," which although it won an award was not particularly effective; you may need to see or learn about your school's program firsthand. Ask about what kinds of evaluations have been done on any program. One new program for secondary schools, called Peace Power, is showing encouraging results. It emphasizes respect in all interactions, and it includes the entire school community (students, teachers, and administrators). The workshop is available to schools for the cost of a donation, or you can read *Peace Power for Adolescents: Strategies for a Culture of Non-violence* by Mark Mattiani to familiarize yourself with the components of the program.

8. Find out what your school does to block Internet access to pornography and chat rooms. Unfortunately, while the Internet is a wonderful resource for learning, it can also be a source of unwanted and inappropriate materials. Children can easily find themselves in chat rooms that are frequented by pedophiles posing as teens. These predators are very clever at disguising their true identities and appealing to all of the vulnerabilities that adolescents feel—shyness, loneliness, and worries about their appearance, not being popular, or not having a local boyfriend or girlfriend. Many schools, aware that pornographic sites and chat rooms can be purposefully or inadvertently accessed by computers, have taken the precautions necessary to prevent this. However, it is important to find out from a knowledgeable person in your school what the status is. Again, your child will know the answer to this question, so you can start there. It is important to pursue this subject with other adults to get confirmation about how safe the school computer terminals are.

9. Remember that the schools and playgrounds will reflect what is happening in our culture and in our own communities. What are your community standards for overt sexuality? Do you have a number of "adult entertainment" facilities in your community? These are important questions because it is impossible to say to teenagers, "Do as I say, not as I do." They are constantly modeling themselves after what they see as acceptable in the adult mainstream, then taking the next step.

10. Suggest that the school administrators and social service professionals look at the Steps to Respect program (or some program with comparable effectiveness) for implementing in your school.

11. If nothing improves for your child, consider legal intervention. The only current recourse for gay students and their families (or other students who are being sexually harassed) is under Title IX, which provides federal funding to schools. Title IX, part of the 1972 federal education amendments, prohibits sex discrimination in any educational facility getting federal money. This amendment was originally intended to prevent school districts from favoring male athletic teams over female teams by providing financial equity for both. All schools receiving federal money can be held accountable for discriminatory practices under the provisions of Title IX. These monies can be (and have been) withheld from schools in cases of discrimination based on sexual harassment or gender.

No school wants to lose any funding and no school wants to deal with federal consequences. As a result, community members can, with legal help, invoke Title IX for protection of their children against discrimination. Families have tried this and won; there is legal precedent.

Chapter 7

Warning Signs:
The System Needs Repairs

S uppose your child does one or more of the following:

- Becomes withdrawn and socially isolated
- Experiences frequent nightmares and cries him/herself to sleep
- Has a significant drop in grades
- Has a significant change in eating habits
- Becomes afraid of walking to school or riding the school bus
- Seems frightened or reluctant to go to school
- Refuses to go to school or is truant
- Attempts or talks about suicide, or purposely hurts himself or herself in some other way
- Displays a marked change in typical behavior or personality

What's going on? What do these "warning signs" mean?

It seems every problem that kids might experience comes equipped with a list of warning signs. Bullying is no different in that way from depression, anxiety, or eating disorders, all of which come with their own "red flags" trying to tell us that a child may be in trouble. At the extreme end of the spectrum, significant changes in behavior could be alerting you to a potential suicide attempt, to sexual abuse, or to drug addiction. If you look at any of the many books and brochures that are readily available to parents and teachers in every high school guidance office, you will find that this same list of warning signs (with minor variations) has been offered for each of these problems.

But a one-size-fits-all approach isn't up to the task of formulating a strategy to recognize bullying, sexual harassment, and emotional violence at school. We need to think about two types of warning signs tailored to our teenagers' emotional lives at school: changes in individuals, and indications that the school as a social system is not functioning well.

System Red Light

Let's start with a different way of looking at the situation. Here is one mother's account in which listening to her son and his friend sounded an alarm.

On a beautiful summer day at the end of August, I was having lunch at an outdoor café with my son and his best friend. As we were finishing our sandwiches and chips, I asked the boys about their plans for the rest of the day. They replied, "We're going to check out the Army-Navy store downtown." Intrigued, I asked, "What are you looking for there?" With some smirking and laughing, they said, "Oh, we thought we'd look at some of their knives for back-to-school supplies." This response seemed completely out of sync with how both boys conducted their lives, and dissonant for how I thought about our "safe" rural school.

I didn't just let this drop as some kind of offhand remark, but instead pursued the subject with, "No, seriously, what would make you even think such a thing?" From that point the boys haltingly, then with ease, began to tell the story of their daily lives at the high school. They told of being pushed into lockers, of being punched by other students that they didn't even know. They reported incidents where their mutual friends had been beaten up in the bathroom by some gang members. They spoke of the number of guns and knives on campus and in students' cars; they knew who had them in the classrooms, and who flashed them during the day to intimidate others when the teachers weren't looking. My son reported on the hall culture in which you were to keep your eyes averted from looking directly at members of some of the groups in the school. If you did not or would not buckle under to this "norm," you risked being assaulted.

The more the boys talked, the more relieved they seemed—finally, someone knew about it. When I asked why they hadn't told me or any other adult about these incidents, they both responded, "Why? There's nothing anybody can do about it." At that point, I knew I had to do something, not only to improve their everyday work environment in the school, but to stop the other insidious aspect of what was happening. These strong, capable, "regular guy"–type adolescent males were learning to be helpless. And they were concluding that the only way around feeling helpless and being abused was to arm themselves.

One minute, I was sitting under a lovely blue sky enjoying the lively conversation of two very funny teenage boys, and the next minute everything changed for me—as a parent, as a citizen. From that day on, my world and my thinking about schools was altered dramatically. The lunch conversation took place almost a decade ago, and for many suburban and rural students not much has changed in the ten years since. In fact, things have gotten much worse for students in many schools, as is evident by the very serious outbreaks of violence at Littleton, Colorado; Santee, California; and elsewhere.

Risks and Opportunities

Listening is the first step. The next stage is to appreciate that the significance of any "warning sign" depends upon what else the child is carrying around in terms of risks to development and happiness. This appreciation brings us back to our understanding of risks and opportunities and how they accumulate in the life of a young person. Research tells us that the presence or absence of any single risk or opportunity rarely tells the story about a person's development. Human beings can handle challenges and difficulties so long as their number does not overwhelm us by exceeding the protective opportunities available.

Risks are the threats to positive development, and they are as varied as factors like suffering from neurological damage, living in an alcoholic family, facing racism, or being the victim of chronic child abuse. Opportunities are the resources and assets we bring to bear in coping with the risks—for example, having a strong sense of optimism, attending effective schools, and having at least one person who is unambiguously and positively attached to you.

These risks and opportunities include internal resources (like an easy temperament) and external assets (like loving grandparents).

What predicts harm to a child's development is the buildup of harmful factors combined with a lack of resources to compensate.

Kids can be resilient, but every teenager has limits. They suffer when the number of strikes against them increases to three or more (for example, poverty, mental illness, child abuse, and exposure to racism), particularly when these hazards accumulate without a compensatory buildup of favorable factors. Once overwhelmed, children are likely to be highly sensitive to whatever additional negative influences they encounter.

Compare this situation to a juggling act. The average person can toss one tennis ball up and down with ease. With two, he or she can still manage by paying close attention. Add a third, and it takes learning how to juggle. Make it four, and the average person will drop them all. Four is too many unless you have a teacher who shows you how to learn more advanced juggling, and you have a special talent for it. It is the same with risks.

The liberating message about this approach is that it tells us life need not be risk-free for our children to develop successfully. As long as we can inject enough compensatory opportunities into the equation of a young person's life, we can expect to see positive results.

When risk factors build up, it serves as an urgent warning to protect our children and to marshal our resources to build balancing opportunity factors. For example, when a parent asks, "Can my child cope with bullying?" we respond, "It depends." What else is in the child's developmental equation? How many other risks are there in his or her life, and how many opportunities are available to compensate?

One area in child development research that illustrates risk accumulation is the study of intellectual development. As risks like poverty, parental incapacitation, mistreatment, and large family size accumulate, intellectual development suffers, and children are less likely to be able to have the cognitive strength to master the challenges they face. In a study by psychologist Arnold Sameroff and his colleagues, eleven-year-olds with two or fewer risks had above-average I.Q. scores (113), while those with four or more had below-average I.Q. scores (93).

Average or above average intellectual competence is important, because it is itself an opportunity in dealing with life. Risk accumulation sets off a domino effect: lesser achievement, increased devaluation, and eventually an inadequate reservoir of the self-esteem needed for dealing with negative peer influences.

So What Are the Warning Signs?

Now that you are equipped with a basic knowledge of the context of risk and opportunity, how can you intervene at school to rectify a hostile or potentially violent environment? Listen to some warning signs from the mouths of students.

Basically a lot of stuff that goes on in school and things that happen . . . there's nothing you can do. Things that you see that you don't like, you can't change it. (Cheryl, 16)

When I see or hear people talking about drugs, I feel helpless. Or when I see it happening. You think some of the people have a better head on their shoulders and didn't do that. (Courtney, 16)

It's not like what you feel doesn't matter, but just that students can't do anything about it. (Greta, 15)

If there's a problem or trouble, it's the students who are going to solve it, not the teachers. I have confidence in the students. (Lynne, 15)

Sooner or later you're going to crack. You can't keep it all inside forever. (Steve, 16).

There's kids in my school who get bullied every day. The teachers know about it. They don't do a thing. (Jake, 16)

It is time for adult intervention when a teenager is heard saying anything at all like the preceding remarks. These statements are *system* warning signs. They indicate dangers inside the kids—helplessness and anger—that arise from adult nonintervention.

Cheryl and Courtney's comments are about feeling helpless, and powerless to make changes in "things they don't like." For a concerned adult, the question to ask is "What are these things you don't like?" Lynne says the students, not the teachers, have to solve any problems. If your child says something like this, you need to ask, "What are the problems that the teachers don't solve?" When "typical" students feel helpless to change the school environment, it is a major warning sign of system distress. When students who function well at school feel these ways, imagine how the more troubled, more marginal students feel.

Systems in Trouble

Students have many important things to say about caring teachers, and about caring in general in the school environment. A critical component of feeling safe at school is feeling that teachers care about you as a person, not merely as someone who produces academically. Students across all academic levels of achievement feel strongly about the connection between caring adults (as the kids define them) and feeling safe at school (as they experience it). The higher academic achievers did not report receiving more caring attention from the teachers and other adults in the schools than the lower achievers. Some lower-achieving students, however, do mention their beliefs that there is teacher bias in policies toward them.

Students are certain that caring adults make a difference in the quality of the school. Those students who did not experience their teachers as caring cite specific examples of how this lack is demonstrated. For example, students talk about teachers "pretending" to care by walking down the hall and saying, "How are you?" when the kids can tell they don't want to know, teachers walking down the hall with "their noses in the air," and teachers turning their backs on trouble (like an actual fight, or one that is brewing).

Counting on Adults

Demonstrations of caring are inextricably linked with the ability to trust adults. Of all topics discussed, students are the most thoughtful on the subject of adult caring and safety. We asked students, "Do you think that teachers and other adults do all that they can to ensure a safe environment here in your school?"

Not really. They should get more involved in, like, how the students see things. (Grace, 15)

No. I think that it's important to them, but there's some things that they neglect, or just maybe because they're lazy or because of their work habits. (Warren, 15)

Well, some teachers tend to just isolate themselves and, you know, like, you go to the class and they give you what you're supposed to do. Then they sit and type their e-mail. (Philip, 16)

It makes a difference, don't you think, when you see a teacher out in the community or after school? They'll, like, show up at the games and stuff, sports games. Teachers that are involved . . . like, they show that they actually care about you as an individual, not just as a student that they have to grade papers for all year. You just can relate to them a lot more. It's a relationship. (Barb, 14)

Teachers are just not involved in our lives. They teach, that's it. That's where they draw the line. (Sandra, 16)

Teachers need to take advantage of the fact that they're with kids and like being there for them. Their job description isn't just teaching us. The other half is they need to be here as someone we can talk to, not just as teachers. (Sammi, 15)

These statements constitute more warning signs of system risk. What else do students have to say about protection? Here's what Latisha, age fifteen, from a large rural school, said:

I don't feel the teachers go in depth enough. If I get harassed, if someone says something . . . it scares you. Earlier, a girl was following me and saying she would beat me up. She's kind of psychotic, and she'll go to any extent to do what she wants to do. I went to Mr. [X], our assistant principal, because it did scare me. All Mr. [X] did was bring her into his office and talk to her. My dad told him specifically, and that's all he did.

That made you mad?
Yes, because it didn't stop.

Respectful and Caring Teachers
Being respected by others and being treated with respect are central issues as adolescents become deeply involved in the process of constructing a self-concept and putting together the outlines of a personal identity. Disrespect from teachers or others in authority can be both very burdensome and difficult to comprehend. Adolescents rarely experience their own behavior as disrespectful or disruptive. Consequently, they take umbrage with any perceived disrespectful remarks or conduct directed at them:

Oh, the other thing is—like, it kind of sounds bad—but we're the kids, so I think we should be allowed to like talk about it if we don't like the teachers or whatever. But I think that teachers shouldn't be so unprofessional, and they shouldn't show it when they hate you. (Traci, 17)

See, the teachers that don't care and the teachers that are mean or rude really sort of cancel out all the teachers that are actually caring. They're just, they're that bad. (Karen, 15)

The government teacher for the eleventh and twelfth grade, she's more like *with* the students. She understands the students because [of] the way she is with the students. She doesn't talk down to people, you know. (Ben, 17)

I think if they made this school more acceptable to people; if they tried to say you have this open-door policy, where people are free to come in and out as they please. And, you know, we want to *love* anybody who wants to come into our school, because it's a public institution. Then, I think kids would feel more at ease in coming in and out, and people wouldn't feel the need to bring in weapons or stuff like that. (Ashley, 15)

Sincere caring by teachers, administrators, and other adults is a critical element for adolescents. It helps them to feel safe and secure while at school. When adults wait too long to intervene in student confrontations, or if they merely stand by while events unfold, teenagers do not feel cared for or safe.

I don't think teachers actually care about kids that much. (Amanda, 16)

Some teachers do, but other teachers, they just don't care. I don't *trust* the teachers who don't care all that much . . . about settling fights and stuff. (Lizzie, 15)

I think we need more teachers that really care. (Chris, 16)

If I ever had a bad day it's nice to know that people care, but you kind of get wondering why the teachers just talk to you when you're having a bad day, and why not on a good day—why don't they? (Ashley, 15)

These students are not alone in their belief that caring is the foundation for a positive social system in the school. Researchers like Nel Noddings and James Comer have documented the importance of establishing a caring environment within the school in order for students to feel attached to the school, to understand and appreciate the school as a community, to develop an adequate sense of self-esteem, and to meet their individual academic potential. An uncaring social system (one that is uncaring from the perspective of the kids, especially) is a warning sign.

Who's in Charge at School?

Helplessness surfaces repeatedly in our surveys and in more informal discussions with students: Who has power to rescue students from a bad situation, either of the everyday type or of the serious, violent kind? It is disheartening to hear over and over again from students about their lack of personal or collective empowerment. Adolescents reiterate the following propositions: "We have no control. No one really has any control." "There is nothing students can do to prevent violence, and there is no way to change anything." Students in one focus group of average academic achievers expressed frustration in their attempts to talk to teachers and school administrators to effect change. Approximately one-third of the students admitted that they had approached an adult in the building with what they considered to be a serious concern, but they were not "listened to" or "taken seriously," and that "nothing had changed" as a result of their attempts. One tenth-grade girl said, "That's how I feel most of the time—helpless. No matter what I say, the teachers and other adults don't listen, they don't care."

This dynamic is a part of the balance of the school as a primarily authoritarian system. All systems strive to maintain balance or homeostasis, even if that homeostasis is unhealthy. It is useful to the maintenance of the status quo of the school as a system for students to feel unempowered, or at least not in charge. Schools as organizational systems change very slowly—and as repositories of societal values, they work diligently to keep doing what they have always done. In that way, they typically meet with public approval, or at least they do not incur much controversy. The main function of the school, as for any organization, is to sustain itself. The system will attempt to do that even if it no longer appears to be in the best interest of its consumers, the students.

Students talk about their sense of powerlessness or helplessness over the possibility of a major catastrophe (like a school shooting) as well as violence of a lesser degree, like bullying and harassment at school. It is evident that some students take control when and where they feel they need to. When a teenager says, "My faith is in the students, not the teachers," this should be cause for administrators to evaluate what is happening in the climate of their school. Remarks about "control" and how "there's nothing you can do" indicate their relative sense of power. Josh, age fifteen, was adamant that there was "not much to stop" a tragedy from occurring in his school. Though adolescents do not admit to worrying very much about the possibility of a major calamity, it appears to be at the back of their minds and shows up in their comments on the illusory nature of safety:

I generally feel safe, but after Colorado I know that that is an illusion. Very little can stop that sort of thing. The teachers had no control about what happened out there. (Jacob, 15)

For me it's sort of like, I don't feel unsafe, you know. I don't walk around the halls thinking somebody might come in and shoot me now. But if I actually think about it, then I know that we're not really all that safe; that we don't really have much control. (Tim, 16)

I feel pretty safe at school, but I think that there is always the possibility for something bad to happen. And right now I don't think there's much to stop that. It would be easy for someone to bring guns to school. No one checks your bags, or anything like that. (Josh, 15)

A few students feel safe and in control when teachers exercise an authoritative attitude. As Simone, age fifteen, puts it, "The teachers and people with authority make me feel safe. People who are more authoritative have more control." Her friend Nikki, age fourteen, agrees: "The teachers make me feel safe. They have some rules but they aren't *really* strict—we don't have to break the rules to have fun."

Adolescents believe that "you can't control other people." The notion that problems have solutions is not yet a part of their understanding about how to take charge in life.

I don't know if there is an actual solution that you can write down or tell people what to do, like, "This is how you solve the problem." It's all about a person that does an act of violence and his choices about what he's doing. If his mind's made up, there is nothing you can do to stop him. I mean, you can't control other people. (Stephanie, 15)

Among the most disturbing replies to the question about feeling helpless at school are those of the three girls below. It is the aspect of giving up, or inappropriate acceptance of poor treatment and acting-out that is alarming.

Our school is safe because people don't go around hurting people for the hell of it. If they are going to hurt you, it's usually for a legitimate reason. (Fran, 16)

I honestly don't care. If I get hurt, it's my problem, not anybody else's. (Beth, 15)

I don't know; there's not really much you can do. I know a.lot of kids who say, "If the administration keeps increasing security measures, I'm just going to be worse." 'Cause I know at home, the more they discipline me, the more I go and do what they don't want me to do. (Molly, 15)

A few of the students feel as though they have a modicum of control given to them by the teachers. Some feel as though they have no control and have no means of accessing any, however, and some take the power or control that they need through fighting (either verbally or physically).

Why Is Feeling Powerless a Warning Sign?

Kids respond to perceived helplessness and lack of safety in diverse ways, including passive, assertive, and aggressive behaviors. A feeling of helplessness or lack of power to alter circumstances is intolerable to many people, so one way to gain some measure of control (at least momentarily) is by responding aggressively. This phenomenon applies to adolescents, perhaps more so because they do not have so many internal resources as adults to resolve the discomfort that results from having little or no control. The basis of most aggressive behavior is a deep sense of helplessness; however, some aggression results from learned behavior, neurological stimulation, and the "kick the dog" syndrome.

In this syndrome, if I have been kicked and the only thing available for me to kick without much chance of penalty is my dog, then the dog becomes an easy target. This implies behavior that originates in abusive families also involves feelings of helplessness. There is not much research about the connections between hopelessness and helplessness, on the one hand, and bullying and violence on the other. But researchers from Europe and Australia are taking the lead in understanding how these connections may operate. In some children, the best indicator of a feeling of helplessness is their aggressive behavior or appearance. Those children who *look the least* helpless, in other words, may in fact *feel the most* helpless. An effective way to ward off feeling fearful inside is to present a fearsome exterior. This appearance bolsters the adolescent and hopefully, like a flower or an animal with a frightening exterior, keeps predators at a distance. Unfortunately, this strategy tends to backfire in that it subjects the children who employ it to further ridicule for their differentness.

Scapegoats: Another Warning Sign of a Sick System

Scapegoats are an age-old concept dating back to times when people literally tied symbols of their troubles to the back of a goat, then pushed it off a cliff in hopes of securing better luck in the near future. They got rid of the goat, and thought they were getting rid of everything that was bringing them bad fortune.

According to psychiatrists Murray Bowen and Salvador Minuchin, systems "choose" scapegoats as a way of maintaining their balance, or homeostasis. These scapegoats are often the people in the system who are most sensitive to what is going on. Systems utilize scapegoats as a means to resist change; if there is someone to blame, then no one has to look to himself or herself for personal change to make things better. Some children are scapegoated or stigmatized based on physical attributes, specific mannerisms, or ways they behave. Others are scapegoated because of some special experience or history they have, like being the new kid in a school or having done something embarrassing that becomes part of the peer folklore.

Children learn from us, and they too engage in scapegoating others. Children tend to blame the kids who are targeted by bullies for the bad treatment they receive. They see the victims as weak, nerds, or as deserving what they get.

At school, kids who are bullied are thus scapegoated by the system many times over—first by the bullies, and a second time by the other kids who see them as causing their own problems. The process continues when the system (in this instance, the school's adults) does not step in and intervene in an effective way on their behalf. Of course, kids are directly scapegoated within the system when they are bullied or intimidated by teachers, coaches, and other school personnel who ridicule or tease for their own reasons. The poisonous process comes full circle when adult participation in scapegoating ensures that the other children will see these kids as "fair game." However confusing or complex this dance may appear to you, you need to believe that you are witnessing a strong warning sign of an ailing system. This is not the kind of system that can or will support the healthy growth of children.

What Can You Do?

1. Listen to your kids. As generic as this advice may appear, your own teenagers, their friends, and the kids who shop in your store, bag your groceries, mow your lawn, or attend your church will know more than you know about how the system is functioning at school.

2. Talk to your kids and the adults at your school about the system warning signs. In summary, here are some of the signs to look for that indicate that your school system is not functioning as well as it needs to for kids to feel safe:

- When teachers and other adults are more concerned about their own safety than that of the kids.
- When you hear kids saying, "There's nothing anybody can do to change it" (whether "it" is bullying, disrespectful interactions, or the school climate). These students are saying that they feel helpless. This encourages them to manufacture their own immature ways of feeling empowered, such as by bringing weapons for defense to school.
- When you hear kids say, "The teachers have no control. I put my trust in the other students." They are saying they cannot count on the adults to protect them. The feeling that they have to take

matters into their own hands encourages students to form groups for self-protection. Some will join healthier groups than others, who may end up in "gangs."

• When kids start saying, "Sometimes the teachers just walk by if there's a fight. And you know they hear all the terrible crap kids say to one another. They don't do anything about it." Kids are telling us that we are letting them down. They know adults are allowing and permitting a disrespectful, emotionally hostile environment.

• When the students (and some of the adults) start to say, "It's the druggies [or the Goths, or any other particular group] who are 'the problem' in our school. If it weren't for them, everything would be okay here." When that happens, the members of the named group have become scapegoats; no one else needs to take responsibility for the disrespectful atmosphere of the school. This encourages continued taunting and bullying of the scapegoated group.

3. Know your child. Try to put together a profile of your child's temperament—as you remember it from early childhood, and as it has been expressing itself over the years since then.

4. Talk frequently with your parenting partner about what you see and hear in your own home and in the surrounding community. Meet with your group of concerned parents and other citizens in the community to discuss these concepts and how a "broken system" is playing a part in the continuance of bullying and violence in your school and community. The group or team needs to decide what actions can and should be taken to change the system—for real change, not just something superficial.

5. Discuss the concepts of "Who's in charge?" and who should be in charge. What should being in charge look like? Discuss the value of student empowerment to counteract feelings of helplessness at school and in the community. How might you, as adults, encourage true empowerment for kids? What is appropriate?

6. Call in an outside evaluator. During this time when so many districts and parents are concerned about safe schools and neighborhoods, sometimes it is advantageous to contact someone from outside the community. An outside evaluator who understands how systems and schools work can see with fresh eyes and make an objective assessment of your particular circumstances. From this assessment, recommendations for effective change flow.

Chapter 8
Taking It

Some kids can get violent, but most just take it and deal with it. The really more mature ones just take it and go, "Whatever." If people turn into, like, 'your worst enemy,' that's like just wrong, and you'll hate yourself for it [being violent]. (Megan, 14)

Some people are really rude and disrespectful; they try to push people around. They make fun of people. You get a nervous feeling in your stomach. There are people that it happens to everyday. A lot of people just try to ignore it. *I think it takes a really mentally strong person to ignore it and forget it immediately.* And I don't think many people do. (Warren, 15, emphasis added)

One of our greatest lessons has been to come to understand what teenagers mean by the phrase "taking it." They mean that everyone must figure out how to interpret and often endure the verbal and physical abuse that is directed at them by other kids. The fact is that few kids' lives are totally free of teasing, and most of them recognize that teasing can be playful or mean-spirited. In the case of mean-spirited teasing, an adolescent has to work doubly hard to determine a course of action. The options seem to include doing nothing and showing no response to the antagonist, saying something innocuous in response (like "Whatever") and going on about one's business, or retaliating in kind.

Retaliation risks an escalated encounter with that person or group, at that moment or at some time in the future. Rarely, though, do students speak of approaching an adult to deal with teasing. Talking with an adult is usually reserved for concern over the perceived threat of physical violence, or the experience of one or more episodes of such violence.

The Ability to Take It

If I get picked on, I don't get upset about it. (Todd, 16)

People tease them and . . . they get all worked up over nothing. They get into a frenzy. They get violent with people over nothing. (Courtney, 16)

You have to deal with those problems on a daily basis. If you let things build up, then of course something might happen. But you can't let that happen. (Nicole, 15)

The outcome for those who cannot or will not take it is that they may strike back in some manner ("They get into a frenzy, they get violent," as Courtney put it). As far as most students are concerned, anyone who can't take it has mental health problems; if he or she acts on their upset, that person is a troublemaker. Adults often agree, at least as far as the necessity of "taking it" goes. What is known about the factors that dispose someone to "take it" or to be unable to continue to do so? While there is little research specifically on this topic, perhaps we can generalize from studies on coping and resilience.

Coping and Resilience

Research on how kids deal with stressful early experiences points to a series of conditions and characteristics that promote successful coping. The factors include the following:

- Actively trying to cope with stress (rather than just reacting)
- Cognitive competence (at least an average level of intelligence)
- Experiences of success and corresponding self-confidence and positive self-esteem
- Temperamental characteristics that favor active coping attempts

and positive relationships with others (for example, activity level and sociability) rather than passive withdrawal

- A stable emotional relationship with at least one parent or other important person in the child's life
- An open, supportive educational climate and parental model of behavior that encourages constructive coping with problems
- Social support from people outside the family

Each of these elements increases the likelihood that a child will be able to manage the difficulties he or she faces. Note that some of these elements are characteristics of the child (like intelligence), while others are characteristics of his or her relationships (like having someone who is "crazy" about you). Still others are characteristics of the child's social environment (like the kind of school attended). There are no guarantees in life, but the research is clear on this point: the more of these elements a child has, the more likely that child is to be resilient in the face of difficult situations.

What Is a Normal Response to "Normal" Teasing?

We asked, "How do you feel about the teasing at school?" Here are some of the responses we got:

I feel fine about it, 'cause it's sort of a way of breaking the ice, and people get talking. (Steve, 16)

Go to any high school full of teenagers. There's bound to be disrespect. (Ryan, 16)

It's just a tease. Not enough to really make me do something about it, but enough to know it's kinda there still. Depends on what it is. Depends on if it's kind of friendly or mean. If it's mean I let it slide the first time, then if they do it again, I'd do something about it. I don't know what. Talk to someone about it. (Tom, 17)

There will always be people who put other kids down to make them[selves] feel superior. There will always be a popular group. There will always be the nerds. (Danielle, 14)

I can see where that kind of stuff would do something bad. Some kids wouldn't know how to react to teasing and might do something violent. Everyone gets teased sometimes—I don't know. I haven't really noticed anyone taking it strange or anything. (Josh, 15)

Kids say stuff. You've just got to ignore it and go on with your life. (Marianne, 15)

I try to ignore it. I'll ignore it and think about it later. Then it comes back. It depends on the person. Usually I can put up with it for a pretty long time, then I just get to the point where I just get sick of it—so I like tell him off and say something to somebody until it stops, and sometimes it does stop. (Warren, 15)

Harassment resides in a gray area between right and wrong. As kids see it, some aggressive responses are justified and understandable, but lethal violence in response to harassment is clearly wrong. Adolescents believe that some of their peers bully and harass to get attention. In that case, they have some effective strategies. As Megan described it, "If someone is busting on you, you just call them a 'scrub' or something. You can't let it bother you. They just want attention. I know that because that's what I used to do."

Anna, age fifteen, agrees with the attention-getting or "positive" aspect of Megan's comments about bullying. She said, "Well, my group, we have a sort of gang that's been made up of us since seventh grade. So then if someone messes with us, even the tiniest bit, we say, 'Do you want to fight about it?' We actually try to get something going. For something to do. This school is so boring."

Adolescents have a lot to say about their own coping abilities, those of their peers, and the kinds of help they think they need. In one focus group, twenty teens from tenth grade in a suburban high school shared their opinions on whose responsibility it is to keep schools safe. Their opinions diverged, but in their answers we get an understanding of how they are attempting to figure this out, and how they use their thinking on this subject to maximize their ability to "take it."

ELLEN: Whose job is it to make the school a safe place to be?
REBECCA: Everybody.
TIM: I think it's mostly the students.

ELLEN: Can you tell me more about that?

TIM: Yeah, if there's somebody punching you, or just making other people feel unsafe, there should be peer pressure against that.

SARAH: Half the time the teachers don't want . . . really don't have a clue about what's going on. So if there's anything—if there's anything that needs to be done about something that isn't right, the teachers aren't going to do it. It's not the teachers, because the teachers don't know what's going on.

ELLEN: Well what do you make of that—"the teachers don't know what's going on?"

SARAH: Well, they don't really need to, unless someone's going to stand up and start throwing punches. Then maybe a teacher needs to be involved. But all the little stuff, you know, that goes on every day is up to the students. Like if someone's going to be stupid, you're going to tell that person they're being stupid. And it's your job; it's not the teachers' job. They don't get paid to do that.

DEENA: Because so many of the teachers don't really want to get involved, because they think it's our job to handle everything.

MATT: Half the teachers don't get involved; they just stand there and watch.

ELLEN: They watch? How do you feel about that?

CLAIRE: Mostly we can handle the little stuff. I mean it's just stupid things that happen every day.

AMBER: Maybe some kids, their parents may not be there to tell them what behavior's right and wrong, so teachers need to let kids know. Some kids need a second kind of parent there to inform them and tell them what they're doing is wrong, because sometimes at home they may not get that.

RYAN: Yes, a second parent.

SEVERAL GIRLS: Yeah, yeah, definitely.

KELSY: I think a lot of why teachers aren't involved is because they're not on our level. They're not a teenager; they're grown up. I mean, yes, they were once a teenager, but they don't want to do that again. And they're not going to go out on a Friday night with you. It's not going to happen, and with that they're just not involved in our lives that way. They teach; that's it. If someone throws punches they might get involved, but that's it. That's where the line is.

LINDSAY: I think that the teachers don't need to get involved,

because I think it's important to really handle problems by yourself.

ELLEN: All right. I would like your opinion on this. Do you think
that teachers ought to be paying attention to when people are
picked on or left out at school?

SHANE: Yeah, it might help prevent some violence.

HEATHER: I can see that. But to me, if I'm going to be told that
something I do is wrong and my parents tell me, then I respect
that, because they honestly care about me. But I don't think
teachers actually care about kids that much.

KELLY: If they tell me *not* do something, I don't really care much
about that, because I don't see how they [the teachers] could
care one way or the other.

NICOLE: Well, I think maybe in elementary school or something,
teachers should teach right and wrong. But if you haven't
learned by tenth grade, then—I mean, you should know what's
right and what's wrong by the time you're in high school.

Peer pressure, a second parent, caring teachers, and trust—these
are the variables that the kids in this focus group brought forward in
discussing how to handle issues of school safety and learning to "take
it" in high school. Some of the members of the group indicate that
even in high school, kids need reminders about what is the right
course of action and what is just plain wrong; they need a second parent during the course of the school day. Other teens aren't so sure.
They believe it is too late for extra parenting on the subject of moral
behavior by the time kids are in high school.

It is particularly interesting to notice how much of the responsibility for safety they place on themselves. Some of this emphasis originates in a belief that they should be able to handle most everyday
hassles themselves. They should, in short, be able to "take it." Some of
their conclusions are based on their perceptions that the adults in the
building don't really care about them all that much anyway. (Whether
these perceptions are "true" or not about what adults actually feel, is
not the relevant point.) These kids say that adults might step in if
punches are being thrown; otherwise, you have to fend for yourself.

The bus is a particularly vulnerable spot during the school day
where kids have to figure out how to "take it." There is only so much
supervision that one adult can provide while driving a bus. This is
what Paula figured out:

There's lots of fights on my bus. I used to be afraid when I was younger. People talk a lot of crap. But I'm one of the oldest ones now, so there's nothing to be afraid of on my bus. But on other buses, definitely.

There's one girl who fights all the time on my bus. Everybody is fighting with her, 'cause she starts crap with everybody. And then she blames it all on everyone else that they're ganging up on her.

Is this verbal fighting or physically fighting?
Both.

What do you do?
I just ignore it. I ignore her. Now most of the time I don't even see it anymore.

Paula believes that she is not as afraid because she is one of the oldest ones on the bus. It probably is true that as a senior, she has less to fear, since it is the younger kids who get most of the attention from bullies. As we will see in Chapter 9, though, some of what allows Paula to feel safer is her relative certainty about the behavior of most of the others on her bus. She can predict their typical actions and reactions. If she had to take a different bus, that might be cause for concern.

One way that kids go about fending for themselves, and trying to take it, is to categorize what happens—all the bullying, sexual harassment, and intimidation—as "stupid things that happen everyday." Holding tight to that perception allows some kids to shrug off much of the unpleasant verbal and physical acts they hear and see. For others, however, this prescription is not so easy.

When Suzanne was interviewed, she was a cheerful, engaging fifteen-year-old who had just completed her freshman year of high school. She was a dedicated and talented athlete. Aside from her sports activities, though, she described her first year at the school as "terrible" due to the lack of safety she experienced. In her interview with Ellen, Suzanne described what made her feel unsafe at school and her strategies for "taking it" for the year.

How much of the time did you feel unsafe at school this year?
Not everyday, but more than half the time.

What were the main things that made the school feel unsafe for you?
The gangs are the main things that make it not safe. They fight
over dumb things, like getting accidentally pushed in the hall or
talking to somebody else's boyfriend or girlfriend.

Is there more than one gang at the school?
Yes, but I don't know their names. They advertise on flyers that
they put up around the school for parties that they hold.

Are there other things that make you feel unsafe at school?
Teachers who can't control their classrooms. My global studies
teacher was really bad. Kids would get into fights in the classroom,
throw things, and talk back to the teacher. It was really bad, and he
couldn't do anything about it. One time in April a kid set off a
bunch of firecrackers right during class.

How old is the teacher?
He's old—like fifty or sixty.

Do you feel like he should have been able to control the class?
Yes, definitely.

What does he do for control?
Just calls a security guard sometimes, or waits for the kids to stop
on their own.

**Is there anything else you can think of that contributed to your feelings of lack of
safety?**
You just see things that shouldn't happen at school.

Like what kind of things?
A teacher with a broken nose, a security guard with a broken nose,
loud arguing in the halls and other places, people in each others'
faces, physical fights with other kids gathered around to watch.

How did the teacher get a broken nose?
She was just in the hall when a fight broke out, and she got pushed
up against the lockers when all the kids rushed by to watch the
fight.

So she really wasn't doing anything—just in the wrong place at the wrong time. How does that make you feel?

Nervous.

What are the most unsafe places at the school?

The cafeteria and the quad are the most unsafe, then the classrooms, then the hallways.

Do you think that the adults could do more to help make the school safe?

They can't really because they can't usually get to the fight, because all the students are standing around the fighters blocking the way. And the teachers aren't strong enough to be able to break up the fights.

Do you think that a Littleton could happen at your school?

No, not really, because the kids who do all the fighting are the gangs, and they keep it mostly between themselves. And they are local gangs, not national gangs like the Bloods or the Crypts.

Suzanne's strategies for combating her unhappiness were to:

• Hope that it would get better

• Immerse herself in her work and her sports

• Try to make some friends who were seniors for protection

• Count the days until the end of the school year

She feels that "it never got better" by the end. When asked about next year, she replied, "I can't think about that now."

As Suzanne sees her school situation, the teachers would have to make their way through a gathering of bystanders in order to stop fights in the hallways or the quad. For her, the fact that responsible adults have great difficulty just physically getting to a violent outburst promotes a strong sense of insecurity; she worries about the stability of the environment, and her own safety in it. In families where children feel that the parents are too weak to protect them (whether as a result of illness or disability), those children are chronically anxious. Similarly, in this case children expect and hope that adults will be capable of intervening for the safety of the surroundings. When they are not, students "count the days to the end of the year" like Suzanne, and they develop other coping strategies to "take it."

Suzanne said she kept saying to herself, "I just have to try to get through to the end of the year."

For concerned parents and adults, questions arise: Why are these kinds of incidents never reported to the parents, or the community, or in the school newsletter? Why should kids have to figure out how to "take it" and count down the days until the end of the school year, for reasons of their safety?

Here is part of a conversation with Natalie, age sixteen. These seemingly "minor" or "typical" childhood issues are still happening for her. She is an average student who began the interview by saying that if she could she wouldn't come to school at all. In listening to her, we get a sense of how she copes, and what can be learned for discussions with other adolescents:

My friends pick on me, just joking around and stuff, but nothing really bad. Sometimes in gym if you don't catch a ball that's coming right at you or something, people say something, but it's nothing big.

Does it hurt your feelings when they do that?
A little bit, 'cause I know I can't play sports anyway. So I try not to let it bother me.

How do you do that?
I just kind of shrug it off and be like, "It doesn't really matter." They don't know me anyway, *most* of the ones who say stuff like that. [emphasis added; this means that some of those criticizing her are her friends, and she is accepting this at some level]

It seems like some kids are able to do that—shrug it off—and some kids are not. Can you help me figure out the difference?
I think that some people really let the words sink in and really have meaning. But other people are like, "It's no big deal. They don't know me. And they're just being stupid."

And that's what you do?
Yeah.

Why do you think some kids let the words sink in and have meaning?
They're depressed, or maybe they have problems. Like they think

badly about themselves, so when people say those things it really affects them because that's how they think, and it makes them feel that way.

Do you get picked on yourself?
Yeah, a little. But they get a smile on their faces, so I know that it's not serious. Like if I goof up a word or say something stupid.

Have you ever seen someone else get picked on or bullied at school?
Yeah, I have actually. Mostly it's just people who are mean to everyone.

Are there people who tend to cause problems at school?
Yes, people with bad tempers. The people who act like they are ticked off all the time.

Natalie's ability to discern between different types of teasing, such as kids who just pick on you and those with more serious problems ("people with bad tempers"), is very useful for navigating the intricate web of adolescent social patterns. She is able to discern that some things are not "a big deal" and so should not be taken that way. She is able to see that some kids do take it the wrong way because they may feel badly about themselves, and being bullied reinforces their already poor perceptions of themselves.

Hopefully, this is the kind of conversation that we, as parents and educators, can strive for with teenagers. It opens the door for discussing feelings and weighing possible coping strategies. Most of all, listening and asking questions in a respectful way validates their experiences and feelings.

Obviously, some children and young people do not "take it." Their responses to bullying and harassment are different from those described above. For example, Shannon, age fourteen, put up with nothing:

I got into a fight last year at school in eighth grade. I didn't start it, but I got ISP [in-school suspension] and they got out-of-school suspension. I was so mad. If somebody hits you, of course you're going to hit back just to defend yourself. So I shouldn't have gotten suspension at all.

You sound like you felt treated unfairly.

Yeah. I think the other people should have gotten ISP because out-of-school suspension is no big deal, it's like a vacation. Adults don't know that because they think out-of-school suspension is worse."

Shannon also confided she "gets in people's faces" and yells back if anyone approaches her with these same kinds of behaviors. Her conclusion is that behaving this way protects her from being pushed around, even though the facts of her life at school don't support it. She ends up suspended for fighting back, but she doesn't see the connection between getting in a fight and earlier verbally aggressive exchanges.

Daniel, from a suburban area, feels helpless at school much of the time. At age fifteen, he does not use these words, but instead says, "-There's nothing I can do about how it is here. There's nothing the class president can do either. Nobody has enough power to make a difference. I don't like it, but that's how it is so . . ." Daniel complained that there are several ways that he gets bullied and taunted during the school year. One way has to do with a girl in one of his classes, who calls him names and threatens him. We asked, "When the teachers hear the name-calling, do they do something about it?" Daniel's face and body language showed the sadness and defeat that he experiences on a daily basis. He replied, "Not usually. Not a great majority of the time. Especially in one class, she tries to annoy me, she yells at me, and the teacher doesn't do anything about it. She'll go, 'Daniel, you're so stupid.'" He continued dejectedly, "It really bothers me after a while. I just try to stay away from her."

This is his strategy for coping with his female antagonist. Imagine trying to learn anything or concentrate in a class where this is what awaits you. Imagine the feelings of trying to bravely put up a façade of not caring in front of your friends, in front of the other boys. Imagine the sense of betrayal a young person feels when no adult intervenes on his behalf. How can he save face? How can he feel good about himself? How long can he actually "take it" without any adverse effects?

"There seems to be a philosophy that 'unpleasantness is cool,'" according to Tyler's analysis. At age eighteen, he has figured out that "if you can take it, the unpleasant treatment, being bullied, then you are cool." On the other hand, he says, "You could be cool, too, by standing up to being bullied. There's a fine line." This line is so fine that even the most socially astute kids have trouble figuring it out. In Howard Gardner's book *Multiple Intelligences,* we learn that social intelligence consists of having an intuitive ability to understand the meaning of social interactions around you. For children without this aptitude, adolescent exchanges can be a nightmare. Their ability to figure out how to "take it" is dramatically compromised.

Tyler concludes, "Of course, nobody can take it forever. Especially if you take school seriously at all. Then there's love and dating. It all mounts up, and it is very, very stressful for teenagers."

Taking It from Adults

We can all remember wonderful teachers and other school personnel who influenced us and shaped our lives forever. Many of us can also remember a teacher who engaged in bullying and belittling behavior toward kids. Even today, kids have to figure out how to "take it" from adults in their schools. While children have an expectation that they will be picked on by peers, they do not accept as "okay" being humiliated by adults. Their rage and frustration over bad treatment by teachers and other school staff burns deeply, complicating their feelings about being safe at school at all. Here is one example:

> A large suburban middle school experienced a serious bomb threat. A note in the mail spelled out the day and time of the "attack" on the school. Parents consulted with one another and with their children about what actions to take, and about one-third of the student population was absent on the day of the threatened bombing. When Jason, age thirteen, returned to his eighth-grade classes the following day, he was met with hostility by several of his teachers. He asked for the assignments to make up the work that he missed, but was denied the information that he needed. His teachers' uniform response: "You weren't here. It was an illegal absence." Jason went home that day understandably very upset. The next day he failed a test in math, his best subject. His parents blame his reaction and his failure on the test to the inappropriate treatment by the teachers.

Frustration on the part of teachers, staff, and other school personnel in these kinds of situations is understandable. However, taking out frustration and anxiety on children is not acceptable. When teachers and other school adults do this, it signals more than their own anger and fears; it points to something greater happening in the functioning of the school as a system itself. It illustrates a significant lack of communication, or a hole in the feedback process from the administration to the staff and back again.

In an instance like this, school staff should anticipate that even with the best of planning for the security threat by administration, some parents will not feel comfortable about sending their children into a potentially risky situation. The school leadership should anticipate that some children will feel too unsafe to risk going to school. Appropriate next-day responses do not include trying to shame the students, especially in front of classmates who may have attended school on the day of the threat. Instead, they should include discussions about any outstanding fears or anxieties, as well as continued plans for the security of the building, the campus, and the children. These talks need to be held on an ongoing basis with the students, and need to consider the valuable input the kids can provide. Otherwise, school personnel continue to make "security plans" that do not feel secure to students and fail to address their needs.

Kids' Solutions

Over the course of hundreds of interviews, we were often surprised at the innovative solutions that kids came up with for "taking it," or for changing the system so there would be less need for them to handle bad behavior from others. Suzanne's solutions involve either "ignoring it" or hoping for a change of behavior from adults in the building:

I don't think the teachers and the principal have a clue. They don't choose to really care. Like the only time they'll really do anything about anything is when they see it going on. Like if they hear about it, they won't really do anything about it as much as, for example, if two girls are screaming at each other and getting into a fight in the hall. That's the only time they'll do anything. Otherwise, if they see someone trying to trip you, they'll pretend they don't see it because they don't want to deal with it. Because they're lazy. The teachers should get more involved, should see the students' perspective. But most teachers are so stuck up, rude, and snooty . . . They're more involved in their life than they are helping us.

Another tenth-grade girl had similar ideas for help from teachers in solving the problems related to bullying and sexual harassment at school: "When the teachers walk around, they just walk around the halls, minding their own business. But have them keep their ears open in case they think something is wrong, then they can ask the students. The students will probably blow up at first, but then we would get used to it. The teachers don't have to be on top of everything all of the time, but be a little more aware. When they're watching in the gym or in the cafeteria or a break, be a little more aware of what's going on."

Janice feels that teachers and other adults can have a big influence on kids who have the most trouble—the ones who get picked on the most. She cited this example from her own experience of watching kids trying to manage in the classroom. Janice was asked, "Do you know of any situation where a teacher or other adult was aware of a kid who was constantly getting teased?"

> I think that sometimes they don't do much to stop that. In all three schools I've attended, the teachers don't really do anything for kids that get teased due to their families or what their parents are, or their weight, or whatever. Sometimes the teachers don't do anything at all. They're like, "Well, I don't really care . . ." I know of one specific teacher in the elementary school. I'm tutoring this overweight girl in his class, and the teacher isn't aware of her self-esteem. She needs to be treated differently.
>
> I don't think most teachers are aware of that, and they don't take that stuff into consideration in how they treat the kids. I think they should try to take a little extra time for people who obviously have trouble in school with the other kids, or have trouble at home.

Janice's ideas and perceptions are important for all of us to be aware of. For one thing, she believes that a teacher she observes on a regular basis (the elementary teacher in whose room she is a tutor) has no awareness that one of his pupils has low self-esteem and is being teased by the other children because of her weight, and possibly other issues. What messages are these perceptions giving to Janice? She has concluded (a) that teachers do not do anything because they "don't really care," (b) that this teacher does not take the variables of self-esteem and peer interactions into account in considering how to treat the students, and (c) that she herself is more aware of what is happening in the classroom than the person in authority.

Clearly Janice is requesting more awareness, more intervention, and more caring, at least on the part of this particular teacher with regard to this particular student. It is admirable that Janice, a fifteen-year-old from a rural community, uses her time to volunteer as a tutor and that she has such a highly developed sense of empathy and justice. As adults with responsibility towards children, we need to step in and support her in the ways that she is articulating.

"Don't rock the boat" is the adage that Chrissy, age fifteen, subscribes to, though she does not express it that way. Here is her sense of how to get by in high school:

> Don't do things to make people mad. Don't get in other people's business, and then there's no fights that way. I respect other people, and they respect who I am. And that's how it is now. When I was younger, in seventh grade, I was better at soccer than the older kids. I started playing varsity, so the older kids picked on me for that. Today, I got picked on for the clothes I'm wearing. But it doesn't really bother me much.

Chrissy is a good example of how feeling competent at something promotes high self-esteem in adolescents.

Psychologists and educators see a link between shame and violence, as well as between confidence or self-esteem and the ability to handle peer disrespect. The developing and ever-changing ego of adolescence has great difficulty tolerating shame, and the shame experienced from being seen as "different" in a bad way. Though we believe that adolescents want to be individuals, they appear from our research to be able to tolerate only a certain amount of diversity among themselves in their school and neighborhood. Shame and shaming appear to act as a means of promoting conformity.

Adolescents rain down shaming behavior on their peers who are different. For adolescents, conformity supports safety by supporting their ability to predict one another's behavior. From a systemic perspective, conformity is, in essence, a cautionary message for anyone even contemplating being different. When asked what would happen if he began to write poetry about sports and other things that he is interested in, an eleven-year-old from Bethesda, Maryland, named Michael Penansky responded, "My friends would think it was weird.

They'd want me to go back to the way I was, 'cause kids want their friends to be just like them." These powerful words have many implications for all kids academically and socially.

In Chrissy's specific situation, she did not knuckle under to pressure to return to her "place" in junior varsity sports. Instead, she stayed on the varsity soccer team and continued to excel despite the intimidation she received from the "older kids." Because she feels basically good about herself as a result of developing her unique talents, she is able to let go of the barbs directed at her by envious peers.

Until schools assume full responsibility for maintaining a positive social environment in the classroom, in the halls, in the cafeteria, in the locker rooms, and on the bus, children will have to be able to "take it." Kids usually separate good-natured teasing, however, from mean-spirited bullying, harassment, and emotional violence. These are five strategies that teenagers have come up with for coping with the mean-spirited attacks:

1. **Learn to discriminate** if the teasing is just playful by the tone of voice and by the peer's usual behavior. Kids are clear that some of their peers have no ability to discriminate. As adults, we can help them learn this. Discerning what is meant by what someone says or does is what psychologists call "meaning attribution," a form of attribution of cues in the environment or in everyday interactions. What is sarcastic and what is real? What is meant to hurt or harm or flirt? These are the questions that a youngster must be able to ask himself and to answer appropriately.

2. **Try not to let it hurt you.** Kids say these things to themselves when they are treated badly:
   - "This is stupid."
   - "This stuff is all crap and it doesn't mean anything."
   - "They don't really know me anyway."
   - "She's just mean."
   - "She's having a bad day."
   - "Try to let it roll off." "Shake it off."

3. **Get philosophical.** Kids try to convince themselves that the problem is about the bullies, not about themselves:
   - "I try to get a different perspective."

- "You can't let these things bother you in life."
- "This won't mean anything after high school."
- "Those people are going nowhere in life."
- "They're losers."

4. If and when it does hurt, talk to a friend. Talking with a friend or adult helps. You feel supported and not so alone. Sometimes you get good ideas about how to handle a bad situation.

5. Don't "take it"—talk to someone in authority. When you can't take it anymore, try to get things changed. Kids find there is usually one teacher or other adult (a vice principal, social worker, or bus driver) who they can confide in and who will help them. They often have to encourage their friends to take the first step to do this.

Why Not Just "Take It?"

Here are some statements we have heard by adults and some responses that you might think about when you hear anything like these kinds of rationalizations for allowing kids to deal with the problems of bullying by themselves:

Statement: "Maybe we should let kids figure it out. Maybe one of the benefits of being bullied and harassed is that you become a stronger person, you learn how to stand up for yourself."

Answer: While it may be true for some kids that they will "become a stronger person" or "learn how to stand up for themselves" as a result of being bullied, we know that there are too many other adverse effects from being bullied and harassed that outweigh the possible "advantages" for this argument to hold water.

More importantly, there are numerous other ways for kids to learn how to stand up for themselves without first being bullied and tormented.

Kids have a much better chance of being a "strong person" if they are raised and taught in a respectful environment. Emotionally and psychologically healthy people respond to being picked on, bullied, harassed, or otherwise tormented differently than unformed children and adolescents. For example, an adult who feels good about himself as a person questions the motives of someone who is attempting to bully him, rather than his own worthiness as a person. A child or teen who is bullied has not had the time and growth necessary to know that he is a worthwhile person with unique strengths and weaknesses, so he does question himself and feel insecure. He is very likely to take the insults personally and to be affected by them. An adult with some ego strength would not enjoy being taunted and picked on, but can recognize that the problem is with the bully, not himself.

Assertiveness training is one component of effective anti-bullying programs, and is one of the best and most effective mechanisms for teaching people how to stand up for themselves. It is not necessary to belittle, torment, or otherwise bully people in order for them to learn how to be tough enough to stand up for themselves in life. In fact, the opposite is true. Well-loved children are the most likely to feel that bad treatment by others is not okay, is undeserved, and reflects the tormentor's own problems. These teenagers are the most likely to ask for help or intervention, and to be open to any strategies that will help them be assertive and proactive in a socially acceptable manner. It is only when adults fail these prosocial, proactive kids that they then believe they have to respond in kind to bullying and other bad treatment.

Statement: "At a time when we are facing attacks by terrorists, I don't want my kid to be some sort of pushover. I think these anti-bullying programs are not such a good idea right now. I want my kid to learn how to be prepared for the worst. I want him to be tough."

Answer: Learning how to "be tough" does not have to happen at the expense of a child's good sense of himself. A child who is subjected to an environment of belligerence, nasty exchanges, and humiliating situations on a daily basis learns to feel bad about himself, which is not a strength in anyone's book. True internal "toughness" comes from feeling good about yourself, from knowing that you can accomplish what you set out to do. The primary thing that adults set out for kids to do and to accomplish is success at school. If we then abandon them to a socially toxic environment while they are trying to accomplish their task, they are not going to get as far with it as they could otherwise. Children forced to develop a false bravado, always ready to just "take it," grow up unprepared to face the important challenges that lie ahead. They are uncertain and fearful. They react defensively instead of positively to one another and to adults.

What Can You Do?

1. Improve the social climate. One way to deal with the issue of "taking it" is to improve the overall social climate of the school at the same time that you are helping to build up your teenager's social coping skills. One of the best guides you can buy is is Myrna Shure's *Raising a Thinking Preteen*. In it, Shure gives step-by-step advice based upon twenty-five years of research developing the "I Can Problem Solve" model. When used with preteens, this approach is quite useful in helping develop the coping tactics for a child *before* he or she enters the extremely intense social environment of the high school. Prevention is a good investment.

2. Teach assertiveness. Children who learn how to be assertive when faced with bullying tend to have less harassment to deal with. In contrast, targeted children are more likely to respond to bullying by crying or giving in than children who are not chronic targets. You can help your child by talking about how to stand up for himself or herself when faced with mistreatment by others. Teach that there is a difference between being passive (a doormat that everyone walks over) and aggressive (being a bully). *What's in between is being assertive—* giving a clear message by one's voice and body language that bad treatment is unacceptable. Teach your children how to walk with a sense of confidence: head up, shoulders back. Teach them that they are somebody to be respected; it is *not* okay for anyone to treat them badly, and they should say so when it happens.

The Steps to Respect program (see the resources at the end of this book) teaches kids assertive behaviors to use in response to bullying. It provides opportunities to practice through role-playing. It also emphasizes that adults need to be involved in order to support and reinforce children's new assertive skills.

3. Promote friends as supports. Research indicates that kids who have a group of friends (or even one friend) to confide in handle the taunts and torments of bullying and aggression better than children who are on their own. As the students we have heard from report, "You go back to your friends and tell them what happened. Then they tell you, 'Never mind. He's in a mood.' And then you feel a little better." Having friends validate the bad experience helps kids feel less alone. They feel there are others who do like them. Some research demonstrates that having a group of friends works to prevent some bullying from taking place at all. Certainly the teens we talked to confirm this in subtle and not-so-subtle ways. If you have your "homies to watch your back," you can be assured that fewer instances of bullying behavior are going to come your way.

4. Support character education. We can see from their quotes that much of what teens struggle with in their interactions with one another is in the realm of moral dilemma. They are talking about what is right and wrong. They are clear that if someone retaliates and becomes "your worst nightmare" as a result of bullying, then that is wrong. On the other hand, they have come to believe that it is right to "take it" and accept bullying up to a point. With a character education program in your school, all children and staff are immersed in discussions and interventions aimed at providing a respectful, caring, and responsible environment for everyone. If your school does not as yet have a character education curriculum, or any program that promotes prosocial values, investigate the idea of advocating for one. See the Resources section at the end of the book for web sites and other reading material on character education.

5. Help increase your child's ability for distinguishing cues. It is useful to talk to your child about how to analyze what happens in interactions with friends or other peers. Some of those, you can see early on—at your home when friends are over, on the playground, or at group activities in the community. When you see something that concerns you, talk it over with your child. Give him or her your version of what you see. Give your child alternatives and other ideas on how to handle difficult interactions with other kids. Don't make the mistake of assuming that he or she will somehow naturally figure out how to manage in the future; for many children, getting along with others is a difficult learning process. You can give ideas and suggestions of what has worked for you.

6. Use Peer Predictability. Help adolescents figure out ways to deal with the worrisome actions of their peers (more about this concept is discussed in Chapter 9). Behaviors that seem outside the normal range of behavior of a particular child must be treated as a red flag. Advise teens to keep some distance from the child they are concerned about, and let them know that you will look into what is going on. Call your school officials and relate the problem as you know it, describing the shifts in behavior in the child. Make sure that you stay on top of communicating with the school—rather than being put off by "We will get back to you," take it as your responsibility to call back again and again if necessary. Communicate all of your proactive interventions to your children so they know that you are working for them, and that something in fact is being done.

7. Understand that discernment is part of being able to "take it." Help your child see the difference between being playful and being mean and hurtful. This is something that all parents can practice at home; if kids have siblings, they will already know the difference. Of course, intervening in "red-flag behavior" also begins at home. It is time to step in when you begin to get a gut feeling of discomfort about what you are observing in your own children's play. Children need our help figuring out moral behavior and attitudes, so take advantage of teaching moments when they come your way (and make others happen). It is in these small moments that children learn how to be good and caring people.

8. Talk about specific situations and specific people. Being available for conversations that include the nitty-gritty of the school day is extremely important and valuable. At the time, the little situations that a child tries to report to us may not seem to be important: he or she isn't chosen until last for teams at school, or is consistently bullied and picked on during gym class. We may be tempted to deny the significance upon hearing this, or to want to turn a deaf ear, because it is so painful to us.

Chapter 9

The Puzzle of Peer Predictability

I think feeling safe is . . . being familiar with people. Knowing what kinds of people are in the school. Knowing what kinds of things they've done in the past or probably would do. (Crystal, 17)

You can't predict other people around you. I mean that's what's bringing everybody down. (Jade, 15)

Some of the weird people at school make me feel unsafe. I think they might get ideas like the kids in Littleton or someplace else. (Amber, 14)

A predictable environment is the safest one, as far as teenagers are concerned. Teens wonder, "Can I count on my friends to help me out when I'm in danger? Can I count on the adults at this school to step in when someone threatens me?" The unpredictability of the environment and of other students is as much a threat as any visible danger to many children. During the course of the school day, they try to "size up" others as potentially harmful or helpful to them.

As Ellen became more aware of the way students adapted to the lack of adult supervision in schools, she began to focus on what she called Peer Predictability, which she explains as a way of measuring how accurately children can predict the actions of their peers in all ways that are important. Ellen identified at least three factors that contribute to effective peer predictability: being in a small school, recognizing people by sight, and being confident about how peers will behave.

What Makes You Feel Safe at School?

Trusting Friends and Peers

Kids count on their friends to feel comfortable and to look out for each other. But more than that, they count on their friends' and peers' typical behavior as a way of interpreting the many interactions that take place all through the school day. Here are some typical examples provided by three boys from three different small rural schools. Notice that Josh is looking for who among his peers has the potential for violence, while Tom determines that by knowing everybody he doesn't have to feel intimidated by their actions. Uriah puts his faith in trusted allies.

> Feeling safe is knowing there's no one for me to be intimidated by. I mostly know everybody, so if somebody is hassling me I know how to take it. (Tom, 16)

> I have my homeboys. We look out for each other. (Uriah, 16)

> I trust my friends; I know everybody. I think I would know which kids have the potential for being violent . . . I *hope* I would. (Josh, 15)

Small Schools Feel Different

Adolescents who attend both large and small schools reflect on the advantages and disadvantages of each. While there is a noticeable privacy disadvantage for teenagers in attending a small school ("Nothing can happen here that everybody doesn't know about in five minutes"), this same element is a major plus for the equation of peer predictability.

In a small school, kids not only have the opportunity for sight recognition of their peers but also the chance to interact with most of them. Even a modest amount of interaction time together—say, in a gym class two times a week—allows kids to compile data about one another. From this data bank, they draw conclusions and expectations about a person's "normal" range of behavior. The range of latitude can be fairly wide; one person may typically, according to adolescents, "lose it" once a week by throwing books in class and swearing at the teacher. But when such actions are taken to the next step—for example, overturning a desk—the peer predictability barometer changes. This change in the peer predictability equation signals a warning to the children. Similarly, in the case of another child whose usual behavior is cheerful and engaging, just being atypically quiet and unsmiling can be unsettling. Internally, his peers will wonder what is wrong. A few may ask about it, while some will begin to assess his risk for harm to himself or others.

Small schools are a safe environment. They shouldn't be big. This school is getting bigger. The big schools, that's a problem. No one knows who anybody is. (Kimara, 17)

I feel safe because this school is so small; you see your friends, you talk a lot—you get things out. You can always talk, 'cause everyone knows each other. (John, 17)

Aaron has attended both a very large urban high school of more than two thousand students and a small rural school. His sense of safety is predicated on familiarity.

In, like, big schools . . . you walk through the halls, and every once in a while you see somebody you know. Like, in this school, you know everybody. (Aaron, 15)

The school is so small, I don't really feel unsafe. Even if I heard there was going to be a fight and I went to it, and it involved my boyfriend, I would still feel safe because I have a lot of friends. But if it were somebody I don't really know who was going to be in a fight, then I would feel scared. When you don't know somebody, you don't know how far they'll take it. (Megan, 14)

Sara is a senior in a relatively small rural school of seven hundred kids. She, like Aaron, believes familiarity with everyone supports her sense of security.

I feel safe because it's small and I know everybody, and it's really friendly. (Sara, 17)

This is the size I like, about five hundred students—so it isn't too small, where everybody knows everybody's business and everything that goes on. This is the size of all the schools I've been in. You have your really close friends, then the friends you hang out with, and then the friends you occasionally say hi to. (Steve, 16)

A small high school allows for fewer unsafe, unowned, or undersupervised spaces, which are unsettling for students. Size is no guarantee of safety, of course. But in general, a small school makes for the possibility of greater adult awareness, supervision, intervention, and caring than a student would expect to have at a large school. Students from small high schools recognize this. Small schools do feel safer.

Besides the chance to know your peers, Ashley comments that small schools allow for bonding with teachers. Kids find this especially important. They don't like to feel anonymous to their peers or to adults at school.

> I think the teachers at this school are really good. In [a nearby school], there are so many kids and so little teachers. In this school, all the teachers have a special bond with the students . . . we're like friends. In the bigger schools, there is just like no way. You can't even remember all their names. Everybody feels close to everybody here. If somebody's going to fight, everybody's affected by it. Here everybody's close and together and knows everybody. [The nearby school] is huge; it's crazy. They have so many halls of lockers. I would be lost there. (Ashley, 17)

> You're going to feel a lot safer if you can know at least that that kid who sits in the back of the class, he knows your name. (Brittany, 15)

The possibility of unwittingly getting into serious trouble with another student is on the minds of kids. Figuring out peer predictability is one means of avoiding trouble.

> If you know somebody, you know how they are . . . and if something happens you know how they are going to react to it. But with other kids you don't know, you could say something and they could just go off and beat you up. (Crystal, 17)

The advantage to the knowing Crystal describes is that you can be prepared for how someone is going to act in the future, a huge advantage in adolescent society. Kids realize that if you do not know someone, you run the risk of saying the wrong thing. The small size of the school promotes this girl's ability to know the other students well enough to predict their behavior and therefore feel safe. This ability to predict each other helps kids protect themselves at school.

Trying to Use Intuition

When schools grow beyond some point of critical mass, students seem to lose their intuitive ability to discriminate among people and groups. Courtney, Lizzie, and Rob each had firm ideas about what results:

> The new renovation—it's going to double the size of the campus. I think a lot of people think that's unsafe, because it's like you get so many more people. It's getting so much bigger. You feel so much less familiar with the people in your grade the bigger it gets. I think I would feel really unsafe if our class was as big as the eighth-grade class is right now. That's the problem with large schools, feeling unsafe because people don't really know each other and stuff. (Courtney, 16)

> If it was a bigger school, like [a nearby high school of 1,500 students], I would be a little more scared. I'm not the kind of person who likes to be around a whole lot of people like that. There's more things likely to happen in a school like that. (Lizzie, 15)

> When you go to a large school, everybody is a stranger. Then you don't really know if someone is behaving not normal, or if they are just normally strange or something. (Rob, 16)

As many students see it, a small school means a safe school, while a larger school equates to a greater likelihood for trouble. Being in a small school, though, is no guarantee of safety and success. In fact, some of the infamous school shootings of the late 1990s took place in small schools—for example, in West Paducah, Kentucky. Nonetheless, researchers have consistently found that small schools have less violence than big schools.

Familiarity: Recognizing People by Sight and Behavior

Roy, age eighteen, attends a large suburban high school. Roy is a tall, good-sized fellow who looks like he could handle himself in any confrontation, if need be. But even he relies on peer predictability to chart a course through the day. His sense of security is partially based on being able to predict certain peers' typically bad behavior. He says,

> I avoid confrontation. I know enough to avoid some groups—especially noisy males, just hanging, looking for trouble. They have a pack attitude. You just stay away from them.

> I think feeling safe is . . . being familiar with people. Knowing what kinds of people are in the school. Knowing what kinds of things they've done in the past or probably would do. Last year, after Columbine, one of the teachers said he wouldn't suspect our school, but it wouldn't be a huge surprise if it did happen here. All schools are equally targeted right now, I guess. (Courtney, 16)

Students believe familiarity is a critical component of their sense of safety, and it is an obvious component of the peer predictability puzzle. Max, age sixteen, is an average student. Here he describes how being familiar with another person helps discern between good-natured teasing and a true threat:

There's always minor picking going on, always. Nothing major.

How can you tell the difference?
It's not that hard. It's usually your friends. It's how they say it. If you know the person, it's not that hard to tell they don't mean anything by it.

So it has to do with their tone of voice?
Yeah. And how they say it.

So you have to be able to distinguish all those things?
Yeah, but it's not that hard to do once you know all the people.

Do you think there are some kids who get picked on that don't get the distinction?
Yeah, you can tell by the way they react. They explode, they cuss at something, they cause a scene.

How come you think some kids don't get the distinction?
Well, for example, this one kid, he doesn't understand sarcasm at all, so he can't really comprehend if you're telling a joke or being serious.

It seems like this guy would be upset a lot.
You have to wait for him to cool down. Then you can explain it to him, and he'll get it.

Why do you think he is like this?
It's just something in his brain.

Does he seem unusual in any other way?
No.

Would you say he's a friend of yours?
Not a friend, really. I mean I talk to him in the halls and everything, but I wouldn't call him a friend.

Nicole, age fifteen, has a similar sense of the safety that predictability affords. She related her feelings:

Is knowing the other kids important to feeling safe?
Well, if you don't know the people, there's always a sort of mystery of what they will do or how they will act. And if you know the people, you're more comfortable with them, obviously, and you won't second-guess yourself at any time about what they would do. There's always people that can hide who they are, but that comes out sooner or later. So I think knowing the people gives you a sense of comfort, 'cause you know what they're going to do. You know how they act.

What if they went outside of the range of how they typically act?
You might ask them, you know, what's wrong? What's going on? Is something at home bothering you? Be, like, their friend. When you

see that, you always ask somebody what's wrong, and especially in girls. You always ask them.

How come especially in girls?
Girls are more sensitive, and they're more emotional. . . . like if something's bothering them, they'll act in a way that people can see it. And usually if something is bothering them, then they'll *want* other people to know. Not all the people, but their friends, so they'll act down or they'll be very angry. And you'll just ask them what's wrong. There has to be friends for everybody and when there's not, people get singled out and people feel like they don't belong, and that could bring about feelings that could be violent. You can't really control if people have friends or not, so maybe creating a friendly environment will let people make friends.

Kids don't seem to need much more than to know someone's name and to exchange a few "hellos" and smiles to consider someone their friend. School administrators who provide these opportunities for everyone will greatly increase their students' sense of safety at school.

Of special concern to adolescents are peers who were once trusted or at least were categorized as predictable within a particular range of activity, who have moved out of that range. Now they are no longer predictable, and that fact calls into question an individual student's ability to keep himself or herself safe. It challenges his or her ability to truly evaluate a peer. One student euphemistically called this "disturbing." Two examples of precipitants for this uncomfortable and unsafe feeling are related here.

> A sixteen-year-old boy urinated in a Pepsi bottle and gave it to a girl. The school suspended him; she sued the school. That is kind of disturbing to some of us. I kind of knew the person—the guy. You don't know who you can trust sometimes. That person's trust fades away from you, and you don't know what to do about it.
>
> You personally feel safe, but this leaves a nagging feeling. . . . I feel safe with my group of friends, but there's other groups of people that I'm not familiar with, and I don't know what they're like. I don't know what their thoughts are, or what they think of and things like that. (Kristin, 16)

Last year there was a fight. I was in the middle of it . . . there was a girl
coming down the hallway after this other girl . . . and these were
decent people that I wouldn't have suspected this from . . . and she
grabbed her and started yelling obscene things at her. I was caught in
the middle. She slammed her into the lockers. I was kind of surprised
and kind of scared that that type of person would do something like
that. This year, that same type of person . . . at a basketball game, a
group got yelling about going over to somebody's house and beating
him up or something. (Tania, 16)

It is disconcerting or "disturbing" to adolescents, as it is to people
of any age, to find out that someone they thought was "decent" instigated or participated in a reckless and abusive incident. Afterward,
everything that has been considered good judgment about that person has to be reevaluated. A whole new set of cues has to be culled
from the person in the environment. A new degree of vigilance must
be brought to bear in connection with a person who could formerly
be trusted to be nonthreatening.

Whether it is the "different kids," the "poor kids," the "hicks," or
even the teachers, the common factor among them that provokes
anxiety for students is that their behavior is unpredictable. Similarly,
several areas of the school outside the classrooms contribute to an
overall atmosphere of lack of security for some students. Why?
Because activities take place in these areas that are not fully predictable, and to which adult response is also not fully predictable.

Jake, a seventeen-year-old senior at a suburban high school of over
1,800 students, told this story about why predictability is meaningful
to him (note that Jake towers well over six feet tall):

It is important to know the other kids around you. For example, there
are some kids who do crazy things in the quad. Like they climb up in
trees and throw pinecones at other kids. They do it every year. And I'm
glad I know that they always do it. Because then I don't have to worry
about them doing some other more crazy thing. This is just what they
do. If you know them, then you know the limitations of their craziness.
You can predict it.

I always look around when I go into the bathrooms. I try to never
have to go in there—for a lot of reasons. One time when I was a freshman, I heard that a kid who was involved in a gang somehow got
thrown through a plate glass window. It was either in the bathroom or

right near it. Ever since then, I have been wary of the bathroom, know what I mean? I always want to know who is in there and where they are in the bathroom if I am in there. You just need to know to take care of yourself, to protect yourself if need be.

One of my teachers said there were some kids in the building that she didn't know. When that happens, I get heightened. I get a little nervous if there are people around that I haven't seen before. Not adults that look like teachers, but sometimes the scruffy-looking ones who are supposed to be security, I guess, or other kids that I haven't seen before and that I don't know.

Predictability is a principal component of safety as kids experience it. If their peers' behavior is predictable, even within a gross range, then the students report feeling more comfortable because as incidents erupt during the day, they know how to categorize such occurrences in terms of potential threat.

The students say, "When you know someone, you know how to think." Predictability is predicated on familiarity. Since predictability is critical for adolescents to feel secure, one solution is to increase the likelihood of familiarity. As many of the students see it, the best hope of actually knowing a peer is through small schools and the intermingling that takes place in class and other school activities. Knowing that familiarity is the key to predictability, even big schools can take positive action by creating a series of "schools within the school," by organizing the flow of students, and by concentrating students into more clearly defined, but heterogeneous groups.

The Impact of Adult Unpredictability

Adult predictability has a different impact. When kids experience teachers as being predictably unaware, predictably late to intervene, or predictably lacking in supervision, many students decide that they need to handle whatever problems arise by themselves. As they conclude that they cannot look to adults for assistance in difficult or dangerous situations, school safety is undermined. The degree of emotional stress that kids feel is made worse by the feeling that no one, except *maybe* their friends, will come to their aid if they encounter violence at school.

As in any system where those who are purportedly in charge do not fulfill their responsibilities, other participants in the system will do what they can to fill in the gaps. In this example, children attempt to protect themselves at school, primarily by continually monitoring and evaluating their peers. When school personnel are not predictable in their means or times of intervention for an orderly environment, students provide this for themselves by observing, categorizing, and eventually predicting the attitudes and behaviors of their classmates. This mechanism of peer predictability lends a large measure of safety and security to teenagers in schools.

Using the language of a systems perspective, we can say that in such a situation the children are "overfunctioning" to compensate for the adults, who are "underfunctioning." From a systemic viewpoint, it is the responsibility of all the adults associated with the schooling of children to create and maintain a safe and secure environment for them to learn and grow. Children can make an important contribution, but it is not their job to ensure safety.

In a family where the parents are not in charge, children feel anxious and fearful for their well-being and safety because, in effect, there is no adult present. In the absence of functioning adults, even young children will attempt to assume leadership and impose routine as best they can. A similar phenomenon plays out at school when adolescents endeavor to protect themselves and even other students by carrying weapons, forming gangs, and using bullying as a means of social control.

Some kids say, "I feel safe at school because I know everyone." For them, knowing everyone is equivalent to knowing what their peers are capable of doing—whether they will be violent, intimidating, or not. For others, it instead conveys the message, "I am protected by the fact that I am friends with everyone, so no one will hurt me."

Is Size Really That Important?

After what happens in their homes, the biggest immediate influences on adolescents are their peer groups and the schools they attend. One often overlooked feature of schools that contributes to the difficulties parents face in raising teenagers today is the size of those schools, most notably the high schools. Put simply, big high schools encourage spectatorship and a "herd feeling" rather than participation, and they exclude all but a small proportion of their students from leadership roles and other developmentally enhancing activities. As a result, they leave the majority of students at loose ends, and the most vulnerable are ripe for the destructive pressures of the socially toxic environment.

By contrast, small schools enhance affirmation and identity because they draw kids into participation and leadership, which in turn offers challenges that stimulate the development of competence—and, crucially, give adults the opportunity to monitor behavior more effectively. All these effects are strongest for the students most at risk for alienation and dropping out, the "academically marginal" students. Parents who are coping with such a child at home have a natural ally in the small school, and a natural enemy in the large school.

Jim returned to his alma mater, East Rockaway High School, the smallest public high school in Nassau County. It is located just outside of New York City. After a thirty-year absence, he found that even academically and socially marginal kids had a sense of belonging there. They said things like, "It's like a family here. You know you can count on everyone. You know everyone." They said, "You can't get away with anything here. Someone always notices what you are doing." That's a good recipe for positive development in teenagers, to act so the kids will think: "People care about me, and they prove it by paying attention to what I do—both the good and the bad." That's about character, a significant lesson to remember as we proceed.

Much of the important research on high school size was conducted in the 1950s and 1960s by psychologists Roger Barker and Paul Gump and their colleagues in Kansas. They documented the superiority of small schools in providing a positive environment for teenagers. Students reported great satisfaction around the development of responsibility, competence, challenge, and a sense of identity. They were drawn into positions of responsibility and activity on behalf of pro-social goals: putting on concerts, organizing meetings, and practicing and working in teams in preparation for competing in athletic events.

The research demonstrated that although the large school provides more settings in which students can act, there are proportionately more kids to fill those settings. Small high schools, in contrast, have more settings than they have kids to fill them. For example, although the large school may have both a chorus and a glee club, together these two settings can accommodate only a very small proportion of the student body, so it is still hard for any given student (particularly one with little talent) to get into either activity. A small high school probably has just one vocal group, but is apt to be so hungry for voices that any student willing to make the effort to participate will be welcomed.

Ironically, just as this evidence for the social and psychological superiority of small schools was becoming available, social forces and deliberate policy were operating to close and consolidate these schools in favor of big ones. This may have been the most unfortunate trend in education of the last half of the twentieth century. Large schools tend to discourage meaningful participation in the social and extracurricular activities of the school, which in turn diminishes students' sense of personal ownership for what happens in the school and thus their sense of responsibility.

Today the costs of being an at-risk kid are so much greater than they were thirty or fifty years ago, when there were fewer kids carrying the burdens of parental separation and divorce, fewer temptations in the form of drugs, and a less sensational mass media. Kids who dropped out of high school could still get on track occupationally. Now, the need for high-risk kids to attend a school that compensates with intact adult authority is dramatically greater.

In large high schools, at-risk kids are superfluous; in the small high schools, they are needed. This is not a matter of the teachers, staff, and student leaders in the small school being nicer or having been to "inclusiveness workshops." Nor is it a matter of the teachers, staff, and student leaders in the large school being mean or exclusionary. It is a matter of social context, a manifestation of the social systems of the school. Psychologist Rudolph Moos uses the term "the principle of progressive conformity" to describe the fact that people tend to become what their environment elicits and rewards. The big school elicits and rewards passivity and marginal involvement among most students, and leadership and activity only among the elite. The small school elicits and rewards participation and responsibility among the whole student body as a matter of necessity.

What is big and what is small? The researchers working in the 1950s and early 1960s concluded that after a school exceeds 500 students in grades nine through twelve, it quickly takes on the dynamics of bigness. From 1955 to 1975, the average size of our high schools grew from about 500 to about 1,500. Just walk into most large high schools, and you can see and feel what the researchers were documenting half a century ago. Many of these schools look

and feel like factories—or, even worse, like prisons. Elaborate security systems are in place to *try* to keep track of students, but even so
the schools leak students all day long. Look at the yearbook and see
how little active participation there is for most students. Then look
at the data on dropping out and delinquency among the high-risk
students.

In contrast, visit a small school like East Rockaway High School. No
look of a war zone. No security guards. No students unaccounted for.
All this despite the presence of at-risk youth and marginalized students. In today's world, the last thing kids need is to go to school and
receive another dose of social toxicity, rather than the antidote.

The Bus Stops Here

School starts and ends on the bus for thousands of kids. The bus
ride back and forth is often the most anxious part of the day for many
students, when bullies are out in force. Bus drivers have the driving
on their hands; they rarely intervene in teasing and fights that occur
in their domain, so students must fend for themselves. Kids depend
upon figuring out the puzzle of peer predictability to provide an
answer about their safety that day on the bus. As adults, we must
examine the impact of a bus ride filled with fighting or verbal abuse
on our children's sense of safety. What are the consequences that
carry over to the next school day? How aware are school personnel
that kids are arriving at school already distressed, based on what they
have experienced during the bus ride?

Kids should not have to run the gauntlet before and after their
school day. Yet millions are subjected directly to abusive behavior on
the bus, while countless others participate as silent observers. In the
absence of safety provided by adults, the ability to predict one
another allows teenagers to conduct their workday with some
amount of emotional ease. When kids get to know someone, they are
less likely to feel threatened, so they are much less likely to avoid,
tease, ridicule, or bully that person—and they are more apt to consider him or her their friend.

Kids need adult help to understand the motives of their peers who
appear different. Difference and diversity can be anxiety-producing
for teenagers. Social workers, counselors, and teachers can advise
and train adolescents regarding appropriate peer interactions,

improving communications between groups of students, enhancing understanding of group behavior, and providing forums for discussions on peer tolerance. Tolerance can begin and end each day on the school bus.

What Can You Do?

1. Be aware that kids are anxious enough at school that they are employing mechanisms like peer predictability to try to navigate the emotional and physical obstacles of their everyday life at school. This takes an enormous amount of energy on the part of our kids. Further, it is time and energy they could be devoting to the academic portion of their school experience.

2. Talk to school administrators. The reason kids use peer predictability strategies is that they don't feel they have enough supervision and intervention from adults to keep them safe. Begin a dialogue with school personnel about how to implement better supervision and intervention techniques aimed at helping kids feel safe. Forms of violence, from what adults might consider mild to the most obviously damaging, should be considered grounds for intervention when adults are concerned with a safe and caring environment at school.

3. Insist on adequate supervision as kids define it. This means parents and school administrators need to get in the habit of asking kids what they need to feel safe. We have seen over and over that students' and adults' definitions of safe and supervised can be vastly different.

4. Volunteer to supervise some area of your child's school. If you are not personally able to commit time on the campus, help organize others who can make that kind of commitment. Kids in a recent poll said, "We're looking to you, the adults, to see how you respond to situations." Kids need and are asking for our awareness, supervision, and intervention in situations that range from plain nasty to physically harmful.

5. Give a lot of thought and attention to bus safety. If the bus isn't safe, the school isn't safe. Typically, bus safety instruction for kids consists of learning how to evacuate through the back door or a window of the bus if needed. Drivers talk to the children about keeping their hands and belongings inside the bus and not sticking them out the windows. Some drivers tolerate a good deal of activity on their buses and others do not; it is not predictable. Drivers need to drive and cannot stop the bus every five minutes to deal with "minor" skirmishes when they break out. With your advocacy group, consider what creative solutions you can generate to provide a safer atmosphere on the bus for the beginning and end of the school day. Are there parents who are able to volunteer their time to ride buses? It is not an unknown concept—parents have been riding school buses for years on field trips. Has the school district considered any plans for addressing these kinds of safety issues on the buses? So many kids mention the bus as problematic that we know it is a precursor of other violent activities that happen in the school itself. We can't afford to overlook this issue, or pretend it doesn't exist. Bus safety problems cannot be considered unsolvable or too expensive to change.

6. Be an active advocate for small schools and small class size in your school district. This issue always comes up for discussion and debate at PTA meetings and open meetings with the school board. Hardly anyone is opposed to small class sizes, yet the issue almost always falls by the wayside the minute budget restrictions comes up. Penny-wise and pound-foolish communities end up paying far greater costs from the impact of school dropouts, youth or young adult unemployment, illiteracy, vandalism, and lower property values as a result of school violence. It is far more economical to pay the salary of the extra teachers it takes to provide smaller classes in your school than the tax dollars required to pay for social services and prisons. You can choose which expenditure makes more sense to you by your vote and your voice.

7. Advocate the "school within a school" concept if your district is not building new schools. This is sometimes referred to as the "house" concept in large schools. What it means is that large schools are divided up into smaller units, each with its own principal and staff. Students have classes with their own "school," though in some instances they share the cafeteria or gym with kids from the other "schools." Communities that have successfully implemented this idea have seen the benefits in less vandalism and a great reduction in the dropout rate.

8. Just as there are community standards for decency, there must be community

standards for safety. As we have seen, for children and adolescents, safety is based on a predictable environment. Some of that predictability is based on getting to know others who are different, and some is founded on the knowledge that adults will set up an orderly environment. Is your community fairly predictable? If yes, why is that? If no, what is your community trying to do about it? Now, apply these same questions to your schools. We learn from kids that their school communities are *not* as predictable as they need them to be. What can the community do to rectify this?

9. Ask yourself, "What does this community do to teach tolerance and encourage diversity awareness?" Gavin De Becker in *Protecting the Gift* describes an interesting strategy for helping kids figure out what they need to know about other people, especially strangers. He suggests allowing young children, under your careful observation, to approach people they don't know. Your five-year-old might approach a policeman or a postal worker to ask a question: "What time is it?" or "Can you tell me where X is?" or "Do you like your job?" After talking briefly with the stranger, you then talk with your child to find out his or her reactions: "Did you feel comfortable with the stranger or not? What kind of person did the policeman seem to be? Did you like this person?" In doing this, you are helping your youngster begin to trust basic instincts, what have been called "gut reactions." If your child felt afraid or uneasy, was that due to a new experience or a true instinct? De Becker contends that over a period of time, with the help of a supportive parent, kids figure out when to be afraid of someone new or different and when they don't need to be. For children at school, this is invaluable. Sometimes the Goths are just kids dressed differently, and sometimes the kids to be wary of look like everybody else.

10. Insist on evaluation to determine the effectiveness of any new supervision strategies in your school or on campus. Any truly sound evaluation must include asking the students. There are pitfalls, though, to watch out for in any evaluation:

- In using surveys, the questions have to make sense to kids. They have to be appropriate for age, and they cannot be asking two questions at the same time.
- Surveys should be field-tested with some students first before administering them to the larger group. Children and adoles-

cents are very able to give good and useful feedback about how a survey is designed and what parts may have confused them.

- Hire professionals who have expertise in working with kids to do individual interviews and focus groups.

- You may need independent consultants to do the evaluations of your school's programs and supervision strategies, rather than having them conducted by personnel employed by the school district.

- All of the different voices at your school must be heard for effective evaluation, including teachers, janitors, administrators, aides, social workers, "at risk" kids, "regular" kids, and the "superstars" of the school. If any group is left out, you only have completed part of the puzzle.

Chapter 10

Kids High at School: Everyone's Affected

drugs and alcohol are a big deal for American kids everywhere. Illicit substances play a major role in every young person's life and identity, whether he or she is using them or not. Drug and alcohol use at school has a significant and direct role in the level of fear and fearlessness among students.

How do drugs and alcohol affect teenagers' sense of safety during the school day? How does substance abuse by their peers, either at school or in their off hours, affect kids? Teens describe classrooms where other students are "high," and hallways in which drug deals are an everyday event, even in schools considered by their rural and suburban communities to be good and safe. Some students seem nonchalant about these things, yet many others maintain a constant anxiety about what could happen, because kids who get high are seen as kids who are unpredictable. Finding ways to make it through this morass of feelings and risky behavior can determine a teen's chances of staying out of harm's way.

Sidney, age seventeen, and David, age fifteen, attend a high school of approximately 800 students in northern New York. Sidney is a senior who is at the top of her class academically. David is a sophomore and a marginal student; he tries hard, but his efforts don't earn him anything but C's and D's. Their comments on kids using drugs represent a starting point for understanding the impact on the school experience:

I don't like sitting next to somebody in class who is all doped up, high . . . saying stupid junk, disturbing the class. (Sidney, 17)

Drugs are bad business. People get killed over drugs. (David, 15)

Kids are concerned about the level of drug use and possession at school, on the school premises, and in the community. Almost half the students we interviewed from high schools in New York State identified drugs as a concern. Fellow students who use or deal drugs make many students feel uncomfortable and unsafe. Unfortunately, the President's Goals 2000: Educate America Act, signed into law on March 31, 1994, has failed in at least one major tenet thus far. Goal Six states, "Every school in the United States will be free of drugs, violence, and the unauthorized presence of firearms and alcohol and will offer a disciplined environment conducive to learning."

The fact is that drugs and alcohol are still prevalent on high school campuses. One way students attempt to deal with others who are using drugs at school is by making fun of them. This has the effect of displacing some anxiety and of calling the teachers' attention to the fact that someone is high. But knowing who the "druggies" are and trying to stay out of their way is not enough. Why? Because they are either high or hassling over drugs—and both produce unpredictability, the bane of high school students' experience when it comes to feeling safe.

Druggies think they're so much better than everybody else. They think they can go and just trash talk everybody and then, like, if somebody trash talks them, they get all offensive and say, "I'm going to beat you up" and stuff. It's stupid. Some people are just mean. I think mostly it happens around people who are doing drugs. (David, 15)

Most of the people who are into drugs think they're all big and macho and the boss. They push each other and say, 'You owe me money.' You try to avoid them the best you can. They come to school all high and everything. They act mean and stupid. (Seth, 17)

Substance use and abuse have a major impact on the school experience. Some of its impact can be readily seen, but other aspects are more subtle and may never come to the attention of adults until it is too late, as we witness in the following exchange between two seventeen-year-olds.

RICH: He's a major drunk [the goalie]. They all are. It's the only way they know how to party or have a good time.

JONATHAN: I think it's half the reason some of the best soccer players in our school quit after one year on the team. Because that's not how they see themselves. That's not who they wanted to hang out with. It's too bad; they were really good, too.

Here we get a glimpse—a sad commentary—into one of the problem aspects of alcohol use for some of the school athletes. It is always sad to think of a young person who is alcohol-involved to such a profound degree that other students already consider him a "drunk." It is also disheartening to realize that some talented and motivated young people are opting out of sports because they experience a social culture that supports substance abuse within their school's teams.

This scenario gets played out all over the country every year. Unfortunately, most of the time parents are totally unaware that their child may be involved, either as an athlete or as a child who might have been one. As parents and educators, we have to ask: What happened to the boys and girls who decided to quit their sports teams? Did they find other positive activities, like drama or band or maybe the yearbook? Or did they find other groups with whom to affiliate that were not so wholesome? Did they begin to disassociate themselves from the school and their peers? Did they start to become isolated? Other students are very aware when kids are high in the classroom or the locker room, even when teachers don't notice. For some students, this situation is very disturbing, because they don't know what to expect from peers who are "high" or "loaded" or "strung out." Kids can be equally disturbed by witnessing drug transactions on the corners of the school property, on the campus itself, and in the hallways.

The fact that adults, both in school and in the community, lack awareness of the true magnitude of the problem makes kids feel unsafe during the school day as well as during out-of-school activities. Katie, age sixteen, an average student and an athlete in her suburban school, puts it this way:

I don't think that people in the district have any idea how big the drug problem is. The students . . . when they go to parties and houses . . . you see so many kids that you wouldn't suspect of being drug abusers. There is a lot of marijuana. A lot of cigarettes and alcohol. The use of marijuana [is] very widespread.

About 15 percent of our interviewees felt uneasiness over drug use in the school building, including in their classes. Fully half of the students Ellen interviewed, as well as those in national studies, expressed concern over drug use in general and "druggies" who hang around outside on the school grounds. A Harris Interactive survey conducted by Edward Gaughan and his colleagues of Alfred University contacted over 2,000 young people in grades seven through twelve during the 2000-2001 academic year. These students reflected a nationally representative sample. They were asked why they thought school violence and school shootings occur. Fifty-two percent of all respondents believed violent offenders drink alcohol or use other drugs, and that this contributes to their potential violence.

Another recent survey (discussed in Chapter 5) asked kids about the connection between bullying and substance abuse. The 15,686 adolescents polled said bullies were more likely than others in the school to drink alcohol and smoke. It is clear that in the opinion of many students, peers who abuse drugs are suspect.

Are Adults Aware of Drug Use or Not?

Good research supports our argument that adults are often in denial or in the dark about the true extent of alcohol use in schools. A survey conducted in 2000 by Rosemary Barrow and her colleagues found that teachers, counselors, administrators, and parents simply view alcohol as "something teens do." The encouraging news out of this dispiriting study is that principals and counselors in small rural schools were better able to spot kids who came to school high or drunk than those in larger schools. (Alcohol is the drug of choice in rural schools.)

What is more, kids are not only uncertain about adult awareness but also about their commitment to doing something. Many kids report that teachers and administrators either do not notice the effects of drugs and alcohol or choose to do nothing about them. They find both prospects equally disturbing. Crystal believes teachers are thoroughly cognizant of "drug kids who are high" in class and are purposefully not attending to them. We asked, "Do you think that the teachers and other adults in this school are aware of what's going on in the school?"

Yeah, a lot. Definitely. Some of the teachers, like, with the drug kids—
if they come into a class, the teachers know that they are high. They
don't pick on them. They leave them alone. They are supposed to go
and tell somebody, but they don't. (Crystal, 17)

Warren, age fifteen, was similarly upset, but for different reasons.
He describes his gym teacher as "oblivious." When we asked him if he
thought his teachers in general were aware of drug use at school, he
said, "No. There's a lot of people that bring drugs to school that the
teachers don't know about. Like in the gym, Mr.———is just doing
his papers and he is almost completely oblivious to what is going on."

What Do Kids Want Adults to Do?

Students are ambivalent about what exactly the school should do
when someone is under the influence. Drug abuse thrives in a culture of enabling disguised as good intentions—whether in the family
or in school. If adults overlook a student who is high in favor of "not
telling" on him or her, that is a clear-cut example of enabling the
behavior to continue. Teenagers are not certain how to feel about the
enabling that takes place within the school.

I think if a kid comes into school high, maybe they should do something about that. I think the teachers are like our friends and they
don't want to go and tell on us, you know. But I don't like sitting next
to somebody in class who's all doped up, high. . . . It's just stupid. Even
the kids who do drugs just once in a while laugh at them and mess
with them. (Rachel, 17)

If the teachers would do something, that would be good. My sister said
there is a kid in her gym class who comes in high everyday. Some
teachers don't do anything about it. They don't care. There aren't any
other problems that are as big as the problem of drugs and alcohol.
(Celeste, 16)

Contrary to what adults may think about teen attitudes toward
drugs, the students we talked to are not blasé at all. They want to talk
with adults about getting substances off campus. They were adamant

that the eradication of all drugs (including alcohol) from the premises would make them feel more at ease in their workplace. Adults with an interest in education must collaborate with students to develop mechanisms to eliminate drug and alcohol possession at school.

We asked several students what they thought could or should be done about the problem of drugs. Warren wants greater stringency about the laws about knives and other weapons and drugs. Alison, a junior from a rural school, was firm:

> More of a crackdown on drugs. There are so many issues about this at this school in particular. Various athletes and individuals and teams have been accused of alcohol or drug abuse by teachers and other students. I know that there's a huge amount of students in this school who abuse alcohol and other drugs. And I think it's a big problem. If you crack down on that, then a lot of people would feel a lot safer.

Brent, also from a rural school, went as far as to advocate drug tests, urine samples, and random locker searches.

We believe there are ways in which the schools have not viewed these issues appropriately or realistically. First, it is apparent from the comments by kids that neither the policies regarding drugs and alcohol nor their implementation have been consistent. Sometimes teachers reported "kids who are high," and sometimes they did not. Of course, all schools currently have policies prohibiting drugs, including alcohol, on the premises. But a zero-tolerance policy lives and dies in the hallways, the bathrooms, the cafeteria, the schoolyard, and the classrooms. Even when adults are not paying attention, kids are. And even when adults are not taking appropriate action, kids are reacting.

Misunderstood and inconsistently enforced policies lead to confusion and ultimately to anxiety. Even if actions on the part of adults are meant to err on the side of tolerance in a spirit of compassion, when students do not understand the reasoning behind decisions made by adults about significant issues like alcohol and drug use, they formulate their own conclusions and subsequent strategies. Tolerance runs the risk of being experienced as neglect and lack of caring.

As David said, "Drugs are bad business. People get killed over drugs." While there may appear to be an element of melodrama in his statement, there is truth, too. Social scientists know that "situations perceived as real are real in their consequences." We must focus on what is true for many teenagers as they observe drug use at all lev-els—from casual use and offhand references to pressured sales and threatening exchanges.

As adults, we would not want to put up with the sale of drugs in our work space. But our kids often have no choice. They see it, it's a part of their common experience, and they have to make decisions about it. These decisions include not only whether to purchase any-thing for themselves, but also how to deal with the emotional impact of feeling this corrosive influence.

Of course, some kids are just mildly curious when they are first exposed to the easy availability of drugs in their school building. Oth-ers never feel comfortable around the sale or the use of drugs, which is a boundary that helps some kids stay on the healthy path—but also causes these same kids to doubt their level of safety on the campus. To tell on another student about this activity is to truly be a "narc" (narcotics officer). This is *not* something that most children are will-ing to risk. David's statements are also warnings: People get killed over drugs. They get killed trying to obtain them. They get killed for not paying for them. They get killed for "narcing" on somebody else.

Is Everyone Else Doing It?

Another issue is the importance of having and communicating accurate information about drugs to kids. Whether it be marijuana smoking or drinking alcohol, the number of kids actually using any given drug is often inflated in the minds of teenagers—and some-times adults as well. Research reveals that while many kids are indeed involved in illicit drugs, most kids overestimate the prevalence of drug use.

This phenomenon in turn precipitates more drug use, because kids think "everyone else is doing it." So communicating accurately can be an intervention in its own right, because it can reduce the per-ception of peer prevalence and thus reduce the impact of the impulse toward conformity.

Most parents and other concerned adults will read a chapter like this and think something like, "I hope my child doesn't get involved with a bad crowd that will be a negative influence." That reaction is natural—but most of the parents of kids who are involved in drugs are thinking the same thing. The truth is, your child may be the bad influence on someone else's child. That's a tough message, but it's true. The cartoon character Pogo said it best: "We have met the enemy, and they is us."

This is important for at least two reasons. First, it generates compassion for other families. If the enemy is us, it is easier to see that "the enemy" in reality is probably a parent or two struggling to do the best they can to raise their kids. Breaking down the stereotypes between "us" and "them" is likely to reduce the impulse to judge, and being judgmental is part of the problem, both within and between families. Second, it motivates a communitywide solution, because we really are all in this together—if not at this very moment, at least in the long haul. You may not feel concerned about alcohol or drugs with your firstborn child, but perhaps a few years down the road it may be something your family has to face with a younger sibling.

The evidence would predict this: one in three high school kids is involved in the illicit drug scene in one way or another. The National Institute of Drug Abuse and the National Institutes of Health have tracked illicit drug use by eighth-, tenth-, and twelfth-grade students since 1991. The 2000 survey of over 45,000 students all across the nation found that 32 percent of tenth graders and 37 percent of twelfth graders had used marijuana in the past year; for eighth-grade students, the figure was 16 percent. For alcohol consumption, the survey results found 43 percent, 65 percent, and 72 percent alcohol use in the past year among eighth-, tenth-, and twelfth-grade students, respectively. In a random survey of 15,877 students, the Jackson Institute of Ethics found that 19 percent of boys in high school and 9 percent of boys in middle school admitted they were drunk at school at least once in the 1999–2000 school year.

How can you know if your child is involved with alcohol or other drugs? We discussed the problems of knowing your child's secret life in Chapter 2. Beyond what we said there, two more things are worth mentioning. First, there are relatively simple tests to determine whether your child is "using." Kids have access to technology and expertise to fake and fool these tests (whole websites are devoted to it), but working with your physician you may be able to finds ways to get an accurate, objective reading of the situation. This is helpful because it takes the debate from the realm of dealing with a teenager who says "You don't know what you are talking about" and "You don't trust me" to that of a parent calmly saying, "Here are the results. What are we going to do about it?"

Second, just because drug use is common among some teenagers today, you must not make simple and drastic assumptions about causes and effects. Some kids really do use drugs (including alcohol) in a casual and recreational way. Of course, they may still become addicted or suffer harm from this particular form of curiosity or sensation seeking. Other kids do use drugs to self-medicate—because they are depressed or have undiagnosed and untreated attention deficit disorder, for example. If you suspect or know your child is using, get some accurate information, take a deep breath, talk it over with a calm adult (preferably one with some knowledge and experience), take another deep breath, and *then* deal with your child directly, as calmly and nonjudgmentally as you can. Here's what an eighteen-year-old who had been through the drug scene said about sixteen-year-olds using drugs:

> Parents need to be calm about it. When they get all uptight, it just makes kids want to do it more. And they need to remember that for most kids, it's something they survive. Don't think "The world is over" or your kid is a drug addict just because your kid is using.

What Can You Do?

1. Find out if your school has a drug task force; if not, work to establish one. A school's drug task force should include professional substance abuse counselors, community mental health professionals, school social workers and a psychologist, a school administrator, teachers, parents, and above all students. It may seem cumbersome to include all of these people, but without them one or more important perspectives on the situation at your school will be lost. Without including the students, you are likely to miss important information about the extent of any problem your children may be facing. Remember that since the school is a system, all of the parts (and people) in it contribute to how it is currently functioning. Consequently, not only do you need to hear everyone's take on the drug and alcohol situation at your school, but in order to succeed in making any real change, all the major players in the system must be involved and committed to a change.

A school drug task force needs to convene to evaluate the level of drug and alcohol involvement in the school, and among young people in the community in general. Once the extent of a possible problem is established, the task force must meet on a regular basis to plan intervention strategies and programs, then evaluate the effectiveness of its work. Have the programs made any noticeable difference? What more should be done? Do you need to bring in consultants from outside the district or from outside the area?

An important element of any drug and alcohol task force is taking a close, careful, and honest look at use in the greater community. When you look at your community from the perspective of someone who has never come to your town before, what do you see? Do bars outnumber any other form of recreation? Are there more liquor stores than churches? What are the statistics in your daily newspaper for DWIs or DUIs? Are there other alcohol or drug-related crimes in your area that you are aware of? Make certain that you find out. Alcohol and drug abuse in a child or in a community is a symptom of dis-ease in a person or in a system. As a parent or educator, you need to ask yourself: "What is this community or school *not* providing that supports an unacceptable level of alcohol and drug involvement for children *and* for adults?"

2. Find out if your school's policies regarding alcohol and drug use are clear. As we have learned, predictability of other kids, of the teachers, and of the environment is central to kids' feeling safe while at school. If adults are inconsistent about removing a young person from the classroom for drug or alcohol problems, kids notice this and wonder. "Can the teachers and other staff protect me? What if this kid does something crazy? Is it right for me to say anything to a staff person?" While all of this wondering and feeling is going on, your child is not concentrating on the material being presented or the test being given. Will you hear about it later? Probably not. In any event, while it is helpful, it is not the kids' job to monitor the classroom or to decide whether to "tell" or not. This is a function and responsibility that belongs to adults—school personnel, parents, and community members. Adults must decide on local policies to comply with federal law mandating "safe and drug free schools," and they must decide how best to intervene in situations where alcohol or other drugs are involved. Deciding not to turn in a student who is high is clearly doing no one a favor.

3. Propose alcohol and drug education for the teachers, administrators, and other staff, as well as for interested community members. While school personnel may have taken past courses on alcohol and drugs, the drug scene changes from year to year in any community. For example, for years heroin may be not seen and not sold in town. Then all of a sudden, it shows up. When this happens, young people are attracted. Drugs can be cool to some kids, and have a kind of cachet. Typically, adults in the same community are the last to know about what substances are available, who is buying what, and what is fashionable in the drug scene. Worst of all, adults do not know the power and serious consequences of some varieties of drugs that are available today. Marijuana is the best example of this. Some adults remember smoking marijuana when they were teenagers and college students, and believe as a result that this drug is not a problem. What they are missing is information about the composition of marijuana today; it is a very different substance than it was in the 1960s and 1970s. Teachers and other school personnel cannot always be up-to-date on the substances in the community and how they typically affect kids. Training on a semiannual basis for teachers, staff, parents, and other community members is an excellent idea and can be provided for free by your local alcoholism council or county mental health association.

4. **Talk to your children about what you are planning to do about drugs and alcohol at school.** Let your child know you are concerned about kids who use illegal substances, especially while those kids and others are at school. It is essential that your child realize you are aware that some kids in the community use drugs, and that some teens are high at school. Kids feel better and safer when they know adults know. Also, your children—especially any that are middle or high school age—will be particularly embarrassed by some actions you *could* take at school. Therefore, it is a good idea to discuss anything you are considering with them first. This is not to get permission, but rather for these purposes:

• By discussing your intentions with your children, you will learn from them what they consider to be essential elements of the problem at school or in the community.
• You will be acknowledging your children as valuable resources who can offer something back to their school community through their discussions with you. You will be validating their expertise.
• You will be demonstrating respect by acknowledging that the

school is their everyday sphere, a place your teens know much more about than you do.

5. Be clear with yourself and with others that alcohol is a drug. This seems obvious to many people, but there are adults who don't think about alcohol this way, because it is a legal and socially accepted drug. It is essential that as a parent you are honest with yourself about it, because otherwise you will tend to overlook the consequences of alcohol use at school. Although we tend to believe that all adolescents experiment with alcohol and other drugs, this is actually not true. While studies show that a significant proportion of teenagers *try* drinking and other drugs when they are still in high school, their use may be anywhere from one time only to occasional use on weekends. Most teenagers are *not* using on a regular basis, parental fear and media hype notwithstanding. That being said, it is still important to remain vigilant for signs of drug and alcohol use by your own child.

Some parents allow their teenage children to drink wine with their meals, believing that it is an important part of their education. These parents often feel that if teens participate in "responsible" drinking in the family setting, then they will not be tempted to get drunk or abuse drugs when the parents are not at home. Research findings are mixed on this theory. We certainly know of many children whose parents adopted this philosophy, but the young people still regularly overindulged at high school parties. If you are a parent who feels it is okay for your teen to drink wine with family meals, it is important to know that—despite your best intentions and explanations—it is not an unlikely leap for him or her to decide it is okay to drink in other contexts as well. Sometimes, unfortunately, this includes drinking or using other drugs during the school day.

And there are also parents who believe it is okay to serve alcohol to minors in their homes. Undoubtedly, you have heard this rationalization. It goes like this: "Since I know that kids are going to drink and party anyway, I would rather they do it at my home so I know where they are." While we can sympathize with a parent's attempts to keep track of his or her own child, this kind of attitude results in many disastrous effects:

- **It gives undermining and inappropriate messages.** The messages are as follows: "I expect that you are going to drink. I basically think it is okay for you to do so; I am cool, and other parents are not. I know it is against the law, of course, but I will collude with you in breaking the law. This law is not for you. I am *not* going to watch how much you drink. You are a responsible person even if you drink to excess."

- **There is a ripple effect.** Not everyone in the school, generally, is invited to the parties. But nonetheless, the message usually spreads to all the kids in the school, and it isn't just that there was a party and the parents bought the beer. The message is, "See, some adults think it is okay for us to drink. They agree with us that the law is stupid." As a result, those adults in your community who do allow parties at their homes where alcohol is served (and other drugs may be present) are giving permission for underage drinking to many more kids than actually attend the parties. As a parent, you need to be aware of this ripple effect and the subtle messages being transmitted to your child.

- **Kids leave these adult-sponsored parties and drive drunk.** Sadly, we all know of young people—talented, wonderful, and aspiring—who have left such a party and either died or killed someone else in an auto accident. The families *never* get over their losses. If the young person survives, he or she *never* truly gets over the guilt that remains from killing someone else while driving drunk. The consequences are felt for the rest of their lives.

6. **Have honest and open discussions with your child about alcohol and other drugs.** As parents we are very tempted to have "the drug talk" once with our child, then hope for the best after that. Sometimes we never have any discussion at all, thinking that there is no need. We say to ourselves, "Obviously our kids know how we stand on the issues; they never see us drunk or high, after all." If our community has a DARE program, we may believe that is enough.

As researchers, though, it is our experience that parents need to basically leave the phone line open on the subject of drugs. Little children will easily talk to adults and parents about what they have seen, or what they know on the subject. So the best advice is to start talking with your children when they are in elementary school. Does anybody smoke at school? Do they see any bottles on the playground? Does anybody offer to sell them any substances when they are at school? On the way to school? Younger children, ages six to ten, will readily have a conversation about these questions. If you ask, and wait quietly for an answer, even older kids will often want to tell you what they have seen and experienced. The trick is to ask and wait, rather than answering your own question. Don't be afraid to hear the truth. A *typical* parent and early adolescent exchange might go something like this:

PARENT: There's not a drug problem in your school, is there?
CHILD: No, there's no problem. Not a *problem* really.
PARENT: Nobody's trying to sell you any drugs or anything, right? This isn't something you have to deal with, right?
CHILD: No.
PARENT: I hope none of *your* friends use drugs, do they?
CHILD: No.

The parent in this scenario did not phrase the questions in any way that would elicit a genuine response, but nevertheless probably believes this was a legitimate "discussion" about alcohol and drugs. He or she could have rescued the exchange by, noticing the child's answer when asked if there was a drug problem in the school. "Not a problem really" is a clue and actually has several meanings:
• Something is happening.
• Your child might not label it as "a problem" on first thinking about it, but you might.
• He or she has noticed something about drugs, alcohol, or something related to it.
• Your child has something to say about this and may just be willing to share it.
Try any of these questions as follow-ups to "Not a problem really":

PARENT: "Not a problem really." Huh . . . how do you mean?
PARENT: When you say, "It's not a problem really," what do you mean?
PARENT: Not really a problem. Hmm. Is it *sometimes* a problem?
PARENT: Have you ever noticed that it's a problem for *anybody* at your school?

The last reply takes the discussion out of the realm of me-and-you (where the child may think, "I don't want to talk about this anymore, because somehow I am going to end up in trouble.") No matter what answer your child may give to any of the attempts listed above—even if he or she gives no answer at all—you can respond with:

PARENT: What have *you* seen?

PARENT: I bet if someone asked you to, you could write a great article for the school newspaper on this subject.

PARENT: Do you ever worry about some of the littler kids at your school and drugs?

Oftentimes, kids have younger siblings (or cousins, or just good friends) at the same school. And, in fact, they do tend to worry about how the younger children will survive the pressures of alcohol and drug use in the school culture. Sometimes, discussing others is a very effective way to get teenagers to talk about problems at school without feeling like they are implicating themselves. In addition, letting your teens provide you with their own form of expertise on a subject empowers them. Acknowledging that they know something you don't is an important way to validate adolescents' growing need for self-esteem. If you listen attentively and respectfully, you will learn about the challenges that your child—and the whole school community—are up against.

It is important to conclude any discussion with your children with the reminder that you are available to talk about anything, no matter how difficult the subject may be. There are always solutions to any problem. Let them know that you will always stand by them, no matter what.

Chapter 11

Principals and Teachers Stepping Up to the Plate

Kids Don't Care How Much You Know,
Until They Know How Much You Care.

d o the adults at school care about your child? One of the most surprising findings of our research was that many kids believe that adults in the school don't really care about bullying, sexual harassment, and emotional violence. Can that be true? Is it possible that many if not most teachers, counselors, administrators, and support staff actually do not care?

Certainly there are adults who really are not interested in your child. There are some adults in our schools who are so burned out they have given up doing anything more than waiting out the years until retirement. And there are certainly adults who are themselves predatory. But most adults in our schools *do* care. They certainly say they do, and we believe them.

So why don't kids see this caring? We think several things are causing this problem. The first is that kids' high expectations for adult support are often hidden behind a façade of demands for independence. This, of course, is a common feature of adolescence in general, and many parents will recognize it immediately. It is captured humorously in the title of a popular advice book for parents of teenagers by Anthony Wolf, *Get Out of My Life, But First Could You Drive Me and Cheryl to the Mall.* But there is more to it than that.

Informally and in confidence, adolescents express recognition and sometimes even acceptance of their need for adult supervision. However, they also indicate that adults underappreciate the challenges they face. Teens we spoke to commented over and over on the lack of awareness, on the part of teachers and other adults at school, about what really happens there. They cited numerous examples of the need for adult intervention and supervision over the course of the school day. They long for it, at least in private and in principle.

Awareness

We asked students the following question specifically about adult awareness: "Do you think that the teachers and other adults in this school are aware of what's going on in the school?" Here are some of the answers we received.

I don't think they have a clue. They don't choose to really care. (Molly, 15)

The teachers often have no clue about things going on in school. They are unaware if someone is about to hurt someone else. (Josh, 15)

No . . . because sometimes there's fights and the teachers are not aware of it, like this morning at morning break. Well, when they walk around, they just walk around the halls, minding their own business. (Liz, 15)

Some do, but I know others who don't. I have some teachers who have no idea of what goes on in their class. It's the type of people they are . . . they're not aware people. [With a particular teacher] you can get away with a lot of stuff, and she has no idea. Like cheating and stuff like that. (Sean, 15)

Half the time, the teachers don't want—really don't have a clue about what's going on. So if there's anything if there's *anything* that needs to be done about something that isn't right, the teachers aren't going to do it . . . because the teachers don't know what's going on. (Natalia, 16)

Only about one in four students believe adults are "aware of anyone making the school unsafe for others." This includes awareness of safety in the classroom, in the hallways, in the restrooms, and in the cafeteria. How do teenagers explain to themselves and others *why* adults are not aware of what students are experiencing at school? We hear two major themes. First, they say that because students keep "their feelings bottled up," teachers and other adults have a hard time figuring out what is going on inside. Second, they realize that the frequently crowded and activity-filled environment of the school day, both in the classrooms and in the halls, makes it unlikely that teachers can be attentive to student behavior. Here are some of their statements:

> Because a lot of the kids I know keep a lot of their feelings bottled up. They think that adults don't really understand, because a lot of the stuff that's happening for us kids today didn't happen back then. Like I don't tell my mom a lot of stuff. I should, but I just don't, 'cause like she wouldn't understand. I don't really think that adults really know what's going on. Some do—the ones that do are really cool about it. But adults like my mom just freak out. (Megan, 14)

> Sometimes the teachers can't, like, see what's happening in all the different parts of the classes. When you have a classroom that's full of kids, you can't see someone being annoying or something. The teacher can't necessarily see that. (Jason, 16)

Steve, age sixteen, represents a minority view of the students we interviewed. He believes adults are very aware of what is going on in the building and on the school property. Why? He feels a strong sense of closeness with his teachers. To some extent, his comments reflect an unrealistic understanding of them, similar to the way young children often ascribe a kind of all-seeing omniscience to their parents ("Mom and Dad know everything"). Here's what Steve had to say when asked how aware his teachers are.

> Very aware. They can tell. They see what's going on, no matter what. Like I'm close to my teachers, so I could go and talk if I wanted to. But there's some [teachers] we have that the kids don't really care about, so that's kind of hard. But I've never really had that, so . . .

Supervision and Intervention by Adults

When they feel free to say so, adolescents are clear that they need more supervision by adults than they are currently receiving. They do not think they, or their peers, are mature enough to interact with one another safely and respectfully on the school grounds with the current level of supervision that they have. We share this belief: *Kids need to live within a structure of adult authority.* In particular, according to survey data and interviews, the hallways are problematic. The following comments attest to this idea:

Maybe some kids, their parents may not be there to tell them, you know, like what behavior is right and wrong, and stuff like that. And sometimes teachers need to let kids know. The kids need a second kind of parent there to, like, inform them and tell them what they're doing is wrong, because sometimes at home they may not get that. (Colleen, 15)

Like the only time adults really do anything about anything is if they *see* it going on. Like if they hear about it, they won't really do anything about it as much as . . . well, if two girls start screaming at each other and getting into a fight in the hall, that's the only time they'll do anything. Otherwise, if they see someone trying to trip you, they'll pretend they don't see it, because they don't want to deal with it. Because they're lazy. (Molly, 15)

I feel pretty safe, but there are many times when the teachers are clueless, and I'm not sure they would do anything to stop us from getting hurt anyway. (Trent, 16)

Little things where you get physically hurt during the day, like punching you in the halls, pinching, and kicks. That stuff adds up and makes me feel unsafe. (Sharon, 16)

Most of the teachers in our school are really lazy, and sometimes I wonder if they would help in a problem. (Susan, 15)

Most people say, "Do you want to fight? Meet you after school on the basketball court." If it was at the basketball court, and no adults heard about it, then there's nothing really anyone can do. But the seniors might try to break it up. (Megan, 14)

The teachers, even the ones that are supposed to be monitors, don't usually pay close attention to students. (Russ, 18)

Teachers walking the hallways make me feel safe. (Joseph, 16)

Potheads hang outside. No adults, no supervision. (Frank, 15)

It may seem strange to think that teens are interested in this much intervention and monitoring by adults. When asked, "Do you think that you would really want this kind of supervision?" kids generally responded, "At first we would have to seem like we resented it, but then we would get used to it. We really need it."

Bill, age eighteen, was more specific about needing greater teacher contact and interaction:

> I need to be heard. When teachers take the time to listen to my ideas, either in class or outside of class, then I feel like they actually care. Otherwise, it is hard for me to believe that the teachers really care about me. It's like . . . here is the task, hand it back to me completed tomorrow. Like I'm a robot. When the teachers do that, it is difficult to believe they care about me as a person.

It is important to notice the rancor with which Bill talked about the adults at his school. It is important because he is one of the "best and the brightest" there. While he is not recognized for athletics or for any other usual student activity, he is a good guy and well-liked by many students. He is also extremely articulate. Consequently, his opinion likely carries a lot of weight with other students and probably taps into their own feelings of disgruntlement about the school and its treatment of the students as little kids. This is a school that would do well to include someone like Bill in its planning and decision making for the benefit of the entire system.

Bill felt that a caring environment could be promoted through "class discussions" that allowed the free exchange of ideas. That way, teachers could see who the kids really are, and it would improve the general atmosphere. Bill also suggested that administrators make a better effort to get to know the students at each high school. For example, he confided that if there was a security threat at his school, he wouldn't even know whom to trust, whom to approach with any information he might have. He reported that he does not see administrators out in the hallways of his school. He never sees the principal, and he admitted to being "disappointed" about this.

Bill's observation is intriguing. Typically adults worry that when kids have information about a threat to safety they won't share it because they don't want to be seen as tattletales or worse. From Bill's comments we learn that, in his school, he feels he wouldn't even know who was trustworthy enough to approach about a potential threat. The idea that an adult has to be trustworthy is important in this context. First, any young person wants to be taken seriously if he or she brings a concern of this magnitude. They don't want to worry about being patronized or brushed off by an adult. Second, the adult must be one that a teen can feel certain will not compromise his anonymity in the reporting process. Without these measures in place, adolescents will not take the risks needed to report on concerns for their peers.

Kids tell us, "Teachers walking the hallways make me feel safe." As parents and school personnel, we need to pay attention to this. It is a simple thing, but it is also something that many schools no longer do. Teachers are busy in their classrooms trying to get ready for the next class. They are answering questions from students leaving the last class and trying to be available to the ones coming in for the next one. There is very little time in between. How can they stand at the door, watch the hallway behavior, and talk to kids at the same time? This is an important question. It cannot remain a problem that is too difficult to solve. It is central to the issue of kids feeling safe and cared for at school, so there *must* be a solution for this problem.

Some districts have considered lengthening the school day in order to reach their academic goals. We would like districts to consider lengthening the time *between* classes so that teachers and other adults could monitor the hallways and the bathrooms properly. Maybe they would even have a minute to get to the restrooms themselves!

Students often feel contemptuous about teachers who ignore or laugh at a serious conflict as it occurs. The following responses were generated by the question: "Do you see adults do anything when kids are violent?"

Last year we had a fight in school over something really stupid like food, and the teachers just stood there. They didn't really do anything until this one teacher came in and controlled everything. The other teachers were just standing there, and they didn't really care. It was really weird. I thought it was stupid. I thought the teachers could have gone back there to see what was going on instead of just standing there and watching them—and I thought it was *right* for the other teacher to come in and settle it down instead of watching it. They should check up on it, at least. (Lizzie, 15)

Most of them, yeah, intervene when there is violence. But I know one that wouldn't do much. He would stand by and watch and laugh about it. I think it's wrong. They shouldn't take sides with anyone. They should just stop it. (Josh, 15)

A lot of the teachers are coaches, and some are of pretty good size. The coaches—it's part of their job. They'll immediately go to it. (John, 17)

Sometimes I think the teachers should just let the kids settle it. If they're yelling back and forth, just let them settle it. You scream to get your point across; a lot of people in our school have big attitudes. But if they're hitting each other, then it should be broken up. (Molly, 15)

Many students rarely see adults taking decisive action when there is a serious physical encounter in the school. This leads them to conclude that adults don't really care. Other children speak more generally of inadequate adult intervention or supervision. We asked students to respond to the following statement: "I can count on it that the adults would stop someone from hurting me or anyone else (in the classroom, in the hallways, in the cafeteria, respectively). The good news is that about 60 percent of kids said yes, but that leaves 40 percent feeling vulnerable.

If adults wait too long to intervene ("Some teachers just watch to see what will happen"), then the student—particularly if he is a boy—must either engage in the fight or lose face. And a kid's sense of how long is *too* long to wait for adult intervention is often different than what adults consider an appropriate amount of waiting time.

Safety springs from a sense that powerful adults care and are willing to help. The surest way to make students feel vulnerable is for adults to do nothing to intervene when a physical fight has broken out. According to students, responses by the adults cover a wide range. Some teachers watch, some turn their backs but still remain in the area, some walk away, and some adults step in to stop the fight. The following comments are typical of what we heard in interviewing kids:

Half the teachers don't get involved, they just stand there and watch. (Morgan, 14)

I feel pretty safe, but there are many times when the teachers are clue-less, and I'm not sure they would do anything to stop us from getting hurt. (Mara, 16)

Male and Female Teachers

While there are exceptions to any general pattern, students say they see a difference between the willingness of male and female teachers to get involved in a problem situation and to intervene if there is trouble. The female teachers who do try to intervene do so with verbal directives, rather than the more physical intervention characteristic of male teachers.

About 30 percent of students consider the discrepancy to be inevitable due to gender-based differences in the ability to physi-cally stop a fight. On the other hand, all the students we talk to are clear that either walking away during a conflict or merely calling out directives from across the room is ineffectual. Most of the stu-dents attach meaning to the teachers' behaviors when they fail to intervene.

Female teachers usually just walk away from any trouble. They just don't care. They don't bother. (Molly, 15)

Megan, age fourteen, is scornful of the female teachers and her perception of their lack of ability or willingness to intervene when there is trouble. She laughed as she explained the gender difference between teachers this way:

The girl teachers, if they see a fight with boys, they'll just walk on by. They're scared to death. If it's a fight with girls, that's different. Last year, me and my friend were in a fight and a girl teacher came, and we said, "Back off, we're going to fight." And she did! The guy teachers, if they see a fight, they'll try to break it up. So, then a guy teacher came and told us to back off, and we were like "okay, okay." Mainly the guy teachers are very scary.

Lauren, age sixteen, shares her thinking on the differences between the teachers and talks about what she thinks should hap-pen:

I see my male teachers as more easily breaking apart the fights than the female ones. I've seen them breaking it apart, and female teachers just yell at people from across the room, they don't get close to it.

Do you think the female teachers should do more?
I don't know if you can really expect them to do more, but if they could, they should try. I think they should . . . be prepared to do that, because most of the time yelling doesn't work. You have to go over and actually physically restrain people.

Teachers' Perspective

What do teachers think about all this? Those we have interviewed mostly believe that teachers should *not* intervene in what they consider to be minor squabbles, even if the students come to them for help. In that event, one teacher said she would try to help the student develop a plan to resolve the problem with the other student(s). Other teachers believe the students themselves have to figure out some way around their problems, however, and those teachers do not offer any help or counsel. Some students say they, too, believe that they should sort out their own interpersonal conflicts.

Of course, teachers are on the front line of the issues of bullying and sexual harassment. They are the first line of defense in keeping the classrooms and other areas of school safe for students. It is interesting that teachers we talk to have so many different perspectives and ideas on the topic of safety, violence, and adolescents. What follows are four examples that are representative of the teachers we have interviewed.

Craig has taught school for ten years. He believes teachers should take a "wait and see" approach with students who look like they might move into a violent episode. At the same time, he is very adamant about clamping down immediately on individual rule-breakers in the school—for example, if someone is late for class without a pass. He agrees with the teenagers' assessment that most teachers are not aware of what is really going on in a school building, and he clearly sees the connection between this lack of awareness and students' perceptions of a lack of safety. Even so, he does not agree with the students' perception that the failure of adults to intervene quickly in a potentially threatening situation contributes to these feelings as well. At his school, he is not happy about the measures the administration takes to try to ensure safety. His sense is that the administration is not doing enough to create an environment of safety and that it is operating in denial about what could easily happen in terms of serious violence in the future. He was frustrated and seemed to feel powerless, however, to do anything about this problem.

Chuck is a man with seven years of experience as a professional teacher. In contrast to Craig, intervention is his forte. He is the first one on the scene when there is a physical confrontation, or even the possibility of one. The students name him specifically in any question about a teacher who can be counted on to intervene if he is aware of a problem in the school. Chuck believes it is critical to do so, and sees it as an integral part of his job.

He feels that there is a clear link between the students' sense of security and their ability to concentrate on learning. Interestingly, his perception is that all of the other teachers in the building feel the same way, and that they all act similarly if they come across an altercation. (The students and the other teachers did not substantiate this belief.) He is also adamant that the administration has done everything possible to ensure safety for everyone in the building, adding that he would not question their approach in any event.

It was obvious from Chuck's responses that he cares about the children, but also that he does not think about this timely issue at a level of any great depth. He opposes the idea of schools with metal detectors, saying he does not want to work in "that kind of environment." Because he is also the coach of one of the boys' athletic teams for the school, we asked about how the athletes behave toward one another in the locker rooms. Chuck answered that he doesn't allow any "hazing," and seemed to be oblivious to the concerns that some students cited about incidents of harassment.

Betty has been teaching for over twenty years, and has very strong opinions about what the administration is doing and could do better. It was essentially at her insistence that the school moved into "lockdown" after the tragedy at Columbine High School in Littleton, Colorado, closing all outside entrances except for the front door of the building. Doing this was a means to decrease random traffic through the hallways, especially by students who had been expelled for bad or delinquent behavior. On the whole, however, students were very contemptuous of this strategy. They were quick to point out that the doors could be (and often were) propped open with a small stone, and that anyone who knocked at a locked door would be let in by any passing student. Even the principal himself violated the policy when he misplaced his keys, according to students in the focus groups and individual interviews. Only one girl thought the locked-doors policy could potentially be useful.

Asked how responsive her school was to issues raised about school safety and the potential for serious violence, Betty answered, "Somewhat." She believes that the administration and other teachers actively resist any real change in procedures that would aggressively ensure safety at school. She wants to see more measures like the locked-doors policy instituted in the school. If students are engaging in problematic behavior, Betty believes in getting involved early. For example, when she once passed a girl hitting a boy in the hallway, Betty stopped and told the student, "Be careful—that kind of behavior can go both ways." When a boy came into her class high on drugs, she took him aside and sent him to the nurse's office. Though this sounds like a logical intervention that any teacher would make, students and other teachers told us it is not routinely done. The teachers we interviewed said many of their colleagues simply try to ignore such a child, even as other students in the class make fun of him or her. Betty does not try to break up physical fights because she does not feel she has the necessary physical strength. Once in the past, her nose was broken as she attempted to stop a fight in the hallway.

Ann has taught in secondary schools for over fifteen years. She does not believe that teachers should intervene in physical fights or other threats of serious violence in the school. She is adamant that intervening in this way is not, nor should it be, part of a teacher's job description. Although this perspective departs severely from what the principal of her school expects from his teachers, it is representative of the view of many other teachers. Unfortunately, this perspective of non-intervention is exactly counter to what students are calling for and saying they need to ensure a secure environment at school.

the variety in teacher responses about their responsibility is intriguing. While they all concur that school should be a safe place for adolescents, exactly how to accomplish that goal and who should do what differs dramatically from teacher to teacher.

Teenagers say what they hear from adults is that they should figure out interpersonal problems for themselves. They should not need an adult to aid in this process, because they are old enough to handle interpersonal conflicts.

The adults are readily available for discussion if a situation rises to a level that *adults* consider serious (for example, two students who engage in ongoing physical scuffles or fights). Short of this, adolescents are mainly left to their own devices, which are often inadequate. Only about half the students we talked to agreed that their peers were able to solve conflicts without physically hurting each other, and one in six said they believed their peers were incapable of nonviolent conflict resolution.

Administrators' Perspective

School administrators, like teachers, have a wide range of responses to bullying and harassment in their schools. Below is a progression of exchanges between students and administrators. The first represents the worst kind of administrative response to the problems and to the students. The last is the best, and it is what we hope for in all enlightened school districts.

School A

STUDENTS: We are being harassed, intimidated, beat up. We need your help.

ADMINISTRATORS: "There is no problem here." [This response is one of total denial.]

School B

STUDENTS: We don't feel safe at this school. Is anybody going to do anything?

ADMINISTRATORS: There may be some slight problems here, but this is the way kids are.

School C

STUDENTS: There are many problems here, but no one can do anything about them. [Kids are expressing helplessness.]

ADMINISTRATORS: We know there is a problem, but there isn't much that can be done about it.

School D

STUDENTS: We still have problems. The school is trying to do something, but they don't listen to what we say or what would really work. [We have no voice. We have no power.]

ADMINISTRATORS: We have problems, and we have some programs that we're using to try to correct them.

School E

STUDENTS: Things are better at our school. The principal and teachers care about our opinions. Everybody seems less tense now. It's hard to know what changed things, but something worked. [The kids have a sense of empowerment.]

ADMINISTRATORS: We are aware of our problems. We have requested some outside intervention. We are evaluating the interventions and programs for their effectiveness. Now, we ask the students for their input and opinions.

Administrators Who Listen

A major and unexpected finding is that teenagers are actually *requesting* more supervision and intervention than they currently have at school. Schools need to accept the fact that adolescents do need more attention, caring, supervision, and mentoring than is popularly believed to be the case. For change to happen, school administrators must design supervision strategies and intervention plans that take these requirements into account. When kids give direct or indirect clues that they feel uncomfortable at school, administrators need to devise a plan to correct this—not do nothing in the mistaken belief that there is no reason for the students to feel insecure. Workable strategies can be arranged to safely monitor problem areas of all buildings, the grounds, and the buses. When administrators actually talk to kids, they find out where the problems are, and they will hear viable solutions from the kids themselves.

Besides listening to students, adults need to be straightforward about what they say. Kids are always listening, and they are very sensitive to anyone being duplicitous. Steven, age seventeen, heard the principal as he gave a tour to some adult visitors from another school district. The principal said to the group that the school was going to change the students' dress code because the school had numerous outside corridors, and administrators were worried about girls wearing spaghetti-strap tops in the winter and getting sick. This reasoning seemed ridiculous to Steven, who commented that none of the girls wear those kind of skimpy tops when it is cold out. The reason put forward by the principal seemed to Steven like a rationalization for changing the dress code against the wishes of most of the students. When students hear adults giving dubious explanations for something, it can be difficult for them to tell if the adults are just uninformed or if they are untrustworthy.

Some administrators have wonderful attitudes about including kids in the everyday process of the running of the school. They truly want to know how their students are doing and feeling, and they want the children to feel involved and secure. The worst administrators believe that teenagers have nothing much to offer in the way of solving the problems of school climate. One such administrator commented to Ellen, "Why would you want to ask the students? They don't know anything; they don't have anything to contribute to this problem." Besides the ignorance that this statement shows, it is also dangerous. Without including students and their ideas, we have only a part of the picture. The ones who really know what is going on— the kids—are also the ones who are telling us what needs to change, if we will only listen.

A Missed Opportunity

We believe the adults in the system are missing an important opportunity to prevent further escalation of conflict, and thus to decrease the potential for serious violence. How? By failing to attend to student requests for help early on in the process of interpersonal conflict. Here's the way one student showed how she dealt with the institutional norm of non-interference:

I think that the teachers don't need to get involved because, like, we're going to be out of high school in three years. So we're going to be out on our own . . . and when you're out on your own, you've got to learn to deal with things. But I think it's important to really handle problems by yourself. (Aliya, 15)

Every day, new teachers are educated in our colleges without benefit of any mention about teacher professionalism as it pertains to student safety, or the expectations that parents have for teachers as guardians of their children. Americans send their kids to school expecting them to learn and to be safe. Teachers are not being trained adequately in our colleges, though, to keep children safe from either verbal or physical abuse, or from more major incidents of serious danger. Is that part of their job or not? The majority of adolescents think so.

When teachers do not live up to this expectation, the safety of the school is compromised. In the meantime, adults have not decided what to think about this subject. Teachers are divided about what they consider to be their responsibility. Those who are unambiguous about their responsibility to protect children from being seriously harmed at school (like some of the teachers at Columbine and other schools where there has been serious violence) are seen as heroes, but not all teachers want to be heroes or to risk their lives. As long as teachers and administrators are unclear or ambiguous about what is expected behavior and what constitutes professionalism, there will be an uneven response in the schools to all levels of abusive and aggressive behavior.

What Can You Do?

1. Strengthen supervision at your school. You, as a parent, need to know that when kids are asked confidentially by outside researchers—not their parents—they admit that they are willing to forgo some of their freedoms in school in order to have better, more consistent supervision. They were able to be quite clear with us about examples of what would constitute preferred supervision.

2. Develop a caring community in a caring climate. In one school we visited, we met with a group of sophomores. Half of the teens in the group said, "The principal doesn't like me," followed by comments like "She gives you the look" and "The teachers do the same thing. They're big on first impressions here." Translation: Adults prejudge them based on their clothing, dress, and overall appearance, according to the kids' perceptions.

What is the cost of these perceptions about adults? They affect children's self-esteem and their ability to trust the adults around them. Ironically, in the very room where we discussed these issues with kids there are two posters prominently displayed on the wall in the front of the room. One begins, "I expect from my teacher . . .," and lists several major themes, such as respect, listening, caring, and expectations for each student's learning. The other is entitled, "I expect from my students . . .," followed by a similar list. These posters claim to represent the "learning contract" in this room for the students and the teacher. Does it seem strange to teens that these posters list elements that are high on their list of what is lacking in their school?

See the Resources at the end of this book for more information on developing caring school communities.

3. Recognize that most students want adults to intervene in situations of violence—for example, when a fight has broken out in the hallway. They differ on exactly *when* they would like the adults to step in. Interestingly, the students' comments suggest they are making moral judgments about the teachers' and adults' supervision and intervention. Many seemed to have a clear sense about when it is right to take action, and all are unambiguous about when it is wrong for a teacher or other adult to merely stand back. Parents should support students in their expectations; kids have the right to look to adults for aid in dangerous or disturbing situations.

4. Challenge old beliefs about what appropriate supervision really is. Encourage discussion. A meeting of parents, students, teachers, aides, coaches, administrators, social workers, and other school personnel can help in getting a clear sense of everyone's perspective on the issue of supervision during the school day and during any extracurricular activities. Representatives from all groups of students are necessary for the discussion to make any sense. Oftentimes, the school "stars" and elites do not see the problems we have been describing. They simply seem to float above all of the troubles that their less successful peers encounter on a daily basis. Consequently, including only the "stars" or the student council president in discussions about school violence may not be enough to gain an accurate picture of what kids are experiencing or of what they would like to see changed. Questions to ask include: Is there any time during the school day that seems more confused or less structured than other times? Are there skirmishes during lunch periods? Some teachers and administrators—as well as some kids—will not admit that there are "fights" at school, but they will readily talk about scuffles or "flare-ups" that occur during the day. Some of these flare-ups are regular occurrences and happen between the same groups, or between the same two or three people. As a result, adults can become acclimated to these happenings, while kids are still nervous about when and where the next one is going to erupt, and if they are going to get caught in it. What is the school's policy on breaking up these skirmishes?

Typically, you will find that either there is no formal policy on what adults are supposed to do about threats to student security, or that a policy exists but is being implemented unevenly (just as the kids cited in this chapter have told us). Where does that leave the adults and the kids in the school? Where does that leave you as a parent? What do you, and your friends, believe is appropriate supervision at your school?

5. Encourage a discussion about alternative ideas of teacher professionalism, and extend the discussion to include other adults in the building. As we have noted, many teachers do not feel it is part of their job description to intervene in the event of fights, physical threats, or when children are being cruel to one another verbally. Along with other educational researchers, however, we believe that in order to educate any child, he or she must feel safe first. And we believe firmly that the adults in the school, and in the community, must provide that security for children during the school day. Consequently, it seems that this is the time for a national discussion on the core elements of professionalism for teachers and other school personnel. Can we as parents afford to pay teachers only to teach course material? Can teachers really convey course material to children who are fearful or anxious? These are critical questions for discussion in your school.

6. Volunteer at your school. The average high school in our country has more than 1,500 children. Even the very best teachers with the highest intentions cannot monitor so many kids as they pass down the hallways or eat lunch or during outside time. Schools have traditionally accepted help from parents at the elementary school level, but it is time for them to begin to accept help at all secondary schools. Some argue that adolescents need more freedom at this point in their lives to make decisions, and so forth. However, our research indicates that teenagers still need adults to create a safe environment so that they can be productive at school. Teenagers are asking for some very specific forms of adult presence, such as the following:

- More monitors in the halls, in the restrooms, outside on the school grounds, and in gym classes
- Adults to sit with them occasionally at the tables in the cafeteria
- Adults to deal with "potheads," "druggies," and drug dealers, either on campus or on the corner
- Action by coaches to prevent the hazing of younger members of athletic teams

Having a greater adult presence on the school grounds can make a big difference. In fact, some schools are beginning to appreciate this. At one large suburban high school, a bomb scare was called in. Supposedly, the bomb was to be detonated the following day, which was the second anniversary of the Columbine tragedy. The administration responded by sweeping the building with police and trained dogs, and by asking for help from community members through their presence on campus.

7. **Insist on educating the whole child.** To support increased and improved supervision and caring, school boards need to furnish the financial means to hire more teachers and mental health personnel, as well as to provide in-service programs for instituting caring communities in the schools. There must be an effort toward educating the whole child. To accomplish this goal, local and state policymakers must understand the place of school safety in children's ability to concentrate and learn. Everyone must begin to see a connection between children who feel unsafe at school and those children who are "troublemakers," who are underachievers, or who drop out of school.

In *The Challenge to Care in Schools,* Nel Noddings writes, "The main aim of education should be to produce competent, caring, loving, and lovable people." And she adds that the schools should "help students to treat each other ethically. Give them practice in caring. Help them to learn how to 'be on both sides.'"

We can no longer accept the thinking that a few "bad" kids spoil the school for everybody, and getting rid of them will solve the problem. The so-called troublemakers are part of the overall system, and they function as part of the scapegoating mechanism we discussed in Chapter 7. Noddings and others call for schools to return to a place of total learning—to be not merely about math, but also about civility, democracy, and diversity.

8. Get administrators talking to all kids. Encourage your school principal and superintendent to listen, actively and regularly, to what their students are saying about the conditions of school climate and culture. How often do they convene a formal discussion with different groups of kids? Are they meeting with kids informally? As Jerome Bruner so aptly and succinctly put it, "If you want to know what children think, ask them!" Children are happy to be involved in any process intended to create a better environment for their days. They are pleased to be considered as having a viable opinion.

How many times have you heard a young person say, "That teacher doesn't like me" as the reason he doesn't do well in class? Most of the time we think, "Well there's another excuse for not taking responsibility." While it is true that the young person is not taking responsibility for his success or failure, it is also true that kids (like the rest of us) learn better when they feel cared about, respected, and acknowledged. They do better in positive surroundings, just like we do.

It is also unfortunately true that some kids just stop trying when they feel we do not like them, respect them, or understand them. For some kids, it is impossible to grow in an atmosphere of non-caring.

We believe that good teachers and school administrators help teenagers believe in themselves, that they can learn and make a contribution to society. They establish a safe space in the classrooms where kids can take a chance to say what they think. Thoughtful and competent adults realize that "kids don't care how much you know until they know how much you care." Teachers and principals can make all the difference in a kid's day by showing how much they do care.

Chapter 12

Epilogue: Final Reflections on the Emotionally Safe School

S tudents often speak with clarity about adults' lack of awareness of the major and minor events that go on in school. The most tragic recent example of adult inattentiveness in the schools occurred at Columbine High School. Though the Trench Coat Mafia existed there and was photographed for the yearbook, the principal stated repeatedly that he had no awareness of the group. Though the perpetrators produced a violent videotape for a school assignment in which they portrayed the shooting and killing of athletes at school, no teachers took action to help Eric Harris or Dylan Klebold.

While the case of Columbine is dramatic in the extreme, it is not fundamentally different from what countless teenagers in many schools experience. In our interviews, students offer "smaller" examples of adult inattentiveness and the consequences of a school being an unresponsive social system.

Part of the ongoing balance or homeostasis of the school as a social system is the lack of real awareness on the part of adults of the events and undercurrents in the lives of students. The "gain" to adults for not being aware may be twofold.

First, when they are unaware, school officials don't have to do anything about a situation or interactions that they believe are, at some level, normal or typically adolescent. Second, they don't have to think about things they feel they can not control anyway. A 1997 study of school social workers by Ron Avi Astor, William Behre, Kimberly Fravil, and John Wallace found that their subjects did not categorize their schools as violent, despite a very high incidence of documented violent behavior on the premises, including major felonies. It seems that one reason for this misattribution is that the social workers had to return day after day to the same environment and could not afford, in psychological terms, to "see" it as unsafe.

Another hypothesis is more systemic in nature. Violent behavior becomes normalized as a part of the everyday workings of the system—that is, part of how the school system stays in balance. For true systemic change to occur, the entire school needs to move out of a state of denial toward a very different state of awareness. This requires a conscious effort on the part of administrators and school boards to instigate and support heightened awareness by teachers and other staff on the front lines of daily life in the school.

Even though in the short run it may highlight conflict and problems, in the long run increasing awareness and attentiveness to adolescents will promote school safety and reduce incidents of violence. A sure way for the institution to be very aware of what is happening is to improve communication between adults and students.

Setting up a student advisory council that meets once a week is a start. To make such a group more than just an exercise in convenient self-congratulation, however, it is important to include members from all groups and cliques in the school. (Only then will you hear *all* of the student voices.) Other means for improving communication include establishing a hot-line or suggestion box so that students can anonymously report their fears, suspicions, and suggestions for change.

Obvious questions can be raised about these latter efforts: What about students who are just trying to get somebody else in trouble? What if anonymous reporting is misused? The response to these apprehensions is twofold. One, it is better to have some misuse of the reporting mechanisms and have the opportunity to intercept a problem that is brewing in the school than to be caught unaware. Two, administrators can receive training from local mental health professionals and local law enforcement personnel to sort legitimate reports from bogus messages. The FBI and Secret Service have developed strategies for "threat assessment" that can be useful in accomplishing this.

What Is Teaching All About?

John Dewey was one of the most influential architects of modern education. His words speak to us a full century after he wrote them.

> Every teacher should realize the dignity of his calling; that he is a social servant set apart for the maintenance of proper social order and the securing of the right social growth.

Today's kids speak to us about the importance of teachers as "second parents," as supervisors in their environment, and as mentors for their social as well as academic growth. When given a chance to say so without the constraints of being cool or defending a position, today's adolescents articulate the need for more supervision and intervention by adults in the school. But if such help is not forthcoming, they will take matters into their own hands—generally for worse, not better.

In some ways this is a core issue of teacher professionalism. Veteran educator Haim Ginott offers the following on this topic:

> I've come to the frightening conclusion that I am the decisive element in the classroom. It is my personal approach that creates the climate. It is my daily mood that makes the weather. As a teacher, I possess a tremendous power to make a child's life miserable or joyous. I can be a tool of torture or an instrument of inspiration. I can humiliate or honor, hurt or heal. In all situations, it is my response that decides whether a crisis will be escalated or de-escalated and a child humanized or de-humanized.

Ginott speaks eloquently of the role of the classroom teacher in creating, maintaining, and preserving a peaceful non-violent climate in the school. The passage suggests that he believes teachers should take full responsibility where they can to "escalate or de-escalate" a crisis, with the humanity of children in mind. We agree.

We have learned that not all teachers agree with this sentiment. Some conclude that it is not their role to step in when a crisis is brewing, or to participate in creating the climate of the school. Of course, by not actively participating, teachers nevertheless contribute to the environment of the system. If the definition of teacher professionalism is to address only the academic child and leave the care of the social-emotional aspects of the child to someone else, then the system fails to nurture the total child.

It confuses some educators when children enter adolescence and give "stay away" messages. But the students we talk to are articulate about their need and appreciation for caring from teachers and other school personnel:

I think we should have more supervision at the lunch tables. Maybe even have teachers sit at the tables. (Warren, 15)

Make the teachers more aware of what's going on . . . and get involved a bit more. (Lizzie and Megan, 15 and 14)

Lower the contact with freshmen and other students. If a building has two floors, separate the sophomores and freshmen from the juniors and seniors. We need more supervision. (John, 17, an athlete)

What Does It Mean to Care?

Caring can take many forms, from sincere inquiry into teenagers' days and lives to showing support by attending school functions. What we hear from students resonates with what others have found in their research about "caring communities" in school. Schools as systems must grapple with the core concept of caring and its impact on the learning environment. Without a definitive resolution to pursue caring in its various appropriate forms, the system engages in empty rhetoric about educating the whole child.

As psychologists Arnold Goldstein and Donald Kodluboy have written, "If the adults don't control the school environment, then the students will do so." All adults connected with the school organization need to accept the fact that adolescents do require more attention and closer supervision than many adults believe.

One place to start is with concrete plans for monitoring student and adult activity on all school premises. Here are some of the essential components of appropriate supervision in high schools:

1. Formulate a uniform plan for when, where, why, and how to monitor and intervene on behalf of students.

2. Develop the plan with the cooperation and input of all players in the school. This includes students, teachers, parents, administrators, counselors, mental health professionals, security personnel, janitors, aides, and concerned community members.

3. Make sure that student input is considered critical, not merely "a good idea."

4. Solicit students' perceptions of what is safe and not safe, and where is safe and not so safe—in the school, on the grounds, and on the way to and from school. Do this through group discussions, interviews, and even surveys by outside evaluators to ensure honest and valid responses from the students.

5. Ensure that the adults who are going to enforce the plan are committed to it and regard it as useful.

6. Make it clear to everyone that adults will intervene in interpersonal disputes quickly (for most schools, this means sooner than they currently do).

7. Train every adult in state-of-the-art intervention strategies to de-escalate conflicts between students.

8. Include a uniform policy in the master plan for intervening with students who are impaired while at school due to alcohol or other drugs.

9. Avoid the temptation of relying too heavily upon technological quick fixes, because in most instances these are not what students want and need to feel safe.

10. Most importantly, obtain continuous feedback from students on supervision strategies that have been or might be implemented.

Students often feel helpless as a result of a lack of empowerment. The authoritarian system reinforces learned-helplessness attitudes and behavior in adolescents by inhibiting their participation in decision making. This in turn impairs their ability to think and act as a

part of the system in a healthy manner. Students who are angry frequently experience a sense of helplessness or powerlessness that is
portrayed in their belligerent attitudes and behaviors.

Why do students feel powerless at times? Their sense of powerlessness flows from interactions with one another, interactions with teachers and other adults in the school, and the inability to make a positive
impact on the day-to-day life of the school. Teachers and other school
personnel often observe adolescent anger, but they typically do not
see the profound feelings of hopelessness that underlie much of it.
Students say they will "take it" as long as they can—meaning they will
handle difficult and disrespectful behaviors directed toward them by
swallowing their anger until they can accept no more. When they
reach that point, they are likely to strike back at someone.

Understanding the connection between feeling helpless and striking out would be useful to all school personnel. Periodic in-service
training programs to address the concept of helplessness and its
impact on adolescents in the school setting can work to enhance the
ability of teachers to deal with the behavior that they see emanating
from these perceptions.

Empowerment is the antidote to helplessness. Happier students
who feel like their voices are heard in their workplace will translate
into a safer school environment for everyone.

Administrators also must provide in-service training regarding the
consequences of allowing bullying interactions among students and
between teachers and students. Educational psychologist Patricia
Kyle found that teachers can "feed [a] potentially violent situation by
choosing inappropriate behavior themselves" such as "yelling, using
sarcasm, put-downs, or humiliation." Several countries already have
successful programs from which adaptations to our schools could be
made; the resource guide at the end of this book identifies some of
them.

Consider the System

In our country, bullying usually is seen in a narrow way as physical
aggression or extortion (for lunch money, for example).

While considered normal by school personnel and many kids
themselves, student haranguing, bullying, and "dissing" of one

another exacts a high price in terms of the atmosphere of the school and in terms of possible escalation, retaliation, or revenge. When "two kids who would not typically blow up at one another at the bus stop" do so, two administrators we spoke to concluded that this was due to "puffery" and "adolescent hormones." Although there may be truth to that approach, it is not enough.

> Yeah, my group is really popular. We're like the only gang. There's like only one group that's ahead of us. That group and our group are, like, kind of friends you know. *We're, like, the ones who usually start the fights.* (Callie, 14)

> *I look out for the younger kids now.* I feel like I'm doing a little something now [like was done for her when she was a freshman]. I don't know what I would do if someone came in with a gun. If I saw somebody going after one of my friends, I'd probably have to go after that person. I can't just stand by and watch. I'd have to do something to help. (Crystal, 17)

Since Crystal (and the other students) did not see bad behavior being interrupted by the adults in the environment, she felt that she should take it upon herself to do so. The silver lining to this dynamic is that Crystal's pride in being able to contribute something to the younger students in the school enhanced her sense of self.

When asked, "Do you have any power to get things changed at the school?" students answered with a mix of responses:

> I have no idea. (Lizzie, 15)

> Yup. I know who to talk to, and what to do. (Steve, 16)

> No I don't have any power so then I have to worry. What if "Joe—I can't handle my problems" comes to school with a plan to take some lives to make himself feel better? Then he is the dumbest ass____ I have ever known. (Sorry about the French.) (Ben, 15)

> I don't think I do as an individual, but if I and other people made teachers and other adults aware . . . then that could probably make a difference. (Courtney, 16)

While student leadership can accomplish some of the goals, there remains a crucial role for the adults. That is where we started, and it is where we finish. When it comes to bullying, sexual harassment, and emotional violence at school, the buck stops with adults.

Resources on Bullying and Violence Prevention

American Civil Liberties Union of Southern California (ACLU)

Contact the ACLU to review the *From Words to Weapons: The Violence Surrounding Our Schools* report (2001). This report contains results of one of the largest research studies on a range of issues related to youths' experiences with violence and weapons possession, and their suggestions for ways to prevent violence and racial tension.

ACLU of Southern California
1616 Beverly Boulevard
Los Angeles, CA 90026
http://www.aclu-sc.org/school.html

National Crime Prevention Council (NCPC)

Contact the National Crime Prevention Council to review the *Safer Schools: Strategies for Educators and Law Enforcement to Prevent Violence Report* (2001). The NCPC website also provides an excellent list of books and links to other organizations for more information on issues related to youth violence and delinquency prevention.

National Crime Prevention
1000 Connecticut Avenue, 13ᵗʰ Floor
Washington, DC 20036
202-466-6272
http://www.ncpc.org/eduleo5.htm

Committee for Children

Contact the Committee for Children for information on the Second Step Violence Prevention Program, the Steps to Respect program for schools, and character education. Their website also provides information on other curricula, videos, and research on violence prevention issues, including the *Bullying and Sexual Harassment in Schools Report.*

Committee for Children
568 First Avenue, Suite 600
Seattle, WA 98104-2804
800-634-4449
http://www.cfchildren.org

National Education Association (NEA)

The NEA's Safe Schools Now web page provides information on education, violence prevention, and several other issues affecting youth. The NEA also provides information on curricula and materials for educators, including BullyProof, a violence prevention program for elementary schools.

National Education Association
1201 16th Street
Washington, DC 20036
202-833-4000
http://www.nea.org/issues/safescho.

Character Education Partnership (CEP)

Contact CEP for information and resources on character education. Their website provides information on issues related to character education, including several links to research reports, curricula, and the *Character Educator Newsletter.*
Character Education Partnership
1025 Connecticut Avenue, Suite 1011
Washington, DC 20036
800-988-8081
http://www.character.org

Education Week

Education Week is American education's online newspaper of record. Access this electronic newspaper to learn more about violence in schools, educational research, and school policies.
Editorial Projects in Education
6935 Arlington Road, Suite 100
Bethesda, MD 20814-5233
800-346-1834
http://www.edweek.org

Harvard Education Letter: Research Online

Access the *Harvard Education Letter* for suggestions on how to respond to some of the most troubling problems affecting children in kindergarten through twelfth grade. The letters review recent research and best practices for violence prevention and conflict resolution.
Harvard Education Letter
8 Story Street, Fifth Floor
Cambridge, MA 02138
800-513-0763
http://www.edletter.org

National School Safety Center

Contact the *National School Safety Center* for information, training materials, and resources on school crime and youth violence prevention. You can review reports on school safety and order videos and books on issues related to school safety by visiting their web page.
National School Safety Center
141 Duesenberg Drive, Suite 11
Westlake Village, CA 91362
805-373-9977
http://www.nssc1.org

Center for the Prevention of School Violence

Contact the CPSV for information on school violence statistics, violence prevention programs, and grants to fund prevention and intervention programs.
Center for the Prevention of School Violence
313 Chapanoke Road, Suite 140

Raleigh, North Carolina 27603
800-299-6054
http://www.ncsu.edu/cpsv

Coalition for Children
Contact the Coalition for Children for information on the Take A Stand: Prevention of Bullying and Interpersonal Violence Program for kindergarten through fifth-grade parents and teachers.
Coalition for Children
P.O. Box 6304
Denver, CO 80206
303-320-6321
www.safechild.org/bullies.htm

National Center for Chronic Disease Prevention and Health Promotion
Access the Centers for Disease Control and Prevention's Adolescent and School Health web page to review research on school violence and other youth risk behaviors.
http://www.cdc.gov/nccdphp/dash/violence/index.htm

London Family Court Clinic
Contact the London Family Court Clinic for information on the prevalence and effects of bullying. They also provide several suggestions for how parents and teachers can prevent bullying.
London Family Court Clinic
254 Pall Mall Street, Suite 200
London, Ontario N6A 5P6 Canada
519-679-7250
http://www.lfcc.on.ca/bully.htm

National Dropout Prevention Center
Contact the National Dropout Prevention Center for more information on model programs, resource materials, and effective strategies for keeping youth in school. The center also provides information on school-avoiders and the link between avoiding school and bullying.
National Dropout Prevention Center
College of Health, Education, and Human Development
Clemson University
209 Martin Street
Clemson, SC 29631-1555
864-656-2599
http://www.dropoutprevention.org

National Association of Secondary School Principals (NASSP)
The National Association of Secondary School Principals intends to promote excellence in school leadership by providing a variety of programs and services to assist in administration, supervision, curriculum planning, and effective staff development. Contact the NASSP for more information and resources on school safety.
NASSP
1904 Association Drive
Reston, VA 22091-1598
703-860-0200
http://www.nassp.org

National Service-Learning Clearinghouse

The *National Service-Learning Clearinghouse* is a collaborative project between the University of Minnesota and twelve other organizations and institutions. Contact them for information and resources on service learning.

The National Service-Learning Clearinghouse
University of Minnesota
R-460 VoTech Ed Building
1954 Buford Avenue
St. Paul, MN 55108-6197
800-808-SERV
http://umn.edu/~serve

Search Institute

The Search Institute is a nonprofit organization that is dedicated to promoting the healthy development of children and adolescents. The institute conducts research, promotes programs, and makes findings on the well-being of youth available to the public. Contact the Search Institute for more information on the 40 Developmental Assets and other issues related to positive youth development.

Search Institute
700 S. Third Street, Suite 210
Minneapolis, MN 55415
http://www.search-institute.org

Early Warning Timely Response: A Guide to Safe Schools

This guide was produced by the U.S. Department of Education and the Department of Justice to outline the qualities necessary for safe and responsive schools. It also reviews some programs that can help foster important characteristics for a safe school.

http://www.ed.gov/offices/OSERS/OSEP/Products/earlywrn.html

National Alliance for Safe Schools (NASS)

The National Alliance for Safe Schools offers a variety of services, including training, school security assessments, and technical assistance for individual schools, school districts, state and national educational organizations, law enforcement, and parent groups. They have conducted security assessments in both large urban schools and small rural schools to provide administrators with a better understanding of their preparedness to deal with a serious incident. Contact the NASS to learn more about their organization, to review publications on school safety and bullying, or to enroll in a workshop.

National Alliance for Safe Schools
4903 Edgemoor Lane, Suite 403
Bethesda, MD 20815
301-654-2774
http://www.safeschools.org

The American Association of University Women Educational Foundation (AAUW)

Contact the AAUW for more information on the *Hostile Hallways: Bullying, Teasing, and Sexual Harassment in School* (2001) report, Title IX, and other research on girls' attitudes toward peer pressure, sexuality, the media, and school.

AAUW
111 Sixteenth Street
Washington, DC 20036
800-326-AAUW
http://www.aauw.org

Information on Title IX and Schools
Federal Title IX of the Education Amendments (1972). *U.S. Code,* vol. 20, section 1681 (P.L. 92-318). This document should be available in most libraries, and certainly in any law library.

National Center for Hate Crime Prevention
The *National Center for Hate Crime Prevention* is a project of the Health and Human Development Programs Education Development Center, the Office of Juvenile Justice and Delinquency Prevention, and the U.S. Department of Education's Safe and Drug-Free Schools Program. Contact them for information on preventing hate crimes and to access *Responding to Hate Crime: A Multidisciplinary Curriculum for Law Enforcement and Victim Assistance Professionals.* This web page provides all the information needed to teach a course on responding to hate crimes, including suggested activities, recommended videos, reproducible handouts, and detailed background notes for trainers.
http://www.edc.org/HHD/hatecrime/id1_homepage.htm

National Mental Health and Education Center
The center provides useful and informative guides for parents, educators, administrators, and policymakers on preventing violence in schools. Pathways to Tolerance: Student Diversity is one such program that teaches youth to value the uniqueness of each individual and to respect student diversity. Contact the center for information on how schools can meet the educational and emotional needs of all students.
National Mental Health and Education Center
4340 East West Highway, Suite 402
Bethesda, MD 20814
301-657-0270
http://www.naspweb.org/center/safe_schools/diversity.htm

Safe and Drug-Free Schools
The Safe and Drug-Free Schools program sponsors a website dedicated to providing information on programs and links to resources for preventing hate-motivated behavior. You can access *Preventing Youth Hate Crime: A Manual for Schools and Communities* through this site.
http://www.ed.gov/pubs/HateCrime/start.html

Protecting Students from Harassment and Hate Crime: A Guide for Schools
The U.S. Department of Education has created a guide for a comprehensive approach to preventing harassment and hate crimes, including identifying and responding appropriately to incidents. See *Step-by-Step Guidance: Creating a Supportive School Climate That Appreciates Racial, Cultural, and Other Forms of Diversity* to learn more about changing the climate at your school.
U.S. Department of Education
400 Maryland Avenue, SW
Washington, DC 20202-0498
800-USA-LEARN
http://www.ed.gov/pubs/Harassment
http://www.ed.gov/pubs/Harassment/climate1.html
http://www.ed.gov/PressReleases/02-1994/parent.html

Teach Tolerance
Teach Tolerance has a helpful website that includes several hate and tolerance news links, suggestions for fighting hate, and self-tests to discover one's own levels of

tolerance and hidden prejudices. Resources are available for parents to learn how they can teach tolerance at home. Other resources for teachers include numerous "Show-and-Tell" topic areas and the 101 Tools for Tolerance, a comprehensive list of suggestions for teaching tolerance in the classroom.

http://www.tolerance.org

Don't Laugh at Me (DLAM)

The Don't Laugh at Me Project is working to transform schools, camps, and other youth organizations into more compassionate, safe, and respectful environments for children. Founded by Peter Yarrow of the folk group Peter, Paul & Mary, the project disseminates educational resources designed to establish a climate that reduces emotional and physical violence. DLAM has developed three curricula: one for grades two through five, another for grades six through eight, and a third for summer camps and after-school programs. All of the program materials are based on the well-tested, highly regarded conflict resolution curricula developed by the Resolving Conflict Creatively Program of Educators for Social Responsibility, and they utilize inspiring music and video. DLAM is a gateway program designed to provide teachers, school counselors, social workers, administrators, and other professionals with an entry point for year-round social and emotional learning and character education programs.

Operation Respect
2 Penn Plaza, 23rd Floor
New York, NY 10121
http://www.dontlaugh.org

Parents, Families, and Friends of Lesbians and Gays (PFLAG)

Contact PFLAG for more information and resources on issues related to sexual orientation, including youth and schools, hate crimes, and civil rights. Additionally, PFLAG provides several links to information, resources, and support groups for parents of gay and lesbian children.

PFLAG
1726 M Street, NW Suite 400
Washington, DC 20036
202-467-8180
http://www.pflag.org

The Sexual-Minority Youth Project

This project was developed by the National Association of Social Workers (NASW) in conjunction with the American Psychological Association (APA) to respond to the claims, "There's no gay youth at our school." The curriculum helps social workers and psychologists counsel students about sexual orientation; address sexual risks of gay, lesbian, bisexual, and transgendered (GLBT) students; recommend HIV testing; and counsel parents about children's sexual orientation. It also addresses issues of harassment of GLBT students, as well as the often-overlooked population of GLBT students of color.

American Psychological Association
750 First Street, NE
Washington, DC 20002-4242
800-374-2721
http://www.apa.org/
National Association of Social Workers
750 First Street NE, Suite 700
Washington, DC 20002-4241
800-638-8799
http://www.naswdc.org/

Gay, Lesbian, and Straight Education Network (GLSEN)

GLSEN is the largest national network of parents, students, and educators acting together to create safe schools for lesbian, gay, bisexual, and transgendered people. The network distributes information on issues related to sexual orientation. Contact GLSEN for more information on school safety, curricula, civil rights, and policies affecting gay and lesbian people.

GLSEN
Glsen@glsen.org
212-727-0135
http://www.glsen.org/templates/index.html

The Child Welfare League of America (CWLA)

The CWLA provides publications on parenting and child development for parents and professionals working with children and families. Visit their web page for free online information on child development and tips on parenting, communicating with your teenager, discipline techniques, and being a friend to children and youth.

CWLA
440 First Street, Third Floor
Washington, DC 20001-2085
202-638-2952
http://www.cwla.org

North Central Regional Educational Laboratory (NCREL)

NCREL is a nonprofit, nonpartisan organization that provides research-based expertise, resources, assistance, and professional development opportunities for teachers, administrators, and policymakers. Visit their website for more information on after-school programs, literacy, educational policies, school improvement, and getting involved in your children's education. NCREL also provides a resource on school climate, including a review of the research, tips for parents and teachers, and links to programs.

North Central Regional Educational Laboratory
1120 East Diehl Road, Suite 200
Naperville, IL 60563
800-356-2735
http://www.ncrel.org/
http://www.ncrel.org/sdrs/areas/issues/envrnmnt/famncomm/pa3lk1.htm

Family Involvement Partnership for Learning

Contact the Family Involvement Partnership for Learning to review the *Partners In Learning: How Schools Can Support Family Involvement In Education* (1995) report.

Family Involvement Partnership for Learning
600 Independence Avenue, SW
Washington, DC 20202-8173
http://www.ed.gov/Family/schools.html

National Parent Information Network (NIPIN)

The National Parent Information Network is a program sponsored by the U.S. Department of Education that provides parents with resources on education, parenting, child care, and child development. *NIPIN* maintains a website where parents can obtain information on issues related to children and education. Contact NIPIN to review the *Exceptional Parent Involvement Programs* (1995) report and other information on getting involved in your child's education.

NIPIN
http://npin.org/index.html
http://npin.org/pnews/1995/pnewd95/pnewd95a.html
http://npin.org/library/pre1998/n00337/n00337.html

The Body Keeps the Score: Memory and the Evolving Psychobiology of Posttraumatic Stress

Contact researcher Bessel van der Kolk to review the literature on the effects of Posttraumatic Stress Disorder.

Bessel A. van der Kolk, M.D.
Harvard Medical School
HRI Trauma Center
227 Babcock Street
Boston, MA 02146
http://www.trauma-pages.com/vanderk4.htm

Suggested Readings

General Parenting

The Busy Mom. Sharon Murphy Yates and Joan C. Waites. Washington, DC: Child Welfare League of America, 2000.

Parents, Teens, and Boundaries: How to Draw the Line. Jane Bluestein. Deerfield Beach, FL: Health Communications, Inc., 1993.

Quick Guide to the Internet for Child Development: 2000/2001 Edition. Sharon Milburn and Doug Gotthoffer. Boston: Allyn & Bacon.

Raising Cain: Protecting the Emotional Life of Boys. Daniel Kindlon and Michael Thompson. New York: Ballantine Books, 1999.

Raising a Thinking Child: Help Your Young Child to Resolve Everyday Conflicts and Get Along with Others: The "I Can Problem Solve" Program. Myrna Shure. New York: Pocket Books, 1994.

Real Boys' Voices. William Pollack and Todd Shuster. New York: Random House, 2000.

Respectful Parenting: Birth Through the Terrific Twos. Joanne Baum. Washington, DC: Child Welfare League of America, 2001.

Reviving Ophelia: Saving the Selves of Adolescent Girls. Mary Pipher. New York: Grosset/Putnam, 1994.

Take Charge! Advocating for Your Child's Education. Jo Ann Shaheen and Carolyn Caselton Spence. New York: Delmar Publishers, 2002.

Special Parenting Challenges

The Family and the School: A Joint Systems Approach to Problems with Children. Emilia Dowling and Elsie Osborne. New York: Routledge, 1994.

Ghosts from the Nursery: Tracing the Roots of Violence. Robin Carr-Morse and Meredith S. Wiley. New York: The Atlantic Monthly Press, 1997.

Lost Boys: Why Our Sons Turn Violent and How We Can Save Them. James Garbarino. New York: The Free Press, 1999.

Too Scared to Cry: Psychic Trauma in Childhood. Lenore Terr. New York: Harper and Row, 1990.

Parenting in Difficult Environments

Bullies and Victims: Helping Your Child Survive the Schoolyard Battlefield. Suellen Fried and Paula Fried. New York: M. Evans and Company, 1996.

Children in Danger: Coping with the Consequences of Community Violence. James Garbarino, Nancy Dubrow, Kathleen Kostelny, and Carole Pardo. San Francisco: Jossey-Bass, 1992.

No Safe Place: The Legacy of Family Violence. Christina Crawford. Barrytown, NY: Station Hill Press, 1994.

Parents Under Siege: Why You Are the Solution, Not the Problem, in Your Child's Life. James Garbarino and Claire Bedard. New York: The Free Press, 2001.

Protecting the Gift: Keeping Children and Teenagers Safe. Gavin de Becker. New York: Random House, 1999.
Raising Children in a Socially Toxic Environment. James Garbarino. San Francisco: Jossey Bass Publishers, 1995.

Talking to Kids

How to Say It to Your Kids: The Right Words for Solving Problems, Soothing Feelings, and Teaching Values. Paul Coleman. New York: Prentice Hall, 2000.
The Parent's Book About Bullying: Changing the Course of Your Child's Life. William Voors. Center City, MN: Hazelden, 2000.
Ten Talks Parents Must Have with Their Children About Sex and Character. Pepper Schwartz and Dominic Cappello. New York: Hyperion, 2000.

Gay, Lesbian, and Bisexual Kids

Lesbian and Gay Youth: Care and Counseling. Caitlin Ryan and Donna Futterman. New York: Columbia University Press, 1998.
Mom, Dad, I'm Gay: How Families Negotiate Coming Out. Ritch Savin-Williams. Washington, DC: American Psychological Association, 2001.
Queer Kids: The Challenge and Promise for Lesbian, Gay, and Bisexual Youth. Robert Owens. Binghamton, NY: Haworth Press, 1998.

School Management

Analyzing Problems in Schools and School Systems: A Theoretical Approach. Alan Gaynor. Mahwah, NJ: Lawrence Erlbaum, 1998.
The Challenge to Care in Schools: An Alternative Approach to Education. Nel Noddings. New York: Teachers College Press, 1992.
School Management by Walking Around. Larry Frase and Robert Hetzel. Lancaster, PA: Technomic Publishing, 1990.
Teacher and Child. Haim Ginott. New York: Macmillan, 1995.
Waging Peace in Our Schools. Linda Lantieri and Janet Patti. Boston: Beacon Press, 1996.

Violence and Bullying Prevention in Schools

Bullying Prevention Handbook: A Guide for Principals, Teachers, and Counselors. John Hoover and Ronald Oliver. Bloomington, IN: National Educational Service, 1997.
Bullying at School: What We Know and What We Can Do. Dan Olweus. Malden, MA: Blackwell Publishers, 1993.
Bullyproof: A Teacher's Guide on Teasing and Bullying for Use with Fourth and Fifth Grade Students. Nan Stein and Lisa Sjostrom. Wellesley, MA: Wellesley College Center for Research on Women, 1996.
Dangerous Schools: What We Can Do About the Physical and Emotional Abuse of Our Children. Irwin Hyman and Pamela Snook. San Francisco: Jossey-Bass, 1999.
Gangs in Schools: Signs, Symbols, and Solutions. Arnold Goldstein and Donald Kodluboy. Champaign, IL: Research Press, 1998.
High-Risk Children in Schools: Constructing Sustaining Relationships. Robert Pianta and Donald Walsh. New York: Routledge, 1996.
The Nature of School Bullying: A Cross-National Perspective. Peter Smith, Yohji Morita, Josine Junger-Tas, Dan Olweus, Richard Catalano, and Phillip Slee. New York: Routledge, 1999.
Peace Power for Adolescents: Strategies for a Culture of Nonviolence. Mark Mattiani. Washington, DC: NASW Press, 2001.
Quit It: A Teacher's Guide on Teasing and Bullying for Use with Students in Grades

K-3. Merle Froschl, Barbara Sprung, Nancy Mullin-Rindler, Nan Stein, and Nancy Gropper. Wellesley, MA: Wellesley College Center for Research on Women, 1998.

Safe and Effective Secondary Schools: The Boys Town Model. Jerry Davis, Cathy Nelson, and Elizabeth Gauger. Boys Town, NE: Boys Town Press, 2000.

School Power: Implications for an Intervention Project. James Comer. New York: The Free Press, 1993.

Schools, Violence, and Society. Allan Hoffman. Westport, CT: Praeger Publishers, 1996.

Understanding and Preventing Bullying Among Children: Viewpoint. James Garbarino. *National Dropout Prevention Center-Network Newsletter, 13,* 2, p. 8. Clemson, SC: College of Health, Education, and Human Development, Clemson University, 2001.

Violence Prevention and Reduction in Schools. William Bender, Gregory Clinton, and Renet Bender. Austin, TX: Pro-Ed, 1999.

Violence in the Schools: How to Proactively Prevent and Defuse It. Joan Curio and Patricia First. Newbury Park, CA: Sage Publications, 1993.

Character Education in Schools

Educating for Character: How Our Schools Can Teach Respect and Responsibility. Thomas Lickona. New York: Bantam Books, 1991.

The Equip Program: Teaching Youth to Think and Act Responsibly Through a Peer-Helping Approach. John Gibbs, Granville Bud Potter, and Arnold Goldstein. Champaign, IL: Research Press, 1995.

Service Learning for Youth Empowerment and Social Change. Jeff Claus and Curtis Ogden. New York: Peter Lang Publishing, 1999.

What Communities Can Do

All Kids Are Our Kids: What Communities Must Do to Raise Caring and Responsible Children and Adolescents. Peter Benson. San Francisco: Jossey-Bass, 1997.

The Vulnerable Child: What Really Hurts America's Children and What We Can Do About It. Richard Weissbourd. New York: Addison-Wesley, 1996.

References

Preface

ix *While there are more plans:* Schubert, T. H., Bressette, S., Deeken, J., & Bender, W. N. (1999). Analysis of Random School Shootings. In W. N. Bender, G. Clinton, and R. L. Bender (Eds.), *Violence Prevention and Reduction in Schools,* pp. 97–101. Austin, TX: Pro-Ed.

xi *In 1986, Jim published:* Garbarino, J., Guttmann, E., & Seeley, J. W. (1986). *The Psychologically Battered Child.* San Francisco: Jossey-Bass.

xiv *Many other books:* Garbarino, J. (1999). *Lost Boys: Why Our Sons Turn Violent and How We Can Save Them.* New York: The Free Press.

xv *In collecting information:* Adelman, C. (1993). Kurt Lewin and the Origin of Action Research. *Educational Action Research, 1,*1, 7–24; Greenwood, D. J., & Levin, M. (1998). *Introduction to Action Research: Social Research for Social Change.* Thousand Oaks, CA: Sage.

Chapter 1

1 *A survey conducted:* Nansel, T. R., Overpeck, M., Pilla, R. S., Ruan, W. J., Simons-Morton, B., & Scheidt, P. (2001). Bullying Behaviors Among US Youth: Prevalence and Association with Psychosocial Adjustment. *JAMA, 285,* 16, 2094–2100.

1 *Other national surveys:* American Association of University Women (2001). *Hostile Hallways: Bullying, Teasing, and Sexual Harassment in School.* Washington, DC: American Association of University Women Educational Foundation; Harachi, T. W., Catalano, R., & Hawkins, D. J. (1999). United States. In *The Nature of Bullying: A Cross-National Perspective* (pp. 279–95). New York: Routledge.

1 *The U.S. Department of Education:* Oliver, R., Hoover, J. H., & Hazler, R. (1994). The Perceived Roles of Bullying in Small-Town Midwestern Schools. *Journal of Counseling and Development, 72,* 416–420; U.S. Department of Education. (1998). *Preventing Bullying: A Manual for Schools and Communities.* Washington, DC: Author.

3 *the principal of the high school:* DeAngelis, F. (1999, April 20). Television interview with the principal of Columbine High School. NBC News. New York: National Broadcasting Company.

5 *Ronald Rohner started his journey:* Rohner, R. (1975). *They Love Me, They Love Me Not: A Worldwide Study of the Effects of Parental Acceptance and Rejection.* New Haven, CT: HRAF Press.

5 *Psychologist Stanley Coopersmith:* Coopersmith, S., & Feldman, R. (1974). *The Formative Years: Principles of Early Childhood Education.* San Francisco: Albion.

6   *At least four others:* Garbarino, J., Guttmann, E., & Seeley, J. W. (1986). *The Psychologically Battered Child.* San Francisco: Jossey-Bass.

8   *Researchers studying the behavioral effects:* Lashbrook, J. T. (2000). Fitting In: Exploring the Emotional Dimension of Adolescent Peer Pressure. *Adolescence, 35,* 140, 747–757.

9   *Researchers such as:* Karr-Morse, R., & Wiley, M. S. (1997). *Ghosts from the Nursery: Tracing the Roots of Violence.* New York: The Atlantic Monthly Press; Van der Kolk, B. (1994). The Body Keeps the Score: Memory and the Evolving Psychobiology of Post Traumatic Stress. *Harvard Review of Psychiatry, 1,* 254–265.

9   *According to science writer:* Ferris, C. F. (1996, March/April). The Rage of the Innocents: Childhood Trauma May Spring the Biochemical Trip Wires That Set Off Later Explosions of Violence. *The Sciences,* 22–26.

9   *Some kids are more vulnerable:* Vorrasi, J. A., deLara, E. W., & Bradshaw, C. P. (in press). Psychological Maltreatment. In A. Giadino (Ed.), *Child Maltreatment: A Clinical Guide and Reference.* St. Louis, MO: G. W. Medical Publishing.

9   *In her book:* Aron, E. (1999). *The Highly Sensitive Person: How to Thrive When the World Overwhelms You.* New York: Replica Books.

10 *Working in Germany:* Losel, F., & Bender, D. (1997). Heart Rate and Psychosocial Correlates of Antisocial Behavior in High-Risk Adolescents. In A. Raine, P. A. Brennan, D. P. Farrington, & S. A. Mednick (Eds.), *Biosocial Bases of Violence* (pp. 321–342). New York: Plenum Press.

13 *Emotional violence is a national problem:* Vorrasi, J. A., deLara, E. W., & Bradshaw, C. P. (in press). Psychological Maltreatment. In A. Giadino (Ed.), *Child Maltreatment: A Clinical Guide and Reference.* St. Louis, MO: G. W. Medical Publishing.

13 *And for some:* Cleary, S. C. (2000). Adolescent Victimization and Associated Suicidal and Violent Behaviors. *Adolescence, 35,* 140, 671–682.

Chapter 2

18 *Most parents are unaware:* deLara, E. W. (2000). *Adolescents' Perceptions of Safety at School and Their Solutions for Enhancing Safety and Decreasing School Violence.* Unpublished doctoral dissertation, Cornell University; Voors, W. (2000). *The Parents' Book About Bullying: Changing the Course of Your Child's Life.* Center City, MN: Hazelden.

18 *Journalist Patricia Hersch spent:* Hersch, P. (1999). *A Tribe Apart: A Journey into the Heart of American Adolescence.* New York: Ballantine Books.

18 *There are millions of kids:* Jacobson, M. (1999, May 17). The Generation Gap in My Living Room. *New York, 32*(19), 26–28.

20 *Swedish Psychologists:* Kerr, M., & Stattin, H. (2000). What Parents Know, How They Know It, and Several Forms of Adolescent Adjustment: Further Support for a Reinterpretation of Monitoring. *Developmental Psychology, 36*(3), 366–380.

20 *Kerr and Stattin learned:* Ibid.

22 *Psychologists call this:* Ross, L. (1977). The Intuitive Psychologist and His Shortcomings: Distortions in the Attribution Process. In L. Berkowitz (Ed.), *Advances in Experimental Psychology* (Vol. 10). New York: Academic Press.

22 *Writing in* Time *magazine:* Dickenson, A. (1999, May 3). Where Were the Parents? *Time, 153*(7), 40.

23 *In* Lost Boys: Garbarino, J. (1999). *Lost Boys: Why Our Sons Turn Violent and How We Can Save Them.* New York: The Free Press.

24 *In their work about school safety:* Astor, R. A., Meyer, H. A., & Behre, W. J.

(1999). Unowned Places and Times: Maps and Interviews About Violence in High Schools. *American Educational Research Journal, 36*(1), 3–42.

26 *The research of psychologist:* Hyman I. A., & Perone, D. C. (1998). The Other Side of School Violence: Educator Policies and Practices That May Contribute to Student Misbehavior, *Journal of School Psychology, 36*(1) 7–27; Hyman, I. A., & Snook, P. A. (1999). *Dangerous Schools: What We Can Do About the Physical and Emotional Abuse of Our Children.* San Francisco: Jossey-Bass.

28 *Their argument is similar:* Goodman, J. (2001, May/June). *Pennsylvania Gazette,* p. 31.

29 *One list of characteristics:* Stennet, N. (1983). Family Relationships and School Achievement Among Boys of Lower-Income Urban Black Families. *American Journal of Orthopsychiatry, 53*(1), 127–143.

31 *As Kerr and Stattin:* Kerr, M., & Stattin, H. (2000). What Parents Know, How They Know It, and Several Forms of Adolescent Adjustment: Further Support for a Reinterpretation of Monitoring. *Developmental Psychology, 36*(3), 366–380.

31 *is what Robert Halpern:* Halpern, R. (1995). *Rebuilding the Inner City.* New York: Columbia University Press; Musick, J. (1995). *Young, Poor, Pregnant: The Psychology of Teenage Motherhood.* New Haven, CT: Yale University Press.

Chapter 3

33 *A majority of middle and high school:* American Association of University Women (2001). *Hostile Hallways: Bullying, Teasing, and Sexual Harassment in School.* Washington, DC: American Association of University Women Educational Foundation; *The Metropolitan Life Survey of the American Teacher 1999: Violence in America's Public Schools Five Years Later.* (1999). New York, NY: Louis Harris and Associates.

35 *For many students, the hallways:* Astor, R. A., Meyer, H. A., & Behre, W. J. (1999). Unowned Places and Times: Maps and Interviews about Violence in High Schools. *American Educational Research Journal, 36*(1), 3–42.

37 *The cafeteria is a problem:* Ibid.

38 *According to a recent survey:* American Association of University Women. (2001). *Hostile Hallways: Bullying, Teasing, and Sexual Harassment in School.* Washington, DC: American Association of University Women Educational Foundation. Available online at http://www.aauw.org.

38 *The school grounds:* Astor, R. A., Meyer, H. A., & Behre, W. J. (1999). Unowned Places and Times: Maps and Interviews About Violence in High Schools. *American Educational Research Journal, 36*(1), 3–42.

43 *They include the 160,000: National Dropout Prevention Center Network Newsletter.* Clemson, SC: Clemson University, College of Health, Education, and Human Development.

44 *According to the research:* Gilligan, J. (1996). *Violence: Our Deadly Epidemic and Its Causes.* New York: G.P. Putnam's Sons; Gilligan, J. (1997). *Violence: Reflections on a National Epidemic.* New York: Random House.

49 *According to researchers:* Fox, J. A., and Levin, J. (2001). Schools' Response to Columbine: A Failing Grade. *Buffalo News,* p. H5.

Chapter 4

53 *One of the early pioneers:* Coleman, J. (1965). *Adolescents and the Schools.* New York: Basic Books.

53 *Decades ago, sociologist Mustaf Sherif:* Sherif, M., Harvey, O. J., White, B. J., Hood, W. R., & Sherif, C. W. (1961). *Intergroup Conflict and Cooperation: The Robbers' Cave Experiment.* Norman: University of Oklahoma Books Exchange.

54 *Social scientist Elliot Aronson:* Aronson, E. (2000). *Nobody Left to Hate: Teaching Compassion After Columbine.* New York: W. H. Freeman.

54 *Aronson's approach is called:* Aronson, E. Blaney, N., Stephan, C., Sikes, J., & Snapp, M. (1978). *The Jigsaw Classroom.* Beverly Hills, CA: Sage.

58 *Harvard social scientists:* Brion-Meisels, S., & Selman, R. L. (1996). From Fight or Flight to Collaboration: A Framework for Understanding Individual and Institutional Development in Schools. In A. M. Hoffman (Ed.), *Schools, Violence and Society* (pp. 163–198). Westport, CT: Praeger.

59 *Children and adults learn:* Peterson, C., Maier, S., & Seligman, M. (1993). *Learned Helplessness: A Theory for the Age of Personal Control.* New York: Oxford University Press.

59 *This attitude of learned helplessness:* Ibid.

59 *Our research supports:* Garbarino, J. (1995). *Raising Children in a Socially Toxic Environment.* San Francisco: Jossey-Bass.

61 *This finding is corroborated:* Crowley, E. P. (1993). A Qualitative Analysis of Mainstreamed Behaviorally Disordered Aggressive Adolescents' Perceptions of Helpful and Unhelpful Teacher Attitudes and Behaviors. *Exceptionality, 4*(3), 131–151.

61 *Ethologist Frans de Waal:* Angier, N. (2001 May 20). Bully for You: Why Push Comes to Shove. New York Times, Sec. 4, pp. 1, 4; de Wall, F. (2001). *The Ape and the Sushi Master: Cultural Reflections of a Primatologist.* New York: Basic Books.

62 *As Ellen found:* deLara, E. (in press). Peer Predictability: An Adolescent Strategy for Increasing School Safety. *The Journal of School Violence.*

62 *A National Center for Education Statistics Survey:* Chandler, K., Nolin, M. J., & Davies, E. (1995, October). Student Strategies to Avoid Harm at School: Statistics in Brief. *National Center for Education Statistics,* U.S. Department of Education, Office of Educational Research and Improvement, NCES 95–203, 1–7.

63 *Self-accepting, self-confident children:* Nansel, T. R., Overpeck, M., Pilla, R. S., Ruan, W. J., Simons-Morton, B., & Scheidt, P. (2001). Bullying Behaviors Among U.S. Youth: Prevalence and Association with Psychosocial Adjustment. *JAMA, 285,* 16, 2094–2100.

63 *Frank DeAngelis:* DeAngelis, F. (1999, April 20). Television interview with the principal of Columbine High School. NBC News. New York: National Broadcasting Company.

64 *Research shows that kids:* Deater-Deckard, K., Dodge, K. A., Bates, J. E., & Pettit, G. S. (1996). Physical Discipline Among African American and European American Mothers: Links to Children's Externalizing Behaviors. *Developmental Psychology, 32*(6), 1065–1072.

64 *Jim Garbarino and Claire Bedard's:* Garbarino, J., & Bedard, C. (2001). *Parents under Siege.* New York: Free Press.

64 *They highlight the finding:* Scales, P., & Leffert, N. (1999). *Developmental Assets: A Synthesis of Scientific Research on Adolescent Development.* Minneapolis, MN: Search Institute.

65 *Service learning projects:* Claus, J. & Ogden, C. (1999). *Service Learning for Youth Empowerment and Social Change.* New York: Peter Lang Publishing.

65 *Research is not definitive:* Brunsma, D. L. & Rockquemore, K. A. (1998, September/October). Effects of Student Uniforms on Attendance, Behavior Problems, Substance Abuse and Academic Achievement. *Journal of Educational Research;* Holloman, L. O. (1995, Winter). Violence and Other Antisocial Behaviors in Public Schools: Can Dress Codes Help Solve the Problem? *Journal of Family and Consumer Sciences;* Stanley, M. S. (1996). School Uniforms and Safety. *Education and Urban Society.*

66   *It is easier to instill:* Lickona, T. (1991). *Educating for Character: How Our Schools Can Teach Respect and Responsibility.* New York: Bantam Books.

Chapter 5

72   *Research reveals that some:* Nansel, T. R., Overpeck, M., Pilla, R. S., Ruan, W. J., Simons-Morton, B., & Scheidt, P. (2001). Bullying Behaviors Among U.S. Youth: Prevalence and Association with Psychosocial Adjustment. *JAMA, 285,* 16, 2094–2100.

72   *As school and military consultant:* Katz, J. (1995) Reconstructing Masculinity in the Locker Room: The Mentors in Violence Prevention Project. *Harvard Educational Review, 65(2), 163–174.*

73   The New York Times: Leland, J. (2001, April 8). Zero Tolerance Changes Life at One School: Columbine Makes a Town Get Tough, But the Students Resent the Scrutiny. *New York Times,* Sec. 9, pp. 1, 6.

74   *However, at Columbine High School:* Gibbs, N., & Roche, T. (1999, December 20). The Columbine Tapes. *Time, 154*(25), 40–51.

74   *School principal Frank DeAngelis:* DeAngelis, F. (1999, April 20). Television interview with the principal of Columbine High School. NBC News. New York: National Broadcasting Company.

78   *Unfortunately, researchers like psychologist:* Hyman I. A., & Perone, D. C. (1998). The Other Side of School Violence: Educator Policies and Practices That May Contribute to Student Misbehavior, *Journal of School Psychology, 36*(1), 7–27; Hyman, I. A., & Snook, P. A. (1999). *Dangerous Schools: What We Can Do About the Physical and Emotional Abuse of Our Children.* San Francisco: Jossey-Bass.

78   *In a series of five videotapes:* Gibbs, N., & Roche, T. (1999, December 20). The Columbine Tapes. *Time, 154*(25), 40–51.

79   *Columbine is a clean:* Ibid.

80   *Organizational expert W. Richard Scott:* Scott, W. R. (1995). *Institutions and Organizations.* Thousand Oaks, CA: Sage.

80   *Researchers like psychiatrist:* Gilligan, J. (1997). *Violence: Reflections on a National Epidemic.* New York: Random House.

82   *Administrators had difficulty grasping:* Bowles, S. (2000, April 14). A Suicide: Devastation Lingers Around School. *USA Today,* p. 13A.

83   *In Atlanta, Georgia:* Jerome, R., Arias, R., Boone, M., Comander, L., Fowler, J., Harrington, M., Mazo, E., Renom, J., Sider, D., & Wescott, G. C. (2001, June 4) Disarming the Rage. *People, 55*(22), pp. 54–61.

83   *In the 1998–1999 school year:* Centers for Disease Control. Youth Risk Behavior Surveillance System, *MMWR,* 45 (No. SS-4), 1-86. Available online at http://www.cdc.gov.

83   *This "suicide by cop" phenomenon:* Garbarino, J. (1999). *Lost Boys: Why Our Sons Turn Violent and How We Can Save Them.* New York: The Free Press; Vossekuil, B., Reddy, M., Fein, R., Borum, R., & Modzeleski, W. (2000). U.S. Secret Service, *Safe School Initiative: An Interim Report on the Prevention of Targeted Violence in Schools.* Washington, DC: U.S. Secret Service National Threat Assessment Center and U.S. Department of Education, with the support of the National Institute of Justice.

83   *According to the 1998:* Speaker, K. M., & Petersen, G. J. (2000). School Violence and Adolescent Suicide: Strategies for Effective Intervention. *Educational Review, 52,* 1, 65–73.

84   *At this time, though:* Ibid.

84   *Social scientists are certain:* Portner, J. (2000, April 12). Complex Set of Ills

Spurs Rising Teen Suicide Rate. *Education Week.* Available online at http://www.edweek.org/ew/ew.

85   *The national survey research:* Nansel, T. R., Overpeck, M., Pilla, R. S., Ruan, W. J., Simons-Morton, B., & Scheidt, P. (2001). Bullying Behaviors Among U.S. Youth: Prevalence and Association with Psychosocial Adjustment. *JAMA, 285,* 16, 2094–2100.

85   *Often, when a child:* Ibid.

85   *Further, our research indicates:* Harachi, T. W., Catalano, R., & Hawkins, D. J. (1999). United States. In *The Nature of Bullying: A Cross-National Perspective* (pp. 279–95). New York: Routledge.

88   *Irene Claremont de Castillejo:* de Castillejo, I. C. (1997). *Knowing Woman: A Feminine Psychology.* Boston, MA: Shambhala Publications.

Chapter 6

89   *In her book* Reviving Ophelia: Pipher, M. (1994). *Reviving Ophelia: Saving the Selves of Adolescent Girls.* New York: Grosset/Putnam.

90   *What is more:* Ibid.

90   *Taking on this issue:* Brumberg, J. (1997). *The Body Project: An Intimate History of American Girls.* New York: Random House.

90   *In* Raising Cain: Kindlon, M., & Thompson, M. (1999). *Raising Cain: Protecting the Emotional Life of Boys.* New York: Ballantine Books.

90   *Similarly, in* The Adonis Complex: Pope, H., Olivardia, R., & Phillips, K. A. (2002). *Adonis Complex: How to Identify, Treat and Prevent Body Obsession in Men and Boys.* New York: Touchstone Books.

91   *One of the best treatments:* Savin-Williams, R. C. (2001). *Mom, Dad, I'm Gay: How Families Negotiate Coming Out.* Washington, DC: American Psychological Association.

91   *This is one of the themes:* Kindlon, M., & Thompson, M. (1999). *Raising Cain: Protecting the Emotional Life of Boys.* New York: Ballantine Books.

92   *A two-year study conducted:* Human Rights Watch (2001, May). *Hatred in the Hallways. Violence and Discrimination against Lesbian, Gay, Bisexual, and Transgendered Students in U.S. Schools.* Available online at http://www.hrw.org/reports/2001/uslgbt/toc.htm.

92   *Research finds that:* Ibid.

92   *Estimates by the American Friends:* American Friends Service Committee. *Gay/Lesbian Youth Program.* Available online at http://www.afsc.org/default.htm.

98   *The Center for Children:* The Center for Children. *Steps to Respect Research Review.* Available online at http://www.cfchildren.org/strres.html#6.

99   *In 2000 the American Association:* American Association of University Women. (2001). *Hostile Hallways: Bullying, Teasing, and Sexual Harassment in School.* Washington, DC: American Association of University Women Educational Foundation. Available online at http://www.aauw.org.

99   *Of the teens who:* Ibid.

99   *Almost 70 percent of kids:* Ibid.

101   *Some adolescents resort to suicide:* Bowles, S. (2000, April 14). A Suicide: Devastation Lingers Around School. *USA Today,* p. 13A; Portner, J. (2000, April 12). Complex Set of Ills Spurs Rising Teen Suicide Rate. *Education Week.* Available online at http://www.edweek.org/ew/ew; Silverman, J. G., Raj, A., Mucci, L. A., & Hathaway, J. E., (2001). Dating Violence Against Adolescent Girls and Associated Substance Use, Unhealthy Weight Control, Sexual Behavior, Pregnancy, and Suicidality. *JAMA, 286,* 572–579; Speaker, K. M., & Peterson, G. J. (2000).

School Violence and Adolescent Suicide: Strategies for Effective Intervention. *Educational Review, 52*,1, 65–73.

102   *Following the Supreme Court:* Gorney, C. (1999 June 13). Teaching Johnny the Appropriate Way to Flirt. *New York Times,* p. 45.

102   *Few experts have studied:* McCann, J. (2001). *Stalking in Children and Adolescents: The Primitive Bond.* Washington, DC: American Psychological Association.

103   *Then a six-year-old boy:* Barboza, D. (2000, March 2). A Life of Guns, Drugs and Now, Killing, All at 6. *New York Times.*

108   *In all of its forms:* Fineran, S. & Bennett, L. (1998). Teenage Peer Sexual Harassment: Implications for Social Work Practice in Education. *Social Work, 43*(1) 55–64.

109   *Read Pepper Schwartz:* Schwartz, P., & Cappello, D. (2000). *Ten Talks Parents Must Have with Their Children About Sex and Character.* New York: Hyperion.

110   *called Peace Power:* Mattaini, M. (2001). *Peace Power for Adolescents: Strategies for a Culture of Nonviolence.* Washington, DC: NASW Press.

Chapter 7

114   *Research tells us that:* Scales, P. C., & Leffert, N. (1999). *Developmental Assets: A Synthesis of Scientific Research on Adolescent Development.* Minneapolis, MN: Search Institute; Rutter, M. (1993). Resilience: Some Conceptual Considerations. *Journal of Adolescent Health, 14,* 626–631.

115   *In a study by psychologist:* Sameroff, A., Seifer, R., Barocas, R., & Zax, M. (1987). Intelligence Quotient Scores of 4-Year-Old Children: Social Environment Risk Factors. *Pediatrics, 79,* 343–350; Sameroff, A. J., Seifer, R., Baldwin, A., & Baldwin, C. (1993). Stability of Intelligence from Preschool to Adolescence: The Influence of Social and Family Risk Factors. *Child Development, 64,* 80–97.

117   *A critical component of feeling:* Scales, P., & Leffert, N. (1999). *Developmental Assets: A Synthesis of Scientific Research on Adolescent Development.* Minneapolis, MN: Search Institute.

117   *Students across all academic levels:* deLara, E. W. (2000). *Adolescents' Perceptions of Safety at School and Their Solutions for Enhancing Safety and Decreasing School Violence.* Unpublished doctoral diss., Cornell University.

120   *Researchers like Nel Noddings:* Noddings, N. (1992). *The Challenge to Care in Schools: An Alternative Approach to Education.* New York: Teachers College Press; Comer, J. (1993). *School Power: Implications for an Intervention Project.* New York: The Free Press.

123   *There is not much research:* Nansel, T. R., Overpeck, M., Pilla, R. S., Ruan, W. J., Simons-Morton, B., & Scheidt, P. (2001). Bullying Behaviors Among U.S. Youth: Prevalence and Association with Psychosocial Adjustment. *JAMA, 285,* 16, 2094–2100; Smith, P. K., Morita, Y., Junger-Tas, J., Olweus, D., Catalano, R., and Slee, P. (Eds.). (1999). *The Nature of School Bullying: A Cross-National Perspective.* New York: Routledge.

123   *According to psychiatrists:* Bowen, M. (1978). *Family Therapy in Clinical Practice.* New York: Jason Aronson; Minuchin, S. (1974) *Families and Family Therapy.* Cambridge, MA: Harvard University Press.

Chapter 8

128   *Research on how kids deal:* Scales, P., & Leffert, N. (1999). *Developmental Assets: A Synthesis of Scientific Research on Adolescent Development.* Minneapolis, MN: Search Institute.

132   *The bus is a particularly:* Glover, D., Gough, G., Johnson, M., & Cartwright, M. (2000). Bullying in 25 Secondary Schools: Incidence, Impact and Intervention.

Educational Research, 42, 2, 141–156; Voors, W. (2000). *The Parents' Book About Bullying: Changing the Course of Your Child's Life.* Center City, MN: Hazelden.

139 *In Howard Gardner's book:* Gardner, H. (1993). *Multiple Intelligences: The Theory in Practice.* New York: Basic Books.

142 *Psychologists and educators:* Gilligan, J. (1997). *Violence: Reflections on a National Epidemic.* New York: Random House; Weissbourd, R. (1996). *The Vulnerable Child: What Really Hurts America's Children and What We Can Do About It.* New York: Addison-Wesley.

144 *Emotionally and psychologically healthy:* Nansel, T. R., Overpeck, M., Pilla, R. S., Ruan, W. J., Simons-Morton, B., & Scheidt, P. (2001). Bullying Behaviors Among U.S. Youth: Prevalence and Association with Psychosocial Adjustment. *JAMA, 285,* 16, 2094–2100.

146 *One of the best guides:* Shure, M. B. (1994). *Raising a Thinking Child: Help Your Young Child to Resolve Everyday Conflicts and Get Along with Others: The "I Can Problem Solve" Program.* New York: Pocket Books.

146 *In contrast, targeted children:* Olweus, D. (1993). *Bullying at School: What We Know and What We Can Do.* Malden, MA: Blackwell.

146 *The Steps to Respect:* Center for Children. *Steps to Respect.* Available online at http://www.cfchildren.org/strres.html#6.

146 *Research indicates that kids:* Hodges, V., Malone, M. J., & Perry, D. G. (1997). Individual Risk and Social Risk as Interacting Determinants of Victimization in the Peer Group. *Developmental Psychology, 33,* 1032–1039; Pellegrini, A. D., & Bartini, M. (2000). A Longitudinal Study of Bullying: Victimization and Peer Affiliation During the Transition from Primary School to Middle School. *American Educational Research Journal, 37,* 3, 699–725.

Chapter 9

149 *As Ellen became more aware:* deLara, E. W. (in press). Peer Predictability: An Adolescent Strategy for Increasing School Safety. *The Journal of School Violence.*

150 *In a small school:* Astor, R. A., Meyer, H. A., & Behre, W. J. (1999). Unowned Places and Times: Maps and Interviews About Violence in High Schools. *American Educational Research Journal, 36*(1), 3–42.

152 *A small high school allows:* Astor, R. A., Meyer, H. A., & Behre, W. J. (1999). Unowned Places and Times: Maps and Interviews About Violence in High Schools. *American Educational Research Journal, 36*(1), 3–42; Barker, R., & Gump, P. V. (1964). *Big School, Small School: High School Size and Student Behavior.* Stanford, CA: Stanford University Press.

157 *Similarly, several areas of the school:* Glover, D., Gough, G., Johnson, M., & Cartwright, M. (2000). Bullying in 25 Secondary Schools: Incidence, Impact and Intervention. *Educational Research, 42,* 2, 141–156.

159 *Put simply, big high schools:* Barker, R., & Gump, P. V. (1964). *Big School, Small School: High School Size and Student Behavior.* Stanford, CA: Stanford University Press.

160 *By contrast, small schools:* Ibid.

160 *Much of the important research:* Ibid.

160 *The research demonstrated:* Ibid.

161 *Psychologist Rudolph Moos:* Moos, R. H. (1979). *Evaluating Educational Environments.* San Francisco: Jossey-Bass.

161 *The researchers working in the 1950s:* Barker, R., & Gump, P. V. (1964). *Big School, Small School: High School Size and Student Behavior.* Stanford, CA: Stanford University Press.

162 *Yet millions are subjected directly:* Voors, W. (2000). *The Parents' Book About Bullying: Changing the Course of Your Child's Life.* Center City, MN: Hazelden.

163 *Kids in a recent poll:* Loven, J. (2001, August 8). Teens Want Parents Involved in Their Lives, Survey Says. *Star Gazette,* 3A. Available online at http://www.horatioalger.com

164 *Communities that have successfully implemented:* Garbarino, J. (1999b, April 26). *Not in My School, Not in My Community.* Video conference presentation, Cornell University, Ithaca, NY. Available online at http://www.cce.cornell.edu/admin/satellite/notinmyschool Nathan, J., & Febey, K. (2001). *Smaller, Safer, Saner, Successful Schools* (pp. 1–64). Minneapolis, MN: Center for School Change, Humphrey Institute of the University of Minnesota.

165 *Gavin De Becker:* De Becker, G. (1999). *Protecting the Gift: Keeping Children and Teenagers Safe.* New York: Random House.

Chapter 10

168 *The fact is that drugs:* Jackson, B., & Muth, M. (2000). *2000 Monitoring the Future Survey: Moderating Trend Among Teen Drug Use Continues.* DC: Department of Health and Human Services. Available online at http://www.hhs.gov/news/press/2000pres/20001214.html.

170 *A Harris Interactive survey:* Gaughan, E., Cerio, J. D., & Myers, R. A. (2001). *Lethal Violence in Schools: A National Survey Final Report* (pp. 3–39). Alfred, NY: Alfred University.

170 *Another recent survey:* Nansel, T. R., Overpeck, M., Pilla, R. S., Ruan, W. J., Simons-Morton, B., & Scheidt, P. (2001). Bullying Behaviors Among U.S. Youth: Prevalence and Association with Psychosocial Adjustment. *JAMA, 285,* 16, 2094–2100.

170 *A survey conducted in 2000:* Barrow, R., van Zommeren, W., Young, C., & Holt-man, P. (2001). School Counselors' and Principals' Perceptions of Violence: Guns, Gangs and Drugs in Rural Schools. *Rural Educator, 22,* 2, 1–7.

170 *Many kids report that:* Ibid.

173 *Research reveals that while:* Jackson, B., & Muth, M. (2000). *2000 Monitoring the Future Survey: Moderating Trend Among Teen Drug Use Continues.* Washington, DC: Department of Health and Human Services. Available online at http://www.hhs.gov/news/press/2000pres/20001214.html.

178 *While studies show that:* Jackson, B., & Muth, M. (2000). *2000 Monitoring the Future Survey: Moderating Trend Among Teen Drug Use Continues.* Washington, DC: Department of Health and Human Services. Available online at http://www.hhs.gov/news/press/2000pres/20001214.html.

Chapter 11

182 *It is captured humorously:* Wolf, A. (1992). *Get Out of My Life, But First Could You Drive Me and Cheryl to the Mall? A Parent's Guide to the New Teenager.* New York: Noonday Press.

182 *Informally and in confidence:* deLara, E. W. (2000). *Adolescents' Perceptions of Safety at School and Their Solutions for Enhancing Safety and Decreasing School Violence.* Unpublished doctoral dissertation, Cornell University; deLara, E. W. (in press). Peer Predictability: An Adolescent Strategy for Increasing School Safety. *The Journal of School Violence;* Gaughan, E., Cerio, J. D., & Myers, R. A. (2001). *Lethal Violence in Schools: A National Survey Final Report* (pp. 3–39). Alfred, NY: Alfred University; Glover, D., Gough, G., Johnson, M., & Cartwright, M. (2000). Bullying in 25 Secondary Schools: Incidence, Impact and Intervention. *Educational Research, 42*(2), 141–156.

183 *Only about one in four:* deLara, E. W. (2000). *Adolescents' Perceptions of Safety at School and Their Solutions for Enhancing Safety and Decreasing School Violence.* Unpublished doctoral dissertation, Cornell University.

184 *When they feel free:* Loven, J. (2001, August 8). Teens Want Parents Involved in Their Lives, Survey Says. *Star Gazette,* 3A. Available online at State of Our Nation's Youth, http://www.horatioalger.com.

185 *In particular, according to survey data:* Astor, R. A., Meyer, H. A., & Behre, W. J. (1999). Unowned Places and Times: Maps and Interviews About Violence in High Schools. *American Educational Research Journal, 36*(1), 3–42; deLara, E. W. (2000). *Adolescents' Perceptions of Safety at School and Their Solutions for Enhancing Safety and Decreasing School Violence.* Unpublished doctoral dissertation, Cornell University.

188 *The good news is:* deLara, E. W. (2000). *Adolescents' Perceptions of Safety at School and Their Solutions for Enhancing Safety and Decreasing School Violence.* Unpublished doctoral dissertation, Cornell University.

189 *About 30 percent:* Ibid.

194 *A major and unexpected finding:* deLara, E. W. (2000). *Adolescents' Perceptions of Safety at School and Their Solutions for Enhancing Safety and Decreasing School Violence.* Unpublished doctoral dissertation, Cornell University; deLara, E. (in press). Peer Predictability: An Adolescent Strategy for Increasing School Safety. *The Journal of School Violence.*

198 *The average high school:* Garbarino, J. (1995) *Raising Children in a Socially Toxic Environment.* San Francisco: Jossey-Bass.

199 *Having a greater adult presence:* Astor, R. A., Meyer, H. A., & Behre, W. J. (1999). Unowned Places and Times: Maps and Interviews About Violence in High Schools. *American Educational Research Journal, 36*(1), 3–42.

199 *In* The Challenge to Care: Noddings, N. (1992). *The Challenge to Care in Schools: An Alternative Approach to Education.* New York: Teachers College Press.

200 *As Jerome Bruner:* Bruner, J. (1961). *The Process of Education.* Cambridge, MA: Harvard University Press.

Chapter 12

201 *Though the perpetrators produced:* Gibbs, N., & Roche, T. (1999, December 20). The Columbine Tapes. *Time, 154*(25), 40–51.

201 *A 1997 study:* Astor, R. A., Behre, W., Fravil, K. A., & Wallace, J. M. (1997). Perceptions of School Violence as a Problem and Reports of Violent Events: A National Survey of School Social Workers. *Social Work, 42*(1), 55–68.

202 *The FBI and Secret Service:* O'Toole, M. E. (2000). *The School Shooter: A Threat Assessment Perspective.* Quantico, VA: Federal Bureau of Investigation.

203 *John Dewey was one:* Dewey, J. (1900). *The School and Society.* Chicago: The University of Chicago Press.

203 *Veteran educator Haim Ginott:* Ginott, H. (1995). *Teacher and Child.* New York: Macmillan.

204 *As psychologists Arnold Goldstein:* Goldstein, A., & Kodluboy, D. (1998). *Gangs in Schools: Signs, Symbols, and Solutions.* Champaign, IL: Research Press.

206 *Educational psychologist Patricia Kyle:* Kyle, P. (1999). Cooperative Discipline to Reduce Classroom Violence. In *Violence Prevention and Reduction in Schools* (pp. 15–30). Austin, TX: Pro-Ed.

Index

About the Authors

Dr. James Garbarino, Ph.D., is Professor of Social Work at Boston College and was formerly codirector of the Family Life Development Center and Professor of Human Development at Cornell University. A Past President of the Erikson Institute for Advanced Study in Child Development, he has served as consultant or adviser to a wide range of organizations, including the National Committee to Prevent Child Abuse, the National Institute for Mental Health, the National Resource Center for Children in Poverty, and the U.S. Advisory Board on Child Abuse and Neglect. He also functions as a scientific expert witness in criminal and civil cases involving issues of violence.

Recognized as a leading authority on child development and youth violence, Dr. Garbarino has appeared frequently on nationally broadcast news and information programs, including ABC-TV's *Nightline,* PBS-TV's *NewsHour with Jim Lehrer,* CNN's *Larry King Live,* NBC-TV's *Meet the Press* and *Today,* National Public Radio's *All Things Considered,* and many more.

Dr. Ellen deLara, Ph.D., is a Faculty Fellow at the Family Life Development Center at Cornell University and a Professor of Social Work at Syracuse University. A winner of the "Just for Kids" Foundation's award for outstanding teaching and child advocacy and the Merrill Presidential Scholars Award, she specializes in the well-being of children and human development. In addition, she has counseled children, adolescents, couples, and families in private practice for more than twenty years. Dr. deLara's research has been featured on national media, including NBC-TV's *Today, The Washington Post,* and National Public Radio.